BOOMERS

TURNING 60 *ish*

WHAT'S NEXT ON...

Are you on the right road?

milestone 60+ Years

The Highway Of Life

Michael Lee

Book Dedication

To my parents, Alyce and Winton
Anyone who is blessed to have good parents is lucky.
I was among the blessed and am very grateful.

Author

Michael Lee is an early boomer and a former educator who
currently works in real estate management. His academic
background includes degrees in history, education,
business, and law. The author and his wife, Dianne, reside
near Riverside, California.

Acknowledgements

Special thanks go to Dr. Melissa Brotton and Kelly Reed,
who graciously edited this book with professionalism, insight,
suggestions, and encouragement. It was a pleasure to
collaborate with them.

Catherine Kent, the talented graphic designer of the book
covers, was wonderful to work with on this project.
Her ability to follow a specific outline and create or arrange
for multiple sketches is greatly appreciated.
catsillustrations@gmail.com

Author contact: michaelleeboomers@gmail.com

Contents

INTRODUCTION

Baby Boomers are shocked that the future keeps showing up faster and faster! Time doesn't just fly; it seems rocket-propelled. Just the day before yesterday we were young and today we are incomprehensibly called "seniors" moving quickly through the 4th quarter of our lives. Incredible!

What you will find in these pages is an engaging and informative look about the 4th quarter of life. It is a glimpse of what is coming up around the corner filled with insights, humor, reality, truth, wisdom, and the occasional profundities that will make you think, wonder, smile, pause, and genuinely reflect upon your life.

It is important for "boomers" (and others) to take stock of where we are on the journey of life by contemplating and reviewing the G.P.S. map of our life. The 4th quarter of life can be great with some wise planning, a little luck, and a clear path of where you want to go and what you want to do.

An alternative approach to reading this book is to browse through the table of contents and skip around to personally relevant chapters that speak to you. The book is not necessarily linear and each chapter is self-contained. Presently, perhaps only two-thirds of this book may apply to you in some way and the good news is the chapters are short and a quick read, even if left in the bathroom. But without question, other chapters certainly apply to someone near and dear to you whether it be a relative, neighbor, friend, or colleague. Consider ordering them a book copy as a personal gift to help illuminate their life journey. As your life evolves, other chapters will become more relevant and have greater personal significance to you. The opportunity to come back and consider all your options and life strategies will be worthwhile as a review.

This book is a wonderful opportunity to share with others over a potluck dinner or as a book discussion on the meaning of a truly "successful" life and what is of real importance. Some people go through life as the driver behind the wheel while others are just bystanders on the side of the road wondering what the heck is happening and where the heck they are going. Include younger generations in the debate as well to help give them more clarity and direction for their future. The goal is to inform each life to make it the best it can be. Carpe Diem. Best wishes for a good trip.

Michael Lee

MAMMA MIA!

A middle-aged couple are sharing a restaurant meal when the husband starts shaking his head and says to his wife, "Wow, see those two old geezers over there? That's what we're gonna look like ten years from now." The wife, with a pained look on her face, says, "Honey, that's a mirror!"

Sixty! Sixty-ish! Wow! The alien landscape of the sixties. For Baby Boomers, it is viewed with awe and sheer amazement. For most Boomers "the sixties" are a flashback conjuring up images of long hair, mini-skirts, rock and roll, protest marches, the Cold War, the counter-culture, landing on the moon, and perceiving themselves as being forever young, full of promise and possibilities to change the world. Being sixty-ish is a whole different dynamic. Such a number rolls off your tongue not so much in celebration but in disbelief. You repeat it to yourself in your head thinking that such a number cannot conceivably apply to yourself. You knew it was coming, but now that it has arrived, you still have a hard time wrapping your head around it. This is a number that you ascribed to your parents and not that long ago to your grandparents. If you are female, you would like to change the subject. If male, you just shake your head in surprise. But you quickly snap to attention with a grin on your face to hear friendly voices of family and friends singing to you with fervor and gusto their off-key rendition of Happy Birthday.

As night follows day, they proceed with jokes that your cake looks like a forest fire of candles and someone snarkily asks if they should call the fire department as a precaution. Young children, if present, are pressed into service to assist your suspected wind power and are eager to oblige in blowing out the candles before the wax melts into the frosting.

More jokes and gags abound about getting you a cane or a rocking chair. The ribbing continues with the inevitable light-hearted comments on various themes of being put out to pasture. It is all part of the ritual scene. Birthday cards in the same vein circulate around the room along with the concurrent hee-haws and hoots of laughter all at your expense. It is all genial fun and games as token presents are offered ranging from bemused sexual aids, thick spectacles, and blue-light luncheons at the local diner. It is, in its own strange way, like the beginning of your last year of high school or college whereby you are officially qualified, promoted, and bestowed with your new title of, "senior." Ruefully, you wince inwardly to yourself and hope "graduation" is decades away.

Trying to come to terms with this new milestone in your life is going to require some psychological heavy-lifting and mental gymnastics. Your first observation is, "Mamma Mia, how did I get here so fast! Where the heck did the time go?" Your second observation is that it all seems so surreal, that this can't really be happening to you. You reflect back and remember the adult milestones of turning 30, 40, and 50. You ruminate that every decade milestone did seem to be more condensed in time, each one showing up quicker than the one before it. It seems a hop, skip, and a jump and boom—sixty-ish is here. When it comes to aging, no younger person can truly understand it, and no older person can truly believe it! Yet, somehow sixty-ish seems qualitatively different than those previous signposts on life's journey. You have a private talk with yourself and promise not to fret about it since there is nothing you can do about it anyway. That little voice in your head tells you to accept it, don't dwell on it, and move on. Quite imperceptibly, often on a sub-conscious level, you rationalize your new numerical status by trying to make yourself feel a little more sanguine about what has just occurred. All the old chestnuts come to the fore. "You're only as old as you feel." "Age is just a number." "Think young, act young." "Sixty-ish is the new 50–or maybe even a delusional 45." You comfort yourself by trying to assure yourself the regular rules of aging apply to others, but not to yourself.

Of course, this new milestone happens differently for different folks. The same reaction is not universal by any means but can cover the entire gamut of emotions from A to Z. Most just take it in stride. No muss, no fuss. It is just another day along life's path. For others, denial, regrets, and foreboding cloud one's horizon. Still others express optimism over the possibilities entering the last quarter of life because they still have big plans with lesser responsibilities. Much is rooted in personality and one's outlook on life and how they feel about their health, finances, and relationships. Yes, a lot of life has been lived, and there is a lot of water under the bridge, but the one shared truth of all members in this new cohort is absolute stunned surprise by how fast the sixties showed up. The whole concept of "life is short" hits home with new meaning like it never did before.

2

FAILING AT RETIREMENT?

*"I get up in the morning with nothing to do and go to bed at night
with only half of it done."*

The lament of a retiree

Failing at retirement? What a joke! This is a trick question,
right? Of course, it seems almost comical to even ask the
question, "how can you fail at retirement," but millions do all
the time. They "take a knee" in the fourth quarter of life and
run out the clock even though there are more good years to
play in the game of life. It is like one of those business maxims
about goal setting that "those who fail to plan, plan to fail."

Here is the upside-down way society looks at retirement.
The traditional view is that you retire *"from"* something rather
than transitioning *"to"* something. It is all the difference in the
world. The popularized and fuzzy view of retirement is that
you are leaving the rat race to "take it easy" by going on a
journey to a strange land. Perhaps the greatest irony of all is
the legendary "gold watch" parting gift in earlier times. The

watch may be unintended commentary since it could be construed in one sense as measuring the little time you have remaining. Today a trendy "smart watch" or fancy cell phone may be the more appropriate and relevant gift of choice, but the wired ubiquity of Internet time is even more pronounced. The world is at your fingertips, but time is still limited.

The common picture of a retiree is taking up a hobby, playing games with friends, leisurely lunches, hanging out with young grandkids, reading the paper, watching TV in a comfy recliner, surfing the Web, and taking the dog for a daily walk. Sprinkle in a long-planned cruise, a foreign trip abroad, or to crisscross America in an RV, and that pretty much sums it up. End of story, fade to black. And this is where a lack of planning trips up so many people. These are the discussions all boomers should be having among themselves before they burn the bridge and make the decision to retire. What are you retiring to? What do you really want out of the Final Act of your own life play? Have you really thought this through?

Of course, there is no right or wrong way to go about it, just your feelings and wishes to consider for a life-changing chapter in your life. But there should be no regrets. So before taking the plunge and handing in your retirement notice to your boss or the head office, it is wise to review a little strategic planning. While many do some planning, others end up more often with an ill-defined "off the cuff" collection of things they believe retirement will bring and an informal feeling of "I'll make it up as I go" process. It is like driving in a strange city without modern GPS or even an old-fashioned fold-up map stuffed in the glove box. It is easier to get lost and go in circles. A little planning can go a long way.

The future is important. It is the place where you will spend the rest of your life.

3

YES! TIME REALLY DOES FLY!

Why did the moron throw the clock out the window?
He wanted to see if time could fly!

There is a proverbial story about a king of days gone by who called all his wise men into his counsel chamber. He asked them to consider the totality of mankind's existence and to come up with a phrase that would stand the test of time and be true in all circumstances for all people for all time. The wise men protested vehemently that such a request was impossible to fulfill. The king ignored the wise men's protests and gave them seven days to report back to him or he would revoke their special status and all privileges in his court. The worried wise men huddled and muddled for days nervously contemplating what to tell the king. At the end of the seven days the King called them to his chamber and asked them if they had been successful. Their spokesman replied in the affirmative. So the king asked of the assembled group, "What say ye?" The spokesman replied, "Oh great King, these are the words that are true for all time ... 'And this too shall pass.'"

Scientists, clergyman, philosophers, and the average person struggle to comprehend the mysteries of time and space. From religious concepts of "eternal life" to the evolutionary study of the "big bang theory" (what came before?) the idea of time is a most elusive concept to understand. Our known "time" only goes back about 5,000 years of the written record. Pre-history, dating before any human records existed, passes on to a geologic time frame of the earth's distant past. Cosmic time dealing with black holes, string theory, multiple dimensions, and quantum and theoretical science bend our minds into pretzels but still intrigue and mystify us at the same time. Even the most brilliant minds among us have a thousand more questions than answers in such research. But we pedestrian mortals on earth calculate time based on the rising and the setting of the sun for our days and earth's revolution around the sun to make up our "year."

A human who lives to 80 gets 80 years, or 960 months, or 29,200 days, or 700,800 hours, or 42,048,000 minutes of life. Those who go into "overtime" do get some extra bonus time, hopefully quality bonus time, before their clock runs out. What an individual does with this time in essence makes up a life story. And mankind is riveted and fascinated by stories. Cavemen depicted them on walls, children ask for them at bedtime, and television is built upon them from situation comedies to gripping dramas to who-dun-it murder mysteries. Books tell stories about individuals, the fate of nations, and the rise and fall of dynasties and civilizations. We create fictional stories out of our imagination, some fantastical and other worldly.

However, a story has a beginning, a middle, and an ending that is always anchored in time. We, too, have a story to tell of our life and times, brief as it may be. Even the word "history" (his-story—and her-story) is just a descriptive story of mankind's past adventures, follies, struggles, and accomplishments over time.

Time for humans is an interesting touchstone for our lives. We can use it, abuse it, waste it, kill it, and even wait on it. In military terms, soldiers are told to "hurry up and wait." We are often reminded that time heals all wounds, to give time for things to work out, that nothing happens before its time, in due time, in God's time, or even that you are out of time. We are told that in time you will get over it, feel better, forget it, or see things in a new light. Older folks reminisce about "special" times or impart stories of the "time of their life." We are even frequently reminded that "time is money." Yet, try as we may, we cannot ignore time. We talk about the "moments" of our lives; we catalogue them as they race by; birthdays, graduations, weddings, holidays, and special events. We try and capture it like an elusive butterfly that is here and then, poof, it is gone.

Time moves on silently, remorselessly, showing no favor to anyone. Rich and poor are subject to its democratic nature of giving everyone the same hours and minutes to each twenty-four-hour-day. Deadlines for business work projects are really all about a race against time. We constantly complain that we do not have "enough time" for work, chores, or pleasure. Only in sports is there a fictitious thing such as a "time out," which is in reality only a delay of the game.

Timelines of nations, events, or famous lives are really just time maps laying out a storyline on a storyboard. Even a bygone commercial admonition to capture a "Kodak moment" is just a human attempt to snatch a second in time and freeze it in amber for posterity. Today, the ubiquity of cell phone camera's and "GoPro" technology with thousands and thousands of captured images and countless hours of video footage means we need another lifetime just to review what we have recorded.

Then there is the perception of human scale time. As we age, people at all stages of life remark on the passage of time and how surprised they are by it. Looking back in nostalgia upon the 8 years of high school and college now looks to most of us like a couple of blips on our life's radar screen. For parents, few things in life give one pause as much as seeing how fast your children grew from baby to toddler to kindergarten, to turning around twice and packing for college and out the front door with a hug and a reminder to drive safely. What happened? Distant family or friends who get together only intermittently over the years always remark, "Wow, your kids have gotten so big since the last time I saw them." It is almost a stock phrase. Yet, when one is in the middle of life and living the day to day experience, the individual chapters of life are less perceptible as the daily present commands our full attention.

Yes, time is constant for us mortals on earth. It drones on - - tick-tock, tick-tock. An hourglass sifts the grains of sand through its tight bottleneck at the same rate. Yet, it is fascinating to watch people watching an hourglass. If it has just started, people will quickly lose interest and move on. But if it is near the end, people will hang around and linger. They are mesmerized as the last trickles of sand seemingly rush pell-mell from the top to the bottom of the glass. It just "seems" that merely observing the last "sands of time" go through the hourglass that they move quicker than before. At the beginning, it seemed more leisurely, more measured, as in "there's a lot more sand where that came from." But toward the end the grains of sand seem to dash through on an urgent mission to pick up the pace and end the process quickly. Of course, this is all our perception, but perception is often reality. For if we see it, think it, believe it, it is our own reality, and it becomes our own truth. The real truth becomes largely irrelevant. So, time really does go faster, at least in our minds. In the same manner as the hourglass, the perception of time, as it relates to our life, appears to rush forward at an accelerated pace.

Perhaps more so than previous generations, boomers, as part of the "forever young" generation, have been genuinely taken by surprise that there is not more sand in the hourglass.

4

THE FOURTH QUARTER (OF LIFE)

GAME OF LIFE				
1st Q	2nd Q	3rd Q	4th Q	OVER TIME
0-20 years	20-40 years	40-60 years	60-80 years	80+ years
☻ Played	☻ Played	☻ Played	☺ IN PLAY	☺ ?

The most exciting quarter in the game of life? Rah! Rah!

Life is like a football game that is divided into four distinct quarters and played against an unforgiving clock. When the gun goes off at the end of the game, it is game over save for those few occasions when the score is tied and "overtime" is allowed to settle the matter. Likewise, life itself from the moment of birth is played against a relentless clock. Unfortunately, not everyone gets the same clock. A few will barely get into the game at all while others are tragically given only a quarter or two. Yet, most people will get to play nearly the whole four quarters, and a few will even get some extra overtime in the game of life, but there are no guarantees. In this game, famous star players and ordinary, no-name teammates alike, can be carried off the field of life at any time.

People in the 60-80 age bracket are what we will call fourth-quarter people. The first three quarters in the game of life (0-20, 20-40, and 40-60) have different game plans. The focus and sense of strategy in the first couple of quarters are designed to get ahead in life as much as possible. But fourth-quarter people (60-80) start to notice a change in their mindsets and outlook on life much as autumn leaves and falling temperatures signal a change of seasons. The days are still mostly bright, and there is a fresh crispness in the air. It can be invigorating after a lovely spring and a long, hot, and busy summer. However, looking at one's face in the mirror, one may notice that while winter has not fully arrived, the signs are everywhere that it is quickly on its way.

The spring days of baseball season characterized in our early life are definitely over with its languid "innings" of unknown durations when time was on our side. We recall fond memories of days gone by, even if they are selectively remembered. But life is rougher and more akin to football, a serious rough-and-tumble business played on an unforgiving field with its triumphal advances and difficult setbacks. The game of life is filled with fighting in the daily "trenches" of life between work, family, goals, and dreams. It requires fortitude to persevere regardless of the blitzes, blocks, bombs, and attempted sacks of what life constantly throws at you. And all of this is played out against our ever-present and unrelenting life clock. Tick-tock. Tick-tock.

At birth, there is no standard one-size-fits-all formal script for a meaningful life. There may be millions of game plans at the start, but certain rules and patterns are in play. Gender, family, nationality, race, income, religion, health, parental education, and economic conditions are all relevant factors that hinder or smooth one's journey in life. Inequality and unfairness can be overcome, but it is like a football game in which a lesser-gifted player must work several times harder than a gifted or lucky-star player to make the team and work even harder to stay on the team. Lots of extra effort is required to be competitive in life.

As your own life coach, it is vitally necessary to review your own current situation in your fourth quarter after the first three quarters of your life have already been played. While the game is still in progress, you are constantly assessing the flow of the game of life and may need to make adjustments as conditions warrant. Bad breaks and lucky opportunities happen unexpectedly in life and must be fixed or capitalized upon as quickly as possible.

Perhaps your life plan has been one of too much caution, and you have been playing too defensively in order not to make any big mistakes. It may dawn on you that perhaps, in your case, you are playing to avoid losing in life rather than to win, by pursuing a boring and uninspired game strategy by being stuck in a comfortable rut. New strategy may demand a push forward with a positive life plan to finish your fourth quarter of life that will be both meaningful and satisfying. You begin to realize that if you do not make some changes right away, the clock will take over and begin to dictate to you, greatly limiting your options.

This is the biggest difference in the fourth quarter compared to the first three quarters of life in the big game. Before, there was always time, or so it seemed, to pull the rabbit out of the hat, change course in the game of life, make new plans, rebuild a career, or embark on a new life. Some of these goals can still be accomplished in the fourth quarter, but it is harder because of the clock and there is little time to lose. The game of life is still in progress, and if you let up too much, it may slip away from you. No one wants to go out in a whimper. In sports, losing a game to a great rival is tough enough to swallow when an unforeseen injury or an opponent's lucky play occurs, but the real heartbreak in life comes when one loses not by unique challenges faced in life, but by losing through inaction, bad judgment, poor play, or no planning at all. Ouch!

5

BABY BOOM TSUNAMI: 10,000 A DAY!

"I have been impressed with the urgency of doing. Knowing is not enough; we must apply. Being willing is not enough, we must do."

Leonardo Da Vinci

The "baby boomers" born between 1946 and 1964 are like the python snake that swallowed whole a fat pig that is slowly moving its way through its digestive track. This is an apt description of the post-World War II generation. However, there are two parts to this group. The first are the early boomers who came of age in the 1960's as part of the Vietnam and Civil Rights experience. The second group are the late boomers of the 1970's Nixon Watergate era, along with gas lines and high inflation.

The crash in birthrates due to the Great Depression of the 1930's was caused by uncertain economic times followed by World War II in the 40's that caused millions of men to be away from wives and family. After the war, couples made up for lost time with a fertility explosion. With an economic boom in full-swing with plentiful jobs and opportunities, the subsequent baby boom was on. The impact of enormous, pent-up demand for housing, jobs, cars, appliances, and more "stuff" of every kind powered America into a golden-age of consumerism. Like our mythical python, boomers through the 1950s, '60s, and '70s would work their way through massive building booms for elementary schools followed by high schools and the fast expansion of colleges and universities to educate this enormous wave of young people. Shopping malls, television, and the interstate highway network tied everything together. In international and domestic affairs, despite turbulent and troubling times; America was still the superpower of the day by a mile. This was true despite very real fretting in seeing a Russian communist behind every tree and under every bed.

Today, the boomers are moving into their sixties at the rate of over 10,000 a day.[1] That is not a typo. 10,000 a day are becoming part of the "senior set," 365 days a year, the equivalent of Miami or Pittsburgh (proper) every month! In just one year that is more people than the population of twenty states! By 2022 their totals will rival the population of California, the largest state in the Union or approach that of New York and Florida combined! The first boomers to hit 65 did so in 2011, and the last of this cohort will be finishing up in 2029, with the mid-point rapidly approaching in 2020.

At over seventy-five million strong, boomers will dominate almost everything as they have from the days they were born. Health care, Social Security, pensions, taxes, you name it; boomers will have their fingers in every pie. Healthier, wealthier, and more educated than any other previous generation in American history, they will control the national discussion for the next couple decades. Because the post-60 crowd has more money, property, and investments than any other group behind them, they naturally have a strong personal stake in wanting to protect what they have. Once retired, retirees feel more vulnerable and cannot make any financial mistakes because they have no time to make up for lost time.

A sizable chunk of this cohort, like all those who have come before, can also be self-absorbed, cranky, obstructionist, and narrow-minded on many issues. The world is changing rapidly, and many seniors generally resist it. They become more conservative both with a small and capital C. Changing social mores and standards of conduct along with generational change and the threat of potential terrorism are unnerving which is all compounded by social media. People like what is familiar and get anxious by too much change too fast. Yet, boomers are also largely educated or skilled and are not Luddites.[2] Like their younger counterparts, they too are often enthusiastic about new techie gadgets and science breakthroughs. Rather, it is the pace and rapidity of change all around them that alarms an older crowd.

If the speed of the 19th century could be characterized by addition and the 20th century by multiplication, the 21st century is destined to be ruled by exponents. And few of us liked algebra anyway. But that is how fast the world is moving. In one lifetime, things have moved from instant coffee to instant everything. No one wishes to be left behind, and seniors tend to object to things they do not understand or that are out of their comfort zone. It is unnerving that a 12-year-old grandchild or wet-behind-the-ears young next-door neighbor is needed when it comes to helping with the latest computer issue or gadget at home. Any electronic device received as a birthday gift is seemingly obsolete before your next birthday.

Often, the word conservative means to keep things the way they are at present or even to go back to the way things used to be in an earlier era. There is always a desire for the simple over the complex, for the assurances and rhythms of the past over the promises of a hazy and fast-paced future. The follow-on generations, the so-named X, Y, (Millennial) and Z generations,[3] will have a tough time getting their fair share of the national pie from the crafty and well-connected boomers. Seniors vote!

Boomers will redefine retirement like they have everything else before them. Indeed, they firmly believe in an active retirement. "Go, see, do," could easily be their motto. They have moxie and attitude and are convinced that the time to "take it easy" is in their 90's. Many of them are also convinced they will be among the divine chosen ones to get there, come hell or high water, despite the lopsided odds. The phrase "Youth must be served" will be turned on its head as society caters to the "seniors" because they have the time, the votes, the money, and the influence. For a young person starting out today, a medical career in gerontology may be a good vocational move that will offer excellent job security with no possibility of being laid off.

Boomers reflect back on the 1960's when the slogan "don't trust anyone over thirty" was a trendy phrase and laugh at it today, chalking up such arrogance to the impetuousness of youth. Boomers today may feel more inclined to a new talking point of "don't trust anyone UNDER sixty!"

6

HOW LONG HAVE I GOT?
THE LONGEVITY PUZZLE

A ten-year-old boy sits at the edge of the doctor's examining table after being routinely checked with the doctor's stethoscope. The boy crosses his arms and stares at the doctor with a penetrating look as he earnestly asks. "Give it to me straight, Doc. I am a big boy, and I can handle it. How much time have I got left... seventy, eighty years?"

How long I will live is one of the great mysteries of life. No one knows, of course, and while it is something we are all aware of, we mostly keep our concern about it in a bottom drawer in a dusty closet in the back of our head. Yet, we are often surprised when we hear on the news of some prominent person of note in sports, government, or entertainment who is struck down by disease or sudden accident early in life. As we age into the fourth quarter of life, we are even alarmed to hear of the passing of people in their sixties or even early seventies (how relatively young we think!) that still seems like a tragedy to us. Even more so for people we know personally that have touched our lives.

Back in the 1950's and 60's an iconic police show, Dragnet, starred a no-nonsense and charismatically-challenged Sergeant Joe Friday who became a cultural touchstone. Recall Sgt. Friday's deadpan persona and dry delivery which has been parodied and adapted in the popular culture ever since over the following decades. His most famous, cut-to-the-chase signature line "just the facts, Ma'am" has become part of the American lexicon. So, in the same spirit as Joe Friday, let's take a quick deep-dive look at the numbers.

One of the greatest misunderstood statistics presented to the public is the concept of longevity or life expectancy. It is routinely misinterpreted by many reporters, academics, and politicians who are math-challenged, or who simply fail to clarify things. Context is very important. Simply put, most of these reports base their longevity numbers on a child born today and compare them to a child born in the distant past, leaving the impression that we are living decades longer than those poor, unfortunate souls who lived in the pre-modern world. While this is true in one sense, it greatly distorts the big picture by confusing average ages of death due to one major factor. The very large rate of childhood mortality in past generations greatly skews the picture.

Child deaths due to accidents, infectious diseases, and childbirth were extremely high when compared to today. The U.S. government of Health and Human Services shows that children aged 5-14 in 1907 died at twenty times the rate they did a century later in 2007 while those aged 1-4 died at a rate just shy of fifty times greater.[4] The lack of vaccines and antibiotics alone, not to mention other simple precautions of hygiene, malnourishment, infection, and timely access to medical care caused an affliction of death in nearly every extended household at one time or another. It is these childhood mortality numbers that give statistics a false sense of relationship when comparing the past and present.

To put this in basic terms consider that if a baby died in its first year of life and another baby lived to be 90, the average lifespan would be 45. But this does not mean that in the general public people who were in the 45-age-range were dropping like flies and planning funerals. Not at all! When longevity is considered in light of one's age as an adult, the numbers and impressions change dramatically. Surviving your childhood was a big deal and made a huge difference. We do live longer than previous generations, but excepting for childhood deaths, we live only years longer, not many decades. For example, the increase in life expectancy at birth in 1900 was 49 years while in 1950 this increased to 70 years (all numbers rounded).[5] Nearly all of these huge gains were due to a great decline in child mortality through improved medicine, hygiene, and drugs.

Today a child at birth is expected to almost make it to the age of 79, (all numbers rounded) with females doing better than males.[6] But a white male who lived to age 60 in 1900 could look forward to living about 14 years more on average compared to today where the average is closer to 21.5 years, the differential being an extension of life of 7.5 years while women would see about 10.5 years' extension of life.[7] Ironically, in light of today's medicine, even the biblical account promises "three score and ten" (70 years) and eighty years if you are strong. (Psalms 90:10)

Of course, any personal view of longevity averages can be influenced by gender, weight, genetics, race, socio-economic status, and lifestyles. Personal choices made about smoking, drinking, and eating habits can greatly affect your numbers either on the upside or the downside. There are many websites on the Internet that can act "as your bookie" [8] and give you personalized odds by plugging in your health data profile to get a more complete picture of your life expectancy from your current age.

Because Social Security tables are based on the standard age of 65 and nearly everyone considers this to be more or less the standard age of retirement, let's consider how the odds stack up at 65. One needs to reset their "life clock" to zero in determining life expectancy from this point forward. Already, for those who have reached this milestone they have lost roughly 20% of their birth cohort, about 24% for men and 16% for women.[9] (Note: If you are at the higher end of the socio-economic scale you will have lost less contemporaries than those nearer the bottom. The difference is largely attributable to health habits, family history, lifestyle, and education.) Amazingly, for a child born in the 21st century these numbers of lost contemporaries are projected to drop by half this amount[10] when they reach their sixties due to technology, advanced medicine, and a better informed society.

Using the mid-20th century (birth) base year of 1950 as an example, a contemporary 65-year-old man can look forward to live on average to 84.3 years while a 65-year-old woman is projected to live to 86.6 years.[11]

About one out of four 65-year-olds will live past 90 (mostly the ladies) and one out of ten will live past 95.[12] The not so good news is looking at these numbers upside down. Half of this cohort of 65-year-old people will fail to even make the "average" numbers just mentioned, and 75% of this group will be gone before age 90, and 90% will be gone before age 95.[13] Perspective!

We are all adults here, and these statistics are not designed to bum you out. Not at all. Rather, the purpose is to inform your life as each one plans for their fourth quarter of life and hopefully beyond. Knowledge is power and it is important to know the score. Optimism should motivate each one of us to treasure the gift of life and make the most of it.

Unfortunately, there is one more joker in the deck that further colors the numbers just mentioned and that is not our life expectancy but something that is even more important, our healthspan expectancy. Because breathing (fogging a mirror) and living independently are two different things, it is important to recognize that the above longevity numbers need to be trimmed down accordingly. While 90-year-old Boomer A dies peacefully in their sleep or from a heart attack on the golf course, Boomer B has a three-year battle with cancer while Boomer C may have a ten-year struggle with Alzheimer's disease. The law of averages must be acknowledged and adjusted accordingly. Likewise, those suffering with severe diabetes, pronounced obesity, or other significant maladies will be impacted with a greatly reduced healthspan[14] and a significantly compromised quality of life.

Have you ever heard anyone express this sentiment? "I ain't so much afraid of the dead part; it's the dying part that scares me to death." Yes, a prolonged and painful health condition frightens everyone. A person who dies at 90 with the last five years confined to a room with severe dementia along with a host of physical woes is a future no one wishes for themselves. Though an individual's death certificate says they died at 90, in reality we all know death really occurred at 85 when mental and physical limitations took away their life by any objective measure. Of course, there is a difference between being physically "challenged" and being mentally "out of it." Physical limitations are feared, but if one still retains their mental faculties and good humor, with some adaptation, life can still be enjoyed and shared with family and friends.

So, what are our odds when we consider our healthspan vs. our life expectancy? Only God knows the odds since they are tough to pin down, being highly subjective depending on one's mental and physical conditions that can suddenly change.[15] There are lots of variables to consider. But we do know our healthspan "average" is a distinct calculation from our lifespan and an adjustment downward from longevity for some individuals must be made to reflect this reality. This is real life.

Some try to quantify life quality based on assistance with ADL's (activities of daily living) that are mostly centered around mobility like walking and bathing or IADL's (Instrumental-ADL's)[16] that require help with finances, cooking, shopping, etc. But we do know that, on average, for some of us, years will need to be subtracted from life expectancy to ascertain one's healthspan numbers the older we become. For example, it is estimated that nearly half of boomers will experience mild to severe mental Alzheimer's impairment if they live past the age of 85.[17] Significant risk factors, in addition to genetics, are poor vascular heart health due to physical inactivity, obesity, smoking and high blood pressure.[18] So your chronological age at death vs. your "health age" of cognitive and mobile ability while alive may be quite different. A special few who go deep into overtime will see age 100 relatively fit and sharp as a fiddle. Others may not be so lucky. Everyone's healthspan longevity factor is a more accurate reflection of what our concept of living really is. It is not just how long you live, but how well (and feeling well) you live. And it is our healthspan that should be the primary focus for every one of us.

7

NUMBERS DON'T LIE–
OR DO THEY JUST SEEM TO?

"There are three kinds of lies: lies, damn lies, and statistics."

Mark Twain

So now comes the fascinating representation in explanatory fashion to prove that time really does "fly" as we age. This will be an "ah-ha" moment whereby many will say to themselves, "interesting, now I get it." Of course, in reality, time does stay constant for us earthlings here on terra-firma during our lifetime, but our perception of it is directly affected to how much life we have lived. It is this ratio that becomes our key reference guide and our own judgment of reality. It is central to our concept of time that is constantly shifting with each passing year.

Since it is true that everything is relative, meaning what it is compared to, start out by trying to recall anything about your childhood when you were four years old. Not a lot, I am sure, but then you were only four. A year represented 1/4 of your life. Remember if a parent told you to wait for something you wanted until Christmas or your birthday and how disappointed you were? To wait that long would be agony and seem like a millennium, even though you had no clue what a millennium, much less a year, was all about?

Next up, you are eight years old. Yes, time remains constant, but a year now represents 1/8 of your life. In relative terms a year now went by twice as fast as when you were four as it represents a smaller fraction of your time on earth when compared to your earlier age. Remember in elementary school when you were told about getting out of school for summer vacation that seemed it would "never" arrive? Moving on to age 16 and despite the treacherous high-school years and being a teen-ager, your perceived idea of a year is now 1/16 of your life. Life is already speeding up. Fast forward to age 32. Your high school and college years are already receding in your mind and are being tightly compressed into hazy and selective nostalgia. Work, money, family, house, and getting firmly established dominate your existence. Now, at 32 a year is only 1/32 of your life. Again, time is constant, but in your perception relative to your age, a year at 32 just flew by twice as fast as it did when you were 16 and four times as fast as when you were 8. Wow, hang on to your hat, for the ride is moving really fast.

Now, consider age 64. A year represents only 1/64 of your life. The years fly by so fast now that you can't remember one distinct Christmas or birthday from another over the last twenty-five years if your life depended upon it unless something really extraordinary happened. Sports nuts who knew every arcane facet of a particular sport when they were younger in their teens, 20's, or even early 30's were like walking encyclopedias (remember them?). But asking the same 64-year old sports addict today who won the Super Bowl or World Series 5, 10, or 15 years ago more often than not draws a blank stare and a befuddled look. So here we are looking at 64, and our "perception of time" has doubled since we were 32 and quadrupled since we were 16, not to mention the 8-fold advance since we were eight years old, which does seem a long, long time ago.

To put all this into perspective, a year at 64 is really six months long when compared to 32, and a mere three months compared to when you were 16. (You can entertain and intrigue friends by telling them that time does "relatively" speed up by taking a piece of paper and drawing a circle followed by drawing two lines dividing the circle into four equal parts. Then add more lines at each life stage dividing the circle into 1/8, 1/16, 1/32, and 1/64 parts representing each doubling of your age in life–see following graph). Is it any wonder that the holidays, the birthdays, and the anniversaries SEEM to whiz by and are coming around faster than ever before? Didn't we just celebrate the holidays and New Year's several months ago, or so it seems. This is the standard observation of all seniors who exclaim with increasing regularity; "where does the time go." And it also expresses their frustration with the younger generation (from the dawn of time) for any perceived idleness, frivolity, and lack of sufficient purpose, ambition, focus, or questionable work or study ethic. Hence the proverbial, "Youth is wasted on the young."

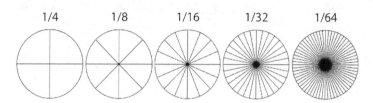

1/4   1/8   1/16   1/32   1/64

8

THE GOOD NEWS

An optimist jumps out of bed in the morning and chirps, "Good morning, God!" The pessimist rolls over in bed and moans, "Good God, it's morning!"

Like any good game of football or basketball, the fourth quarter is often the most exciting quarter of the whole game. Life after sixty can also be the most exciting and important part of one's life as well. This may sound delusional for some or like a mind game for others but true nonetheless. In sports, the first three quarters have seen ups and downs, ebb and flow, thrills and spills, amazing plays, dumb plays, lucky plays, and a see-saw score constantly changing on the scoreboard. As the commercial time-out has been taken and the fourth quarter is about to get under way, worry, doubt, and expectations for both players and fans becomes more palpable. This is crunch time. Things are really serious now as the clock keeps ticking.

The last quarter of the game just has an entirely different flavor and feeling to the game. A new urgency takes hold. Like a poker game with a big pot of money on the table, the fourth quarter concentrates the mind. A renewed focus and determination and eyes on the prize is what is now required for you to be at your best. It is, in many ways, as if the first three quarters of the game of life were yesterday's newspaper. It is old news. History!

Regardless of how the game turns out and the final score, the fourth-quarter ending is often what people remember and what sticks mostly in their mind. The next few days after the big game, time is spent discussing the players, the smart strategy, the "key" play, the gutsy call, the blocked ball or broken-up pass, the "bad call" by the ref, the amazing can-you-believe-it play, which is all magnified exponentially because it was the fourth quarter, and the game was still in doubt and on the line. Win or lose, it was a thrilling game packed with emotion, adrenaline, prayers, superstition, and passion. Likewise, so too should be the lives of fourth-quarter people in the game of life.

The good news about being sixty-ish is that for most of those already in or entering the last quarter of life it presents many new possibilities. Yes, some are constrained by health, finances, or family setbacks as each walk in life is different. But for the majority who have made it to the fourth quarter, there is positive news that should be viewed with appreciation and perspective.

First however, everyone should take a few respectful moments remembering those loved ones, friends, or colleagues lost over the years that did not make it to their fourth quarter. One should not complain too much about getting older: many others didn't get to have that privilege. Gratitude is in order. Consider all the famous people who never saw a fourth quarter. Abraham Lincoln, John Kennedy,

Martin Luther King, Elvis Presley, Steve Jobs are just a few random names among thousands. An entire book of notable and recognizable names could be filled who were denied a fourth quarter of life.

Next, let's recall our parents, grandparents, and even those who remember their great-grand-parents. With few exceptions, these previous generations "seemed" old. Even discounting our perceived bias and distorted view from our younger selves, things are just different today. Back then almost all "white collar" men wore formal suits and ties. Blue-collar workers also dressed up outside of work, putting their "Sunday Best" foot forward. Today, Grandpa is just as likely to be wearing jeans and a T-shirt and may be found at the gym, not rocking on a porch.

The Depression and World War II Greatest Generation[19] always had an air about them that seemed older, more formal, stable, responsible, and perhaps a touch boring in their grown-up way of approaching life. Most likely the life-changing experiences and challenges of the Depression and WW II made them grow up faster, mature quicker, and take life much more seriously. Nobody coddled them. Furthermore, much of the work force of yesteryear required more physical labor in the agricultural, industrial, and manufacturing sectors of the economy, which, over time, takes its physical toll. Life was harder.

Despite the obesity problem of today, people of the past smoked in much larger numbers, rarely exercised outside of work and ate foods high in fat. At the same time, they did not have the amazing options offered by modern medicine and drugs so common nowadays. So we are indeed more fortunate when we consider our situation in light of those who have gone on before us. We should all be thankful.

In TV-land, Prime Time[20] is the sweet spot for network and cable executives for television audiences. The evening audiences are the largest of the day because that is when most people are at home, and the war of attracting eyeballs, and therefore selling lucrative commercials, begins in earnest. But in the ordinary lives of most human beings we think of prime time as when we are at the presumed heights of our powers in looks, achievement, vitality, energy, and most of all, possibilities. And if most people could go back in time, they invariably choose the age range of 25-50 as their prime time. Of course, many peoples' greatest successes take place after this, but this is where most adults place the prime-time label.

But do not be dismayed, for if prime time falls in this category, the post-sixty, fourth-quarter crowd should be considered like a "special guest" on television. Generally, a seasoned and well-known performer will attract a following to help goose the ratings. As a "senior," you can be seen as taking this time to run your own "specials" show with dramatic plot twists. Indeed, some of your best material is now being written, produced, and directed by you. So ---break a leg–on the stage of your own life.

9

NEVER TOO LATE:
SHOULD'VE-WOULD'VE-COULD'VE

Fall down seven times; get up eight.

Japanese proverb

You can still do anything you want! Okay, this is a partial lie for fourth-quarter people. For women, it is too late to become the drop-dead, 25-year old, top magazine cover model. For guys, it is too late to become a professional athlete. Yet for most everything else the idea that you can still catch the boat before it sails is mostly true. Age is not always a handicap, and in many instances a decided advantage, despite some biases among younger people. Experience, self-discipline, and insight are all traits that should be acquired as a young person although some people never do and are stunted in their development. These traits must be honed and refined to establish an edge over the competition, and even more critically, over one's self.

It is like the revealing story of a teacher, who, when asked by a parent how much experience they had in the classroom, responded with pride and a smug smile that she had spent over 30 years in the teaching profession. Another teacher, however, upon overhearing the conversation, later told the parent in private a different story. The teacher in question had only one year of experience repeated 30 times, just basically going through the same repetitive motions year after year. It brought to light the fact that this teacher showed no growth in her career and in essence was no better than a rookie teacher. On the other hand, older individuals with a good number of miles on their lives' odometers, who have embraced lifelong learning habits, are critically valuable assets. Not only to any particular business, profession, or organization, but to themselves as well.

A practiced and wily old pro can outfox a new rookie every time. Making a "rookie mistake" is nearly universally expected as part of the learning process. The key for seniors is to never stop learning and growing in knowledge and wisdom. While time may be a factor in one's plans, it can also refocus and redouble one's efforts to accomplish a goal or a dream. Carpe Diem - seize the day - cannot be emphasized enough. Too often, the biggest stumbling block is our self. Paralyzed by doubt, fear of failure, and hobbled by procrastination, far too many let their dreams slip away like water dripping through their hands.

So how do we get off the dime to make our move? First, we must do a rigorous and honest self-assessment of our own strengths and weaknesses. It is essential to get out paper and pen and literally write them down in two columns. This should not be a mental exercise in your head but really putting pen to paper so you can see it in black and white. It is really that important, and the self-analysis has real value. But don't beat yourself up with unnecessary negativity. That is not helpful and can be self-defeating. Then spend twice as much time improving your weaknesses as refining your strengths. A chain is only as strong as its weakest link, and an individual cannot let this hold them back.

Next, make a short list of the top four things you would really like to do in your 4th quarter whether a hobby, a business, an adventure, or some worthy cause (or all four). Upon determining what you are interested in pursuing, it is imperative that you follow through with additional steps. First up, there are always people close by who can be mentors or at least steer you in the right direction. (Don't be afraid to ask. The absolutely worst thing they can do is say no. You just go on and ask someone else.) It can also be a thrill to hit the road by taking some field trips to meet and greet people who actually do what you want to do. Most of them will be only too eager to help. One, because they are flattered you asked and delighted to play the teacher role to such an eager student. Secondly, they are excited about the same things you are and anxious to share their passion.

Finally, do your homework. Ouch, Ouch! This is where a lot of people fall by the wayside. Spend hours on the Internet learning all you can in detail. Get advice not only on what to do but also what pitfalls to avoid, which can save a lot of time and grief. And then follow through and give it your best shot. This is all about you and making your 4th quarter meaningful and rewarding.

If you are not willing to do these things, it shows that you have the interest for pie in the sky but not the passion and drive to succeed. Sadly, your dream will not have a chance to become a reality if you are more of a dreamer than a doer. It is like someone who wants to be a great pianist but never wants to practice or the young person who dreams of becoming the hero of the big game but never wants to go to the gym or to be yelled at by the coach. If you are allergic to some committed work, success usually proves to be most elusive. Success is only partly about opportunity but far more about execution. No guts, no glory! Discipline, will-power, and the persistence of the turtle will beat the distracted rabbit every time. When opportunity knocks, one still has to get their butt off the couch and answer the doorbell, or it just leaves and moves on to knock on somebody else's door and wait for a response. Tragically, a lot of people have an out-of-order doorbell or are too lazy to answer the door.

10

DON'T QUIT YOUR JOB... YET!

"Making a living is not the same as making a life."

Maya Angelou

Work defines us. So don't quit your job unless you are absolutely sure, and even then think about it some more. For every person who rejoiced and was glad they quit the rat race or felt it was time to go, another has later wished they had stayed just a little longer since retirement has not met their expectations. However, while in some cases it is about the money, it is also frequently about being needed as part of a team and having a sense of place. There is also the self-satisfaction that comes with a job well done. Co-workers really represent a second family which many people spend more time with than they do their real families. For a few, they are their family. So, if you have even the slightest doubt, wait since there are rarely any "do-overs" with this decision. When you are gone, you are gone. The door swings only one way, and you are replaced in a heartbeat since no one is indispensable. And if in rare circumstances, a return is possible after some time has gone by, it never feels quite the same. Many of the old familiar faces are gone, and the work challenges have often changed.

Work is where we spend most of our time. Consider a 24-hour day. If you are smart and get your 8 hours of sleep or close to it, one third of your day is gone. An eight-hour workday takes up even more than an additional third if we factor in lunch and the hour long, round-trip commute. Throw in errands and chores, and we are left with just the "remains of the day."

Meet any stranger at a meeting, party, function, or just on the street and within minutes, the question is posed, "And what do you do?" Generally, this question is asked to find common ground between two people. Simultaneously, we have already made our pre-stereotypical assessment based on gender, dress, age, height, color, looks, and body language. It all happens in a flash as we build a mental composite picture of this new person for ourselves. It is shorthand for sorting new people into our little boxes of preconceived opinions of the individual based on their work title by making snap judgments regarding power, authority, associations, wealth, or even political leanings. It is almost like speed-dating for people with A.D.D. It becomes our handy little reference guide.

Meantime, our opposite number is doing exactly the same thing to us. If there is an obvious mismatch based on class, education, or personality assumptions, the strangers move on. The encounter can only be quickly salvaged if the parties find common ground in hobbies, family, business, sports, or other interests beyond just the work title constraints. But work histories are often the starting reference points.

One option to pursue is a pre-retirement try out. If you have vacation time, ask in advance for an extended break of a few more weeks if you can get the boss to agree. The dress rehearsal will be a dry run to get a feel for having an extra 45-50 hours a week of unstructured time at home along with no commute. However, being away on vacation does not count. For some, that much time on their hands at home without planning is refreshing and liberating, for others, after a few weeks, it is slightly distressing and they get antsy.

Many potential retirees don't want to quit work just yet but would prefer to slow down and catch their breath. The ideal for some is a fade-away plan whereby they could continue working on a part-time basis. This means money is still coming in while one is still connected to the dynamics of the work world with a little more personal time to smell the roses along the way while reducing stress. Unfortunately, few job descriptions allow for this. Most require a full-time commitment to keep the company position running efficiently. However, a highly valued employee may be lucky as a boss will not want to lose all that expertise, experience, and institutional history walking out the front door. Plus, a wily and calculating employee may let slip a less-than-subtle implied threat that a competitor may be willing to make accommodations regarding hours and work assignments. Smart employers will want valued employees to mentor a replacement, work on special projects, or maintain special relationships with key people in or outside of the organization. They may be willing to bend a little.

Professional individuals in fields of medicine, law, engineering, and consulting have an advantage in that these fields lend themselves more easily to scaling back their work hours rather than being forced to quit because of the demands of a 40-hour or more work-week. Self-employed individuals can also scale back by delegating more responsibility to a few key employees. By working part-time, a would-be retiree will be able to realistically assess different options going forward.

Another tactic to try is getting another job that may have better hours or work requirements that are more interesting or less demanding. Often, many individuals who have worked quite a few years for the same employer may be unaware of alternative opportunities in the market place. A few may even be intrigued to take a leap of faith in a different field or area of work that may be more appealing. Quietly spend six months or a year outside of work (off the radar screen) testing the waters before your target date of retirement looking into what the potential possibilities may be for a new adventure. Of course, one needs to remember that age discrimination is a not-so subtle factor and is tough to prove. Besides, employers don't like paying top dollar, or even medium dollars, for someone at the top of the pay scale who will leave them in the next few years. Such a search will require more time, patience, and some luck on your part. However, it will help you clarify your options. There are many dreams in life to pursue that may only require a shift in emphasis to be both satisfying and fulfilling.

Another option is to be your own boss and strike out on your own as an entrepreneur working as many or as few hours as you choose. You call the shots relying on your own skills and background. Just be careful not to get fired by yourself as your new boss!

11

QUALITY WOMEN

"Who can find a virtuous woman?
For her price is far above rubies."

Proverbs 31:10

Women are better human beings than men. It is just a fact. On every level of character, women come out on top. To be sure, there are women who are scheming, cheating, and contemptible everywhere, but in any random sample of a hundred men and a hundred women, the women will win easily. To be more precise, they are more responsible, mature, nurturing, collaborative, and virtuous across the board when compared to men. This is not to bash men at all, of which there are legions of noble and upstanding examples worthy of great emulation. It is just that women outnumber them overall with a higher sense of morality and duty. It is a matter of superior quality. In the larger society, men may always fancy themselves to play captain and steer the ship, but it is often women who are relied upon to run and maintain it to avoid sinking. Increasingly in modern times with each passing generation, women also want to have a greater say in navigation and to aspire to be captain. Critically, hospitals and education of the young would collapse overnight without women–and perhaps modern civilization. More than ever, women are leading out in a wide swath of middle-and-upper-management talent that makes business function in the twenty-first century. Even the glass ceiling is showing more and more cracks.

Women often need to be tougher than men. Many women in their early years do "double duty" by holding down a job and running a home. They regularly step up to the plate as caregivers to others, often out of expectations and sometimes simply by default. Many are squeezed as the "sandwich generation," looking after parents and children. Because women have a longer life expectancy and generally marry men a few years older, they may spend a number of their fourth-quarter years alone and some overtime (past eighty) fending for themselves. So will millions of other women due to divorce or having never married. All of them need a game plan if they find this is their lot in life. Too often, a dying husband has a younger or healthier wife to look after him, but when he is gone, it is a different story for the wife who is left behind. Children may try to step in but may live far away or face pressing issues in their own lives with their own children or other life events and become unavailable. It's not fair, but it is reality.

Many baby-boomer women were brought up in the transitional generation between traditional female roles that confined their options in life and those of the coming-of-age era in the feminist vortex of the sixties and seventies that promised a world of possibilities. It was an exciting, if conflicted, time to be young and female. Feminism, to some, is a polarizing word that implies that women want to be like men. But that is not true. At its core, feminism is about fairness, choices, respect, and opportunities for women—no more and no less. That's it.

The twentieth-century transformation in the role of women in Western society is among the most revolutionary changes in all of human history, arguably the greatest change of all time. Its profound effect cannot be overestimated in every aspect of society from marriage and birth rates to education, the workplace, and government. It is a power and paradigm shift that is still underway. Consider an average wife and mother of five children more than a hundred years ago, married to an alcoholic husband in a home where domestic violence was the norm. The wife's choices were basically none. With little education, no marketable skills, a biased legal system, and no way to provide for herself, much less her kids, she absorbed the abuse of a drunkard husband and stayed. Or, more accurately, she was trapped. There was no practical option, and divorce was not a rational choice and often a social death sentence in small rural communities.

The difference for many women in the twenty-first century is that with an education, many finally have choices for the first time in history. On college campuses today, fifty-eight percent of all students across the nation are female, compared to forty-two percent of men on campus, so the dynamic of change continues onward. Nearly one-third of married women today make more money than their husbands.[21]

Ironically, for many young women today who are armed with a solid professional education, they lament the fact that when looking for a life partner that there is a pool shortage of quality young men who have their act together. In generations past, women generally tried to "marry up" by looking for a "good catch." These days they worry about having to "settle" by marrying down.

In dealing with poor countries, a sea change in recent years has taken hold in favor of a new standard model for third-world development. It is the belief that to truly transform poverty, it is critical to improve the lives of women. They ensure better outcomes for their own children by becoming advocates for better education, health, nutrition, cleanliness, and public order. In America's past, it was men who pushed into the frontier and explored the West, but it was women who followed and civilized it. In a different context today, nothing scares radical conservative Muslim men more than the liberation and equality of women. It terrifies them to their very core. It threatens their power and authority. They see it in nearly existential terms. It is fundamental to some who thus lash out in destructive and deadly ways.

Fourth-quarter women need to look ahead, regarding their future plans, even more so than men, due to their longer lifespans and the fact that most of them will be on their own at some point in their life. According to the U.S. Census, almost half of all women over the age of sixty-five were widows, outnumbering widowers roughly five to one. Furthermore, men on average have more risk factors such as smoking and drinking, along with poorer nutrition habits that compromise their health earlier than women. Many wives end up becoming in-home nurse caregivers.

It is important for women to be proactive by making sure they know what the current family score is in regard to family finances. If, as in many households, the wife attends to the major bookkeeping of family accounts, this is all to the good in that there is intimate knowledge of the current situation and confidence to continue on in the future. However, for those marriages where the husband takes care of nearly all the finances, it is imperative that a wife who is passive, disinterested, or marginalized gets serious about learning where all the money they have is located, knowing the amounts, and speaking up about the general plan going forward.

The first item of business is to secure long-term housing. If the current house or condo is paid off, great. If not, extra payments need to be made quickly to pay off the mortgage. It is a great stress reliever. Those paying rent at older ages on a fixed income will be in a more difficult position. Rent will continue to rise and, depending on the market location, could double over the next ten or twenty years.

The next item on a woman's agenda is to review if there is a life-insurance policy with her as the beneficiary. If so, she should make sure those premiums are paid monthly on an automatic deposit-withdrawal schedule so the policy never lapses. If there is no life insurance, it needs to be considered even though it is more expensive in later years. Next, review any pensions, Social Security benefits, and any savings accounts to know where they are located and the balances.

For women of very modest means, options are limited, unfortunately. One consideration, if possible, is to seek a room accommodation with one of your offspring. For some families, this works out great as part of one's fixed income can go to help an adult child build equity in a home, and the trade-off of helping with the grandkids or household chores is a win-win situation. For others, geography, personalities, and privacy issues make this a nonstarter solution or may devolve into a toxic relationship. Still others may try to share housing expenses with a friend, which can beat living alone but also comes with the downside of having to live with the foibles of a roommate.

Smart women need to think ahead and plan ahead in order to stay ahead of any contingencies that life throws their way.

12

THE HAPPINESS TRAP

"I'm bored. There's nothing to do."

When parents are asked what they most wish for their little tyke, the response is predictable: "I just want them to be happy." Oh brother, what a burden. What a trap. What an impossibly high bar to achieve. Indeed, under this expectation, a child or even a senior in the fourth-quarter of-life who is not happy nearly all the time becomes a tragic figure. They are consumed by looking for happiness under every rock. The search is on to be in a state of Nirvana when traveling through Utopia by way of Shangri La on the way to Seventh Heaven. Disappointment awaits them.

Kids will mope and fuss to parents and grandparents in order to get attention but also as a command that somehow they must be entertained. "Come on," they demand, "put on a show for me to keep me distracted or amused. When does this circus start?" In order to keep them pacified and from throwing a tantrum or hissy fit, stressed-out parents and grandparents almost always cave, partly out of love and partly to avoid going ten rounds of crying and theatrics.

Adults can do the same thing sometimes but are just a lot sneakier about it. They get on the phone to a friend who asks them what they did last weekend and the reply comes back, "Nothing, same-ol'-same-ol' routine." They moan about the mundane: work, family drama, watching television, errands, chores, or the wretched state of the world in general that is going to hell. Often, they consider themselves in a rut, either one forced upon them or the one they have chosen by taking the path of least resistance, but it is at least a familiar rut. Certainly, the feeling by lots of people is that everyone else's life is far more exciting than theirs. And even those who feel they are doing okay in being engaged with life still worry it does not measure up to others who are "really" having a good time. You can't win at this mind game.

It can be compared to "Facebook envy" of others where fun pictures, scads of "friends," witty comments, and many "likes" are posted and make some feel that their lives are somehow less than their friends'. It can become competitive one-upmanship. I'll see your Grand Canyon and Disneyland vacation pictures and raise you with mine of Paris and Rome along with my kids are more awesome and my pet is cuter than yours. Facebook can leave more than a few mildly depressed. There is even a new twenty-first-century acronym made up for all of this angst, called FOMO: fear of missing out. How wonderful—we get one more thing to stress over!

We all know some seniors who, in some ways, are just big kids still going in circles on the happiness merry-go-round. Few are immune to this siren call instilled as a child. It is a cliché about a fortyish-year-old man in a midlife crisis who buys a red sports car and may embark on an affair because he is "not happy." Men are advised to pay attention to their wives because "happy wife, happy life." Children are admonished to heed Mom's fluctuating moods because "if mom's not happy, nobody's happy." If nothing else is working, we can all go to Disneyland since it is "the happiest place on earth." This happiness trap is like being on a hamster wheel, always running faster but not getting anywhere, or like a junkie afraid of coming down from a high.

This is the snake oil that is also pushed by the media. Many people of all ages swallow it hook, line, and sinker: Buy this to be happy, wear this, drink that, vacation here, party everywhere on your way to blissful happiness. Be entertained and jaded by the latest, coolest, hottest thing going.

It is your full-time job to be happy. Indeed, it is your birthright and duty to be happy, and if you are not, it's your own stupid fault because you are not trying hard enough. In order to achieve this exalted state of perpetual happiness, it requires that all your endorphins are firing on all cylinders, the adrenaline is pumping at full speed, and the hormones are running wild. Maintaining this "rush" at peak levels requires full-time stimulation with your foot on the accelerator of life during all waking hours. If I let up, I may find myself unhappy, and this is against my belief system and all that I have been taught and led to accept as gospel. It is a disease that must be eradicated at all cost. Caffeine is my best friend, alcohol my companion, and pills my out-of-town guests. My smart phone is my new religion, work is my alternate universe, and the Internet is my lifeline. My fear is that if I slow down, I may get run over by someone behind me—and that would surely make me unhappy, so I must run harder after happiness.

Many seniors, having accumulated life experiences, finally realize the shallow and superficial nature of this trap. But not all do since some remain enthralled and trapped in "happiness quicksand" by its seductive power. A minority of adults turn to alcohol and drugs chasing the ephemeral "high" of an altered state of mind and consciousness. The core of substance abuse is predicated on how it makes one feel right now, in the moment. It is a momentary short-cut high that leads nowhere.

Family or friends in casual conversation ask, "Are you happy with your new car, house, job, or move to the city?" Its close cousin, pleasure, also takes its cues from outside of ourselves, all based on our physical senses, primarily food, sex, and endless entertainments of sight, sound, touch, and frenetic action. It is almost exclusively external in nature. Pleasure, although fleeting, has its place and is wonderful, but it is not a "destination place" and often feels like a mirage just beyond our reach. Rather, the proper place for pleasure on life's journey should be the occasional pit stop for cake and ice cream.

In many ways, pleasure is a drug high that people try to replicate over and over. But you can only touch it, taste it, feel it momentarily. You can't buy it, bottle it, or keep it. It is effervescent. It goes away almost as quickly as it arrives. It is like trying to keep a raindrop in your hand from evaporating after a quick morning drizzle on a hot summer day.

What is often missing is joy, which is different from happiness and pleasure because it largely comes from within. It can last a long time, much like a warm fireplace with lots of wood stacked up beside the fireplace. Unfortunately, in life there are no required classes in school that teach the differentiated fine points of happiness, pleasure, and joy. These are intangible subjects that society just assumes everyone will learn like walking and talking as a toddler. It's not that simple or appreciated.

The real human quest (and the least understood) is for the desired state of joy. It is an internal experience as opposed to the transitory nature of mere pleasure or the mystical state of nirvana that always seems to be elusively around the corner. Is this just semantics, splitting hairs between happiness, joy, and pleasure? Perhaps to some degree, but consider that joy comes from somewhere deep inside us that gives off a special glow, that lights us from the inside out rather than the outside in. Most of this comes from real accomplishments, from the mundane to the sublime, rather than just material stuff or passive entertainment. There is a qualitative difference in the joy of being able to play the piano in comparison to just the pleasure of hearing someone else play. Hearing the boss praise you with an "Atta boy" or an "Atta girl" for a job well done gives one pride and a sense of being valued with inner-joy and approval that mere money by itself cannot always satisfy. We all want to be validated.

Joy is felt just watching the sheer delight of a young grandchild's birthday party that makes the heart skip a beat. Just the act of silently sitting with a loved one on a beach on a moonlit starry night makes the heart sing with joy. Doing an act of kindness gives an inner sense of satisfaction. Watching two kittens or puppies play-wrestle on the living room floor is pure joy. A sense of inner-satisfaction can even be found sitting in an armchair after cleaning the house and observing a job well done. The hours of preparation for a Thanksgiving family celebration may be a chore, but the sweet feeling of joy and gratitude as you look around the table at loved ones near and dear is irreplaceable. The afterglow is what is retained in one's joyful heart.

Our genius founding fathers who wrote the Declaration of Independence wrote the immortal words of "life, liberty, and the pursuit of happiness." These were promised guarantees to the people, but it is important to note that they did not promise a state of happiness, only that every man and woman would be able to chase that elusive butterfly (that never stays still for long) as they saw fit. Besides, it is like a barking dog that caught a car he was chasing. Now what? Even bliss is ephemeral and tough to capture for long. Some philosophers of mankind even go so far as to say the human experience demands bad times, trials, and tribulations in order to appreciate their opposites of victories, successes, and triumphs. If every day was sunshine in paradise, how could one truly appreciate a beautiful day without the contrast of rain, storm, or winter? The problem with joy is it requires so much more internal development. Chasing stuff and entertainment is a much easier road in order to keep score between friends and others. Joy requires more effort. It involves introspection, self-reflection, and an outlook on life that focuses more on what makes us tick along with the beauty in the world in many forms. It is a higher calling. So if happiness, pleasure, and joy are a three-legged stool, joy is the most important one to work on, which means becoming a better person from the inside out.

We all know people who just light up a room by their mere presence. They bring the joy of being a cheerful, good soul with warmth, grace, and good humor. They are a joy to just be around. They have an inner-love that keeps everyone else warm with a soft magnetism that draws people to them regardless of their station in life. So when asked what one wishes for their grandchild in life, (or yourself) the answer should be; joy, wisdom, integrity, self-discipline, grit, accomplishment, and compassion. These are the traits of a truly remarkable human being and a life of real meaning and purpose. Seek joy before pleasure.

13

I WORRY THAT I WORRY

"Blessed is he who expects nothing,
for he shall never be disappointed."

Alexander Pope

This is the beatitude of the pessimist, the cynic, and the skeptic all rolled into one. All bases are covered. If the sky is not falling today, just wait till tomorrow. If the bogeyman failed to show up last week, it just means he got delayed, but rest assured he is on his way. If my cup in life is not even half full, it is because there is a slow leak in the bottom of it, and I am doomed to never get ahead. Nearly everyone knows someone in their social circle who worries about everything.

Of course, there is so much to worry about, one hardly knows where to begin. It is an exhausting job that has many on edge all the time. Incredibly, as you read the newspaper and watch TV news, you find to your dismay that there are so many new things to worry about that you didn't even know about before. There is a premonition that something or someone is out to get you, lurking behind every other corner. Crime, disease, accident, or tragedy is nearly omnipresent. Hypervigilance is necessary to avoid calamity. Where will it all end? We are drowning in media that hypes everything to the max because our attention span is that of a fruit fly. Some just want to take a nap and pull the covers over their heads. And so it goes...

Anxiety seems to be a special malady of the modern world. In one sense, it is an epidemic that afflicts nearly everyone. We worry about image, money, jobs, relationships, health, and terrorism. Just listening to Oprah, Dr. Phil, Dr. Oz, or surfing the Internet, you are a wreck by either doing it all wrong or being foolish in ignoring 101 other important things you should be doing but aren't. Talk radio's central focus is about anger, fear, outrage, ranting, conflict, and how terrible things are in the world today. Without stirring the pot nobody would listen. We further stress about our own phobias and personality shortcomings that compound our worry. We worry about falling behind our friends and social groups. There is no pressure like the pressure we put on our inadequate selves.

Take a deep breath, sit down, and have a talk with yourself. Nearly all of our fears are unfounded. Instead, they are gut emotions not based on logic or even math. Not every shadow outside the campfire is a wolf waiting for you to go to sleep. This is not to be Pollyanna-ish, for bad things do occur since there is evil and tragedy in the world, but it is not the whole story.

The good news is that there is plenty of good news if you look for it. There is a cute Ziggy cartoon where he is lying in bed and can't sleep. He is worried and can't relax, just staring at the ceiling. The phone rings, and Ziggy learns the other person on the line is wide awake, worrying about the same things. Ziggy hangs up, rolls over, and goes to sleep, content that someone else is worrying about it all.

It is interesting to observe in our lives that ninety percent of everything we worry over never comes to pass, and another five percent that did come to pass was one hundred percent out of our control. There was absolutely nothing we could do or could have done to change the outcome. Of course, telling someone not to worry is like telling a child in a candy store not to think about candy. Hard to do! Take, for example, someone who has a fear of flying. The chance of dying on a commercial plane is so remote that a passenger is more likely to be attacked by a shark or to die in a bathtub, along with driving to the airport. And if they are among the extremely small handful of the unlucky fliers, there is nothing they could do about it anyway. So why worry about it?

While all worry cannot be cured, it can be better managed and set aside as much as possible. By knowing the score on anxiety, we should set aside our worry beads to a lowly five percent of our mental time and address the things we do have some control over like our health and personal self-improvement. Less angst, more joy is the goal. But we even worry that we are not getting enough fun out of life. To paraphrase H. L. Mencken's observation, "a Puritan is one who worries that someone, somewhere is having fun" (or at least more fun than we are). Heck, we even sometimes worry about dying but not anytime soon because we worry we don't have time for it in our schedules.

One of the best antidotes for worry and negativity is to practice a daily habit of looking for good things. It needs to be a conscious "pick me up" like a cup of coffee in the morning or a quick kiss to a loved one on the way out the door. Actively look for the good and the positive. Flowers, sunshine, pets, a kind word, a good deed, etc. can set a tone throughout your day. If you can magnify it with some uplifting music, positive reading, and genial conversation, it all helps to keep things in balance.

Generally, one finds what they are looking for whether it is good or bad. It is a choice we all make. In order to reduce our worry, it helps to look at the world in a different way. Another strategy to help curb our anxiety levels is by "doing." When we are engaged in something, our minds refocus on the task or activity at hand. Idleness tends to be the time when spooky thoughts come out of the woodwork to nibble away at the mind. We all need to spend more time counting our blessings rather than moaning over troubles and disappointments. We actively need to be careful not to let social media and television dominate our time or warp our sense of well-being.

Motivational speakers talk about taking persistent action in one's life as they know that this is the most likely route to change any present condition. The paralysis of analysis is a huge killer of dreams. Anyone can be a wannabe, a daydreamer, caught up in process. But it is the execution of any plan that is critical.

It is also important to be aware of mind games. Another good trick to reduce worry is to short circuit your mind by becoming hyperconscious of your worry track and quite deliberately changing channels in your head. You literally become self-aware of your line of thought and you intentionally move on to think of something more pleasant. This even applies to visuals on the movie or TV screen that are graphically violent or grossly disturbing. Just close your eyes. It's that simple. You have chosen that you do not need those visuals haunting your sleep at night or even desensitizing you in any way to the horror displayed. This is a good strategy to teach grandchildren and to even younger adults. You are the guardians of your own mind. No one or no visual can pass through your optic gate without your express permission.

Of course, better yet is becoming more selective in what you expose yourself to in the first place, both visually and in your surrounding life's environment. Far too much of entertainment is consumed by the rude, the crude, and the lewd that people become desensitized to it all. It becomes a new normal, particularly among the young today. In the words of the late Senator Patrick Moynihan it is "defining deviancy down." Throw in the gross, the crass, and depraved cruelty depicting gore, horror, and buckets of blood and it should give everyone pause about what it means to be entertained these days. Indeed, studies show consistently that those who consume a lot of violent media are more fearful of the world and its dangers and thus worry more about their personal safety. The world would be a far better place if everyone strove to be more aspirational, inspirational, and uplifting in the choices one makes.

Finally, there is the issue of medications prescribed by a doctor. Just by virtue of taking pills, our worry can increase over our health. Of course, there is no one-size-fits-all in this area, and medication certainly has its place. However, there are always side effects that are often little understood. Often, long-term meds can become more habitual than medically necessary. Check with your doctor for periodic reviews to reduce or stop medications whenever possible. Less, if medically possible, is always preferable. Generally, if you can get off (or greatly reduce) meds, it makes you more responsible and empowered by removing a crutch, and the big bonus is there is one less thing to worry about!

For seniors in the fourth quarter of life, a new attitude needs to take place that is best expressed as follows: "I worry less about what others think of me and more of what I think about them."

14

LONELY OR ALONE?

"To thine own self be true."

Shakespeare's Hamlet

These two words, lonely and alone, are often confused with each other. But they are worlds apart, and many people fail to make the distinction and realize the significance of each word.

Many people fear growing old and being lonely. Being lonely is seen as being a sad, sad, commentary on a life that has been shunted aside, cut off, and largely devoid of joy or happiness without much meaningful contact with others. It is kind of like being deserted on a desert island.

Strangely, there are also a lot of people who feel very lonely even in a crowd, or even in a marriage. This says even more about their internal feelings and perhaps the lack of connections they have been able to make with others. Some who are clinically depressed also feel a sense of isolation even with caring family and friends about. Loneliness can also strike those who wallow in their own despair (woe is me), letting dark clouds and negative thoughts crowd out the good in life. It immobilizes them, and they feel trapped inside their own heads and hearts. One of the most painful causes of loneliness is the loss of a spouse, parent, or child. Some of those left behind can retreat inward and begin to dry up from the inside out. The loved one is gone, and aside from the grief of the loss is the hard reality that they have to drive on in their journey of life without them. Some just break down by the side of the road and never fully recover. The same can sometimes be true for those who have lost their closest friend. In any case, life is just not the same without them. They are sorely missed and, it is keenly felt, can never be replaced.

Dealing with loss in life is always tough and is a nearly universal experience. It is a tragedy of being mortal. But consider the loved one who has recently departed. Would they really want you to spend the rest of your days building a shrine to their memory, wearing sackcloth and ashes, and feeling miserable day after day with a broken heart as a way to honor them? Of course not—if they really cared about you. Conversely, what would you want for those you left behind and deeply cared for? Would you want endless pining over you or for them to keep you close in their heart but also return to life. Would you not wish for them to be joyful and looking for happiness wherever it might be found? The difference is often between a very deep scar that will always remain as a reminder or an open festering wound that never heals and hobbles a life.

Loneliness is hard to cure since it is an internal battle waged deep inside the soul. It can, however, be mitigated by turning one's thoughts and feelings as much as possible from the internal to the external world, where life is happening all around. A change of focus toward others is the key to keeping the blues away. One should never forget the past, but must work hard to keep their mind oriented to the future.

Being alone is a whole different discussion. It is just a description of a neutral state. One can be alone and be as happy as a lark. Being alone is often a state of mind and should never be construed on its own as a negative condition. Many people enjoy their own company. Lost in their own thoughts, projects, reading, chores, routines, and activities, they are basically content in their lives. This does not mean they are hermits. It simply means they are comfortable in their own skin, have a rooted sense of identity, and are interested in the world around them. They can enjoy socializing with others but are also quite comfortable being by themselves. These are people who are alone but are rarely lonely. If, on occasion, the blues do show up for a day or two, they know these feelings will pass away soon. They do not need, nor do they expect, other people to have to entertain or to engage them.

Yet being lonely, feeling starved for attention and companionship, can be debilitating and sad for many. Human beings are naturally wired to be social. We want to share companionship with others, with sharing being the key word. We desire to share our stories, hopes, and dreams. Finding a simpatico mate or friend is icing on our cake.

If we use the analogy of a cake, the different ingredients that go into the cake mix determine who you are as an individual. Baked in are your talents, virtues, values, and personality. Also, unfortunately, all of one's shortcomings as well. These are all the internal aspects of your traits and character that make you tick. The icing on the cake is represented externally, outside of yourself. Family and friends add sugar, spice, and flavor to your own cake. However, if your cake is missing several ingredients or did not rise properly by being undercooked in the oven, there is a problem. Few people are going to like your cake.

In practical terms, you must first become your own best cake. This means working on yourself to become your own best friend. If one does not like oneself very much, why would others like that person any better? Ironically, a lot of people try to avoid self-improvement by being maniacally busy or distracted all the time to avoid much self-reflection. Others withdraw into themselves or lean on drugs, both legal and sometimes illegal, as an escape. Where many fall short is that they go through life with a nearly empty cup while expecting others to fill it up for them. You can learn to become your own best friend or your own worst enemy.

Many would argue that for fourth-quarter people all this talk of improving themselves is a fool's errand. They firmly believe it is far too late to change their ways. Nonsense! It means no one else can make a life for yourself but you. No one is suggesting you undergo a personality transplant at the local hospital. However, it does require continual self-development to become a better all-around person than you were last year and the year before that. Progress is like taking a walk, one foot in front of the other.

It takes work and effort improving your own cake with the right ingredients. Like life itself, the hard work needs to be put in so that one can enjoy the icing when it comes into balance with the cake. Stunted personal growth has frustrated many a life that could have been better lived if only the work of personal investment had been made. It is never too late, but it helps to be self-aware and have a plan.

When learning to fly a small plane, the moment of truth comes when it is time to fly solo. It is just you and the airplane, nobody else. Everything rests on your shoulders to fly the plane and to land it. It takes confidence for sure, but if one has put in the many hours of ground school, done their homework, and won the full confidence of their flight instructor, flying solo is not scary but exhilarating. Indeed, avid small plane pilots will tell you with almost religious fervor the joy of flying among the clouds and the birds along with the rush of the wind and the hum of the engine. They describe it as magical, even bliss.

If you are lonely, or alone, can you fly solo by going to see a movie on your own, have a restaurant meal by yourself, or even take a heavily discounted last-minute trip on a cruise ship and enjoy them all internally along with meeting strangers? For some this sounds terrifying–for others, no problem. Generally, most people fall somewhere between these two groups and just need to be assured that, as with flying an airplane, the more hours you do it, the easier it becomes. Admittedly, it is much easier for secure people who are alone than for the truly lonely. But there is a partial cure for that as well, and it is to make other people or activities a priority in your life.

The best antidote, if you are feeling isolated, is to "join up" to every organization you can that is in sight. You must go out and meet the world, for the world will not come to your door. Sign up to book clubs, church, and community groups. Start hobbies, hit the gym, mentor a student, take a college class, start a sideline business. By pursuing this course of action, you will have jumped back into life in making friends and having a schedule of events to worry about rather than having only navel gazing scheduled on your calendar.

Involvement is the greatest cure for feeling needed and being a part of something. If one is isolated due to a disability, do the next best thing, which is to get on the Internet and make friends around the world. There are hundreds of groups dedicated to every topic under the sun, even how to combat loneliness and isolation! Taking action is imperative.

Many seniors who have had pets when they were younger as a child or with their own children have vowed to have no more. Some wish to be free to travel and come and go as they please. There is also the time and care required along with the guilt at leaving them for long stretches of time. Also remembered is the pain at losing a great friend and companion that was heartbreaking. But at a certain stage, you may wish to reconsider. For when it comes to unconditional love, having the love of a pet is often beyond words. They often disappoint us far less than family or friends. Sure, you provide your four-legged friend with food and shelter, but they wag their tail in delight or purr in contentment as a sign of approval and appreciation. They become family. They truly know how to live in the moment, where a past and a future do not exist. Curling up on the floor or in your lap for a nap, they are at peace with the world. Having their belly or chin rubbed, they are transported into a state of bliss.

A beloved pet gives us so much and in proportion gets so little in return. It should be a heart bond of unconditional love going both ways. However, pets need to be attended to with proper care and respect. Some have suggested that in a just world, if there is a belief in reincarnation, a human should come back as a pet and be treated in the same manner they treated their pet. That would be justice.

Pets are not for everyone, and it is a life commitment that needs to be taken seriously. If you cannot make the commitment, don't do it. It is completely unfair to the animal. So think this through carefully. But if it is right for you, consider adopting an older dog or cat at the local animal-rescue shelter. (Note: If your mobility is limited, stick with cats who are more independent since dogs deserve to be walked daily and require much more attention.)

Generally, an older pet is more mellow and manageable and will be eternally grateful. Sometimes they are at a shelter only because their owner died. They can be a wonderful pet already and you will be giving them a second chance at life. Take your time to find the right match for you. At the shelter ask for help and suggestions from the staff about personality and ask them to call you if a certain breed of dog or cat comes in that you may prefer. Also, and this is important, seriously consider adopting two. Another one is relatively little extra trouble, and by bonding, they also keep each other company when you are out of the house. They may have less anxiety when being left alone. They often become buddies.

Moving one's focus from the inward turmoil of loneliness to an outward expression for others and possibly bringing pets into your home can make a profound difference in many lives. Certainly, of all the traits to improve on the most, cheerfulness is critical. Few things lift one's mood and attracts those around you since people love a jolly ol' soul. But they run from grumpy curmudgeons who are forever complaining about everything under the sun.

May you never be lonely again, and if you are, recognize it is just a passing rainstorm, and the sun will shine again. When you are merely alone, may your heart be at peace with itself and counting its blessings. Recognize that your internal feelings and thought patterns need to be adjusted in a positive way to see the light and not just the troubles of the world. It will require personal effort and a sustained plan. But those who do this will be more joyful for it. There will be more sunshine in their world.

15

SEX! SEX! SEX!

Just because there is snow on the roof,
doesn't mean there isn't fire in the furnace!

Made you look! Got your attention, right? Other chapters may be browsed through or skimmed over, but this one about sex has slowed you down. Bazinga!

Don't you wish you had a dollar for every Viagra, Levitra, or Cialis ad you have seen on television? Who knew that E.D. was a twenty-first-century medical crisis that seemingly rivals cancer? It is perhaps a testament that captures male angst about one's virility, masculinity, and capability to hold off Father Time from robbing him of his youth and sexual vitality. What it says about women is another matter entirely. Both men and women can be all over the map when it comes to sexuality, and as we age, it can morph in many directions.

Sex sells. Sex titillates. It even has its own "drive," much like a car. And when it is out of control, it tends to propel itself forward almost of its own volition and can cause all kinds of grief and trouble by metaphorically driving off the cliff. More than a few seniors shudder in retrospect when thinking of their sexual history. Many wish they had left their "drive" in "neutral," thereby avoiding a lot of regret. They mentally compartmentalize and try to practice selective amnesia.

Sex captures one's attention and is unavoidable in our day and age. In earlier generations gone by, sex was largely confined to the bedroom and in private discreet conversations. In television's early days, even couples like Lucy and Desi had single beds. And they were married! Lucy could not even use the word pregnant on television. Times have changed.

Over the last two generations every soap opera plotline is almost exclusively built around who did who and who did what to whom. Sex and betrayal are the main drama storylines in some form or manner. Television comedies these days do not even waste their time on innuendo any more, but rather thrive on in-your-face explicit sexuality for cheap laughs. Today, in the public square, from movies, billboards, and ads of all kinds, sex permeates nearly everything, and pornography is in great demand on the Internet.

In the movies and general media, sex is often coarse and cheapened in its portrayal as an obligatory construct. Sex in the media and advertising world is often reduced to either gender-power games or just general horniness of two people on the make. It is often less about "making love" than "making lust." Yet like the sex drive, it drives ratings and sales. Indeed, the only thing different about cable TV from network television is actors are allowed to swear like a sailor and flash a lot more skin. It's pretty shallow, manipulative, and unimaginative, but whatever sells, sells. Madison Avenue will pimp out anything that can make a buck. The voyeur of the lowest common denominator trumps everything. Many decry the coarsening of the culture, but the public is also at fault by still tuning in.

So why is sex so ubiquitous today in the media landscape today? One of the consequences of our modern world of plenty is that sex has been elevated up the ladder from fourth place to first place in our perceived personal hierarchy of needs when comparing the past and the present.

In first place is mankind's fight for self-preservation. If an enemy, predatory animal, or disease is out to get you, it wonderfully concentrates your mind. Everything else is secondary, or you are dead. In second place was the acquisition of water and food. Historically, this required lots of time, effort, and labor in an agrarian society to insure food access to life-sustaining supplies. If you failed in this endeavor, you died. In third place was the quest for shelter from the elements. Yes, one can live and sleep under a tree, but not in winter. Neither is survival assured in extreme heat, flood, fire, or storm. Consequently, without proper shelter, an individual is likely to die. Next in line came our hormonal sex drive. Designed for the propagation of our species and, in the case of humans, as a pleasure response, it generally ranks for many as number four in a list of needs or desire.

But today in our modern world, if you are not worried about dying from a wild animal or a stalker criminal your first concern is taken off the table. Also, if you are more worried about losing weight than obtaining your next happy meal while having a home with a roof over your head your top three concerns are now largely irrelevant. Our number four concern, one's hormonal drive, now becomes number one for many individuals. However, some may rightly contend that, in most cases, it still trails behind the obsession over money, thus moving the concern about sex down to fifth place.

An unwritten rule of our sex-fueled society is that sex is for young people. Just the thought of older people having sex is, well, creepy and gross for the younger set. For young adults, just thinking about their parents having sex is a visual that makes them clammy along with a visible shudder. "Quick, change that mental channel!" The funny thing is that fourth-quarter people think the same way. Sixty-somethings don't view themselves as particularly old and have pretty much the same type of reaction in wanting to avoid a mental picture of ninety-year-olds possibly still doing it. Please change the subject–fast! We will pass on what ninety-year-olds think.

So what about senior sex? Despite the ubiquitous nature of sex in society, it is highly personal and makes most people squirm. While it can be joked and gossiped about with relish, few people want to open up clinically about themselves. It just hits too close to the bone. Some things are just meant to be private. Yet everyone seems to be insatiably curious about everyone else's libido. From celebrity gossip magazines to tell-all books to over the backyard-fence whispers about the neighbors down the street, enquiring minds want to know.

The most common question seniors ask of themselves on this subject is, "Am I normal regarding my sexuality in light of my advancing years? Is there something wrong with me because I want too much, don't get enough, or don't care at all?" And the most important answer to this question is you are fine. Relax. Wherever you are on this continuum from lots to none at all, if it is right for you, don't stress out about what others think or do. Critically speaking, it is none of their business, and the old saying "different strokes for different folks" applies in spades on this subject.

Of course, that is not the end of the conversation since life is often more complicated. If you are widowed or divorced, your sexuality may be problematic without a partner. Only you can work through this and come to terms with it. Those with strong religious convictions will also have to rely on their faith to make decisions that are compatible with their principles.

Those who are married know that in every area of their lives, compromises and negotiations are the order of the day. Sex is no different. However, with age, the "urge to merge" has usually shifted over the years. Sometimes, with a house empty of kids and worries of birth control left far, far, behind, sex can take on a different flavor which may be more special than in the recent past. For others, companionship and shared interests take a more predominant role, and sex is a minor or even a non-issue. However, problems arise when one of the partners is "out of synch" on this issue with the other. All couples will be different and must find their own pathway to resolve this.

Open communication is important and a spouse who avoids it is not playing fair. Sometimes counseling with a neutral third party professional is a good idea. If it works out to the satisfaction of husband and wife, it is a plus. If it doesn't the money was worth the try. The key is to approach the subject in the proper spirit. But marriage does have its obligations, and one partner should not try and dominate the other in this area regarding frequency either on the upside or the downside.

Too often, sex is used improperly in being granted as a reward or withheld as a punishment in a power contest within the marriage rather than fostering shared intimacy. A spouse who shuts out their partner is being selfish and a partner on the flip side who is unreasonably demanding is showing a lack of respect. Remember that on the subject of sex, attitude and especially enthusiasm are everything along with romance and common interests and goals. Apathy or indifference are the big red flags that cause trouble in all areas of a marriage. Sexuality in a positive relationship requires a meeting of the minds and the hearts as well as the bodies. Avoidance of the topic can lead to resentment and spill over into other parts of the relationship that hurt both spouses.

Contrary to popular mythology, genitalia are not the organs of intimacy. The organ of intimacy is the ear. It is even highlighted in the word end-ear-ment. Only the lucky few really get the profound importance of such a distinction. This is a skill that if not learned or if forgotten, needs a refresher course and more generally for men than for women. In the end, it is what is said, expressed, communicated, and shared that makes a relationship special. It must be heartfelt and sincere and not out of any sense of duty or obligation. Everyone wants to be wanted and appreciated. Both men and women desire romance, touch, and acceptance. Patience, a loving heart, and a willingness to really listen can only heighten intimacy. It brings couples closer together. Both partners need to be reminded that the key word is us, not me, not you, not what others think. Sex is like dynamite–handle with care and lots of respect.

16

THE BUCKET LIST

"Life is what happens while you are busy making other plans."

John Lennon

In more recent years, you begin to notice that your spouse or close friends begin to bring up the topic of "The Bucket List" more often in casual conversation. The Bucket List concept is now an ingrained part of the zeitgeist of the twenty-first century and has been embraced by the baby-boomer set as just another checklist in life. The term went mainstream with the 2007 movie, starring Jack Nicholson and Morgan Freeman, about two terminally ill patients and their last fling at life to see and do all those wild and crazy things they had never gotten around to doing before. Boomers have latched on to the idea with gusto and have been composing their own bucket lists with what they would like to do with the remaining fourth-quarter years that hopefully lie ahead.

Many seniors find themselves taking more mental notes of offers for destination packages, cruises, adventures, or articles on a host of interesting projects or hobbies. Starting a new business, writing, taking a college course, or considering some missionary or public-service work that would be personally satisfying. The spoken and unspoken vibe is that there are so many things yet to do, places to go, things to see, experiences to be had, life to be lived, and the rational realization that the clock is ticking and there is only so much time to pack them all in. A feeling of "Let's get this show on the road" becomes more pronounced.

About your bucket list–don't fret about it. It is only an aspiration and a desire, not a be-all or end-all test that will determine the entire course of the rest of your life. It should not be a contest to check each item off the list as quickly as you can by rushing through it.

Okay, we saw the Eiffel Tower for five minutes–check it off the list, now let's hustle quickly over to Notre Dame cathedral, the Louvre, and Napoleon's tomb. Then we'll take the train to Versailles before it gets dark so we can catch the plane and be in Rome for tomorrow and London the following day. Check, check, and check. This is travel by A.D.D. (attention deficit disorder).

Whatever is on your list, soak it all in, and try to be in the moment. It is less about the list and all about the joy. It is not about just showing up and quickly skipping through rooms in some musty old museum that show old stuff in order to rush on to the next item on your list. It is also about reading and doing a little research before traveling to appreciate the experience.

One good illustration is visiting a historic site such as Independence Hall in Philadelphia, where the Declaration of Independence was signed. For most visitors, they may have only a very rudimentary understanding (a mostly forgotten class or two in history) and even less of a true appreciation for what transpired in that room (rebellion with their lives literally on the line) where the course of the world was changed for billions of people in and outside of America over the following centuries. What took place there was a very big deal. However, only by reading in depth beforehand is a connection made with the foundations of our democracy. Viewing the eighteenth-century main chamber with its desks and chairs displayed in the setting of the day is hollow unless one knows the men and the details of the story of what transpired. Some tourists, armed with a visitor's pamphlet or an audio guide, are attempting a fifteen-minute, cursory cram course. In a way, they are trying to learn calculus and trigonometry over lunch. For people who are frenetic about their bucket lists, it should be remembered that it is not about the bucket but what is in the bucket.

Everyone should also take the time to have a mountaintop experience. It can be a small local mountain (or big hill) that only requires a few minutes or a few hours' walk to accomplish. Or if need be, drive to a local lookout point. A quiet couple of hours on a clear day while overlooking a valley and munching on a sandwich and trail mix is soul restoring. The air seems to be fresher, and the view is great. It gives a different perspective on the small world below.

It is also important to take time to not just smell the roses but to take inventory of your life. This literally means getting away from home and daily routines for a few days: no phone, no computer, no TV, no interruptions, just you and the mountain or perhaps a deserted ocean beach where you can drink in the beauty of nature and think in peace. It is a chance to reset your GPS life map.

17

WHERE DO I FIT IN?

Where you sit often determines your outlook in life

Faced with looming retirement, it is good to consider what category of retirement each individual fits in. There are six variations of retirement scenarios, so feel free to pick one from the following choices. They are delayed retirement, early retirement, late retirement, partial retirement, care-free retirement, and forced retirement. In general, all of the following groups cluster together around one of these possibilities. Much of this is defined by our own opportunities and circumstances. Some we get to choose; others are chosen for us. But it helps to focus on the highway of life what lies in front of us.

Group A (delayed retirement) is characterized by those who feel they have to work for income because they are stuck. Often the decision is self-evident for this group who has had financial reverses in life. Reasons may include layoffs, low wages, change of careers, bad investments, a health setback, perhaps a divorce or death of a spouse, children who need assistance, or simply a failure to save over the years and living paycheck to paycheck. For this group, work is a given in order to pay the bills and keep their boat afloat. They do not see any other options that are financially viable to survive. They stress out that they will have to work until they drop or financially go down with the ship. So, for the foreseeable future anyway, retirement will have to be delayed indefinitely, case closed. As long as they are physically able to respond to the alarm clock, they will be back at work tomorrow morning. The one upside is they are thankful they still have a job to go to when so many others have been forced out for a variety of reasons.

Group B (early retirement) have worked over their financial retirement spread-sheet many times, checked with a financial planner, and like a green-eye-shaded-accountant considers every angle to insure they and the family will be okay. The job they trudge to every day has lost its luster and has become a chore or a bore simply to get a paycheck. They are burned out and are tired of bosses, deadlines, and commutes. There is a strong desire to have personal control over their own time that belongs to no one else. For Group B they feel it in body and soul that it is time to "hang it up." With a sigh of relief, they are more than ready to say good-bye to this chapter of the rat race. While there is uncertainty about what retirement will bring, the urge to escape the present situation is the dominant emotion.

Group C (late retirement) feels they are in a good place. They could quit work tomorrow if they chose to do so. Financially they are okay, but they are skeptical of retirement. They feel fine physically and are in good form, at the top of their game and like being part of the action. Work is still satisfying and provides structure and identity to their lives. Colleagues, staff, customers, and projects all bring a sense of continuity and place in their world. Group C types are not burned out but often energized by the possibilities of what they can still achieve in the workplace. Some who have risen to a position of authority are reluctant to give it up. Did you ever notice that Type A creaky old politicians and driven CEO's are often loath to step down from the commanding heights? It is good to be King! Or Queen! These "bigwigs" fear moving from being a "big wheel" to a spare wheel and finally to a forgotten flat tire in a matter of weeks. It can happen fast. For a smaller subset of Group C, work is not even work to them, but is fun, interesting, and challenging. They would do it for free–okay not really, but money is not the prime motivation. Besides, they know themselves well enough that they will never be content with some forced activities in retirement for its own sake. They feel the need to be plugged in and like the "rush" of accomplishment and meeting lofty goals. In their bones they believe, for them at least, that it is better to wear out in life rather than rust out. In their mind a potted plant just collects moss, mold, or mildew, which is not for them. Given a choice, Group C much prefers working as long as they can and going out with a bang on a high note if possible.

Group D (partial retirement) is a hybrid of Group C with just a touch of Group B in them. Work is okay, but they are leery of quitting. However, there is also a feeling of "been there, done that" repetition after decades at the wheel. The nagging question in the back of their mind is; "Is this all there is?" Highly engaged, this group does not want to be sidelined or marginalized at all, but is looking for one or two more big adventures in life. There is that feeling, "now or never" which is played over and over in their head and says that there should not be any second-guessing in life and to follow your heart and "go for it." This group is not interested in parking in the shade of leisured retirement, but just in pursuing another back road of life while they explore where such an adventure may lead. It may involve a host of interests, dreams, and possibilities. But if they do not pivot quickly to this potential new challenge, the opportunity may be lost.

Group E (carefree retirement) has worked hard and put in their dues. Kids raised--check, house paid off--check, retirement pension/401K secured--check, bucket list in hand--check. This happy band of retirees is not as interested in being carried out the office door one day in a coroner's ambulance. They believe that after a lifetime of work and responsibility, that this is now their time. They want to "hang out" with friends, visit, travel, laugh, play, see, read, putter around, and do whatever the hell they please. Some retirees are so busy; they marvel at how they had any time to cram in a 40 or 50-hour work-week when they were younger. This group does not feel they are being lazy or irresponsible, but that this is now a time for their day in the sun. Their biggest fear is that recess will be cut short and they will not have enough time to play. Retirement is simply cake and ice cream after eating one's vegetables in the form of a lifetime of schooling, work, parenting, and being a good, responsible citizen. Retirement was justly earned, and I deserve this "me time." Any questions?

Group F (forced retirement) is the toughest group to be in. Members of this group did not get to choose their future, but circumstances chose it for them despite many of them trying to do their best. With a forced retirement the situation is taken out of one's hands that they are ill-prepared for and will struggle to meet the adjustments that lie ahead. Forced retirement situations include company layoffs, aging out in some fields, new technology coming in, a health crisis, "downsizing" or "restructuring." A company bankruptcy, merger, or re-location out of state or country comes as a blow. Any way you slice it, they are out of a job, and the alternative possibilities to replace it are not apparent. There is a strong feeling of bewilderment, even a betrayal of the American dream, and a deep sense of loss of control. This was not the scenario in life they had planned for. Reduced expectations and a scaled-down lifestyle is their new reality. Life is not fair.

However, one needs to "stay up" and try as best as they can to keep despondency from their door and focus on making the very best of things. Health, relationships, and circumstances are sometimes beyond one's control. But one's financial well-being is not always set in stone and can be improved upon only by being pro-active.

18

PERSONAL INVENTORY

Who are you?

Walk into the bathroom, look into the mirror, and proceed to explain yourself to yourself in as much detail as possible what kind of a person you are.

#1 First, a personality checklist is in order. Are you outgoing, reclusive, social, grumpy, a follower, a doer, a volunteer, a leader, a whiner, a dynamo, a tinkerer, a scholar, or a couch potato? Only you can identify you although your family and friends will be glad to chime in, perhaps a lot more objectively. This is crucial to begin to identify your personal assets and liabilities when you retire. Just dying on the vine is no plan at all. There are a number of websites that can give you a personality test by asking you a series of questions to ferret out a composite sketch of who you are. You may be surprised by some of the feedback. It is a worthwhile exercise even for those who have done this many years ago. Personalities do shift over time, for good and bad. You can't fix anything if you don't measure it and know what needs repair. This is not to assume there is anything wrong with you at all. Many people are well-adjusted, confident, and have arrived at the start of the fourth quarter with a lifetime of honed skills and earned wisdom. Still, it is a good idea to consider. Just like with a trusty older car in the garage, some preventative maintenance by a timely check-up may be in order to ensure optimum performance. Everyone can learn something to up their game.

At halftime, every football coach will review the game in play with his staff of what is working and what is not. Likewise, at the start of your own fourth quarter, you, as your own life coach, need to be evaluating a dozen different strategies for yourself. Like in any game, if the team is doing great and firing on all cylinders, a sound strategy may be to play it safe and conservative. Stick with what is working. However, if things are not going well and one needs all the time on the clock available, perhaps changes may require a higher risk/reward type of plan. By glancing at the clock and taking stock of your current situation every coach begins to make last-minute adjustments. The time for subtlety and nuance is over. Similarly, each new player turning sixty-ish in joining the fourth-quarter club needs to make necessary revisions to their life-game plan.

#2   Married? This is reality-check time since marriage is... well, it is marriage. It is wonderful, frustrating, liberating, confining, comforting, nostalgic, loving, and a confounding mystery all wrapped up at the same time. But the reality check is that in retirement there is a lot more "togetherness" than some marriages can cope with. Wives are not happy if a man is suddenly under foot deciding that he can improve the running of the household. Neither spouse likes being bossed around.

Spouses should not be taken for granted as even long-married couples can decide to go their separate ways as evidenced by increasing divorce rates in this age group. Nearly everyone was stunned in 2010 when former Vice President Al Gore and his wife Tipper separated after forty years together which from the outside looked like a model marriage and family. For other couples, it is just the opposite that occurs that allows space for a marriage to rekindle into a second romance. One can fall in love all over again with your best friend over shared joys and the special "moments" of life. So everyone should do a pre-retirement check-up on the state of their marriage to see if it is up to the challenge of this new phase in life. And just like a houseplant, it needs to be cultivated and cared for with TLC. It is said by some that absence makes the heart grow fonder. But, if not attended to properly, the neglected spouse's heart may not grow fonder, but wander.

There is also the room-mate marriage model where resources and history are shared, but each spouse pursues their own lives, interest, friends, and hobbies. For good or bad, familiarity can be a double edged sword. Sexual chemistry may be on life-support or dead, buried in apathy. Although daily life is predictable and follows a pattern which can be comforting for some, it can lead to contempt and unhappiness in others. One's mannerisms, habits, and personality can become overbearing after decades of walking around them (or putting up with them) because there was so much else of life to contend with.

Rule #1 for men: The house is still the queen's castle---you are just a boarder. Don't forget it. Go and build a spaceship in the backyard, but don't mess with the furniture, the kitchen, or long-established rituals by the wife except to be really quick to help out with the chores. Real men know how to vacuum, do dishes, and clean up after themselves. However, women also need to be considerate in return for a smooth functioning household that is comfortable for everyone. There needs to be give and take. Rule # 2: A husband should be kind and listen to her more than talking to her. Rule #3: Fuss over her in a heartfelt way, not at her. Rule #1 for women: Don't nag or boss around a man like a child with your agenda. Men chafe and resent it. Rule #2: Be kind and patient. Rule #3: Fuss over him in a pleasing good-natured-fun-way, not in a cloying way.

For both spouses, cheerfulness, courtesy, and lots of humor go a long way. If you have lost laughter or misplaced your humor gene, "google" it on the Internet and take a night class to get both of them back. There needs to be laughter. It is like sunshine. A humorless house is a place very few want to visit, much less live there. People want to escape. Finally, putting "The Golden Rule" into practice is instructive for both partners.

#3   Single, divorced, never married, or the death of a spouse have left millions literally on their own to make their way forward in an uncertain world. Most did not contemplate finding themselves in the fourth quarter of life doing this on their own. But reality is the present, the past is gone, and looking to the future is imperative. While each individual's situation is different, singles, as a group are more vulnerable financially, emotionally, and can often feel more isolated. When with couples, they often feel like a third wheel and are sometimes left out of social occasions because a hostess does not want to feel awkward in small, mostly couple, gatherings or make an invited guest feel uncomfortable. Some insecure married women also see other unattached women as threats. On the other hand, profound changes in society over the past generation have caused more singles than ever, and there are more opportunities for platonic and romantic friendships than in the past.

However, this is where personality is critical. Outgoing and gregarious people have a real advantage in this regard. They like people, feel confident, and enjoy the social interactions that groups both large and small bring. They are also more likely to initiate activities, events, and "happenings" for everyone to enjoy.

Those who lean more as timid types can easily slip into isolation and a slow withdrawal from others. They have less confidence, see themselves more as wall-flowers, do not like to be in uncomfortable situations, real or imagined, and often feel inadequate. Individuals in this category have to be extra reflective and realize that they need to "push" themselves to get out more often for their own mental and social well-being. One suggestion is to make friends with an extrovert (an odd couple) so you can ride on their coattails—and act as their wing-man or as a sister act. You are part of the show without having to star in it. The pressure is off, and you can enjoy all the benefits by coasting along in your friend's slipstream. A really good friend who is outgoing will understand your personality and make sure you are under their wing and included. It is a win/win situation. But you must be pro-active as hard as that may sound.

#4   Children: Your adult kids are adults and have their own lives. While a part of them will always be your small child in your heart and mind, the only current evidence for that is in the family photo album on the shelf or on an old CD disk. It is wistfulness from days gone by. Boundaries (on both sides) need to be set so that general harmony can reign. Much will depend on whether children live close-by or far away. It will also depend on whether you have approved of their life choices and shared history while they were being raised and how you get on with their spouse. Tolstoy said it best. "All happy families are alike; each unhappy family is unhappy in its own way."

We can choose our friends, lose our friends, or get new friends. But family, for good or bad, is forever. Perhaps the best thing to remember is that human nature with all its wonder and joy, along with all its shortcomings and disappointments, is in the end what makes us human. So start with the premise that all families, every one of them, including yours, (and you as an individual) is dysfunctional in some way. It is all just a matter of to what degree, large or small. Some families are quirky, some are crazy. It is observed that most families are like fudge with a few nuts sprinkled in. We are all works in progress.

#5   Kids, grandchildren, and money: The bank of Mom and Dad is closed. For those seniors who are on fixed incomes and do not have much discretionary income, this is just a matter of survival, your survival. Your offspring have the youth, energy, and opportunity to go out and meet the world to make their own way. For those seniors who have extra funds and resources, the bank should still be closed. Metaphorically, progeny should be given a life preserver, not a yacht. They should be assured of a parachute, but not an airplane to fly over and above life's trials and challenges. Self-reliance, self-denial, and some struggle helps to build character or at the very least creates some empathy for those less fortunate.

Life's lessons are never learned or taken to heart on a bed of rose petals. Of course, many seniors want to smooth the way for their offspring, which is a natural impulse. There is nothing wrong with that. However, while helping vs. giving may sound the same, there is a huge difference. Help is always the loving thing to do and many times has nothing to do with money but rather being a shoulder to lean on while imparting wisdom and values and being a cheerleader.

Giving is much trickier. Motivation on the part of the giver and the receiver are critical in this dance. See if you can relate to any of these scenarios. Parents who are stuck in that they feel "obligated" in the context of "I am selfish if I don't fork it over to the kids. Others feel "guilty" acknowledging some mistakes in parenting along the way and this is a way to make up for it for those shortcomings. Some parents look back on their own personal history and reflect how little they had growing up and do not want their kids to struggle like they did.

Then there are the money games of manipulation to buy love. Giving money is a way for some seniors to get attention from family members who keep coming around hoping for some more "goodies;" otherwise it is felt the kids would not have time for them. If this scenario is true it says more about your kids' superficial values and lack of character than anything else. So, instead, if this is the case, befriend a community neighbor as a surrogate son/daughter who is truly worthy and appreciates your time and help.

Money can be a blessing or a curse and for those who do not have enough of it, they always joke---"Bring on the curse," convinced beyond a shadow of a doubt they would know how to handle it and be wise about it. Money is seen as always good and to the positive upside. It has been said by many a successful person, "I've been rich, and I've been poor, and rich is better." Yes, it certainly is, but if money is all about stuff, bling, and me, it carries with it a very shallow outlook on life. Money is just a tool much like a knife that can be put to a thousand good uses, but as evil, it can be used to kill and destroy. If money is used only as an expression of selfishness, the end result is triviality and banality, if not harm.

The next trap to be aware of is the phony guilt trips laid on by adult children (they are good and know where to hit below the belt), which is just a form of extortion, unless, of course, they are right, and you are guilty as sin.

While parsing the difference between helping and giving may sound like semantics, the best "gift" a parent or grandparent can give is not a gift of money or material goods per se but an investment. Education is the one item grandparents should enthusiastically support if there are funds available. Cars depreciate; houses can be lost to divorce or a job layoff, and all kinds of stuff fades away in time, but an education is forever. No one can ever take it away. And if your offspring have it, coupled with strong values, they are more likely to find joy, meaning, and wonder in the world.

19

EVERY AGE HAS ITS COMPENSATIONS

"I aspire to inspire before I expire."

Eugene Bell, Jr.

Every age has its compensations. This is such a critical sentence that many can easily pass over it, but it says so much. What we lose at one age, we are often compensated for through different gains later in life. For example, very few older people, if asked, would choose to go back to their high-school years. The good memories are often highly selective and mask the naïveté, angst, and confusion of the teenage years. The adolescent years are a netherworld of being neither a child nor an adult, not always a desired state of being.

Seniors today, when looking back at their thirties and forties, depending on the drama, may wince over the rough times of raising their own children or some of the personal choices they made. Throw in marriage challenges or woes, financial struggles, job-related stresses, or some ethical lapses and few would really choose to go back in time. To be sure, there were past good times, laughter, and special memories that are sweetly treasured. However, as time goes by, it is a mystery of the human mind how we block out as much as possible the pain, hurt, and negativity of the past. What usually remains is nostalgia, a warm and fuzzy place of all our fondest memories but only a partial picture of a complicated puzzle. We remember the dessert in life, but try to forget about the tummyaches.

Many of the mistakes you made in life when you were younger, you would never make today. Lessons are learned in the school of hard knocks over the years. For some, it only takes one time to metaphorically (or literally) burn a hand on the stove to learn to be more careful. For others, they have to get hit over the head repeatedly with a two-by-four before they begin to "wake up" and see the light that certain behaviors need to change. Some never learn. The story of the young man who left home to attend college for four years is instructive. Upon returning home, he remarks to a childhood friend that he can't believe how much his Dad has changed while he was away at school.

Regrets are stored in everyone's mental closet. Everybody has some tucked away in the recesses of their mind. As with old toys kept in a shoebox covered in cobwebs, we sometimes take them out and play the game of what-might-have-been. Yes, there are those individuals with great regrets of bad judgment. They wish certain chapters in their life could be changed or erased that may have involved drugs, the law, career choices, or screwed-up relationships. But for the majority, it is more about regrets of omission—missed opportunities, both personal and professional, good advice not heeded, risks not taken, being stubborn.

Most people, as they age, see (and feel) their youth, vitality, or opportunities as things they have lost or as things that are fading away. Yet on the positive side, most seniors have gained a lifetime of maturity, insight, understanding, and wisdom that escapes most of the young. These are no small compensations.

People often wonder what their lives would be like if they could live them over and make different choices. What and who would you be if you had taken a different path in life? Work, education, spouse—they all come into play, and these little mind games can go both ways. A romanticized old flame makes you speculate on what might have been. On the other hand, you might reflect on that girl/boy that you were crazy about and that dumped you, "Wow, would that have been a disaster, and did they ever do me a favor! What the heck was I thinking?" Dodged a bullet there! Or what if you had gone to college, had not gone to college, or had started working in a different field or started your own business? Would it have been more rewarding? And what would it have been like had you moved to the exciting big city or had you done the opposite and gotten out of the rat race of the big city to Small-town, U.S.A., a more peaceful and friendly town. The variations are endless and unknowable.

Our innate personalities, habits, and outlook are largely set by our twenties, and fundamentally, they rarely change much except perhaps around the edges. Yes, we all know a few people who have made some dramatic U-turns on life's highway and have changed for better or for worse. But for most of us, our identities are clear for the most part and we have generally stayed in our own lane in life.

Here is the thing: if you dwell on this replay game too much, you will start to run in circles. Just like in a time-travel sci-fi movie, everything you change changes everything else, and you are no longer you. In sci-fi Trekkie-speak, you have upset the time continuum. So you need to give yourself some slack and lighten up. The appeal of a do-over is having foreknowledge of where the land mines of life are and walking around them in the belief of a better life. Indeed, by swerving to avoid one land-mine from our past that hurt us deeply may have caused us to go over a cliff we did not see. We will never know. But many of the traumas and struggles of life have molded who you are into someone tougher, more resilient, and appreciative because of your life journey. Failures and early defeats for some have been the catalysts for later success. You cannot capture the past when looking back from your current age with the added benefit of wisdom and experience.

Here is the acid test when looking backward over your life: if you could have become your own mentor by having your current sixtyish-year-old self-counsel your twenty-year-old version of yourself, would you (at the age of twenty) have even listened? Odds are, probably not. As it was, we selectively tuned out portions of our parents and teacher's admonitions at that juncture of our life. So at each stage of life, whether thirty, forty, fifty, or sixty and onward, we live life in the present under current circumstances. Life is lived going forward but only understood looking backward. Remember that every car has a huge windshield to see where we are going but only a very tiny rearview mirror to view the road we have already traveled. None of us have a crystal ball in life, so crying over spilt milk from our past does not do anyone a whole lot of good.

Doing a postmortem on a failed relationship or bad decision, past or present, has value to see what can be learned. But don't dwell on it in an endless loop since it is so profitless. Just vow to do better next time around. Remember that after any postmortem, there is a burial. Don't keep digging up the past. Let it rest in peace. Life reorients itself to the future. Anxieties and troubles just come with the life manual of being a human being. You already know the well-worn adage by heart that the definition of insanity is doing the same thing over and over again and expecting a different result.

So the good news for a fourth-quarter person is to embrace the lessons of the past and apply them to the remainder of the game. And let's take a general review of a list of regrets along life's journey. You may wish to add or substitute a few that are personal to you. Here are the "top ten" although we will approach this in reverse order in the same manner as David Letterman, the retired TV host of The Late Show. These should also be shared and discussed with younger generations.

Here we go—drum roll please:

10. The wish that we had learned to be more forgiving toward others and ourselves.
9. The wish that we had worried less.
8. The wish we could have been better parents.
7. The wish that we had appreciated and acknowledged more the struggles of our own parents, who often did the best they could as imperfect human beings.
6. The wish we had learned better the value of patience and especially delayed self-gratification.
5. The wish we had developed better money sense at an earlier age.
4. The wish we had taken more risks by being less fearful.
3. The wish we had taken our education more seriously regardless of our grades.
2. The wish we had been more self-disciplined.
1. (Big drum roll please, with a rim shot!) And our biggest regret in life is: All the precious time we procrastinated!

Seniors, by and large, have developed insights into human nature that often escape the young. They have learned that life is not black and white, right and wrong, left and right. It is nuanced, contradictory, and often messy. Yes, there is luck and cruel misfortune in life, but most often it is "what you sow, so shall you reap" and "the harder I work, the luckier I get" gems that determine the trajectory of most lives.

20

CRACK UP OFTEN

Yuk it up...

A generation ago, the late Norman Cousins's book *Anatomy of an Illness* became a best-seller in which he describes his experience with a debilitating medical condition and how humor made such a positive impact in his recovery. While definitive medical science has not weighed in completely, some anecdotal reports are linking a patient's resilience and improved psychological health to humor. A positive outlook on life also helps. Laughter does wonders for both body and soul. Besides, if you are not having fun or including some laughter in your life, you are really missing out. It is like sugar on the family table. It gives flavor and zing to your life.

Fourth-quarter people need to make sure they schedule as much laughter as they can into their day or week. It is the "fun" part in fundamental, and if you don't do it enough, you can become "mental." By being some somber old fuddy-duddy or cranky ol' lady, people are pushed away from you by your suck-on-a-lemon demeanor.

The late actors Jack Lemmon and Walter Matthau made a couple of movies titled *Grumpy Old Men* and *Grumpier Old Men*. Of course, this was science fiction that these two old buzzards would attract the likes of Ann Margaret and Sophia Loren, but hey, it's the movies. It was played for laughs with truth, humor, and pathos along with the creative license of exaggerated hyperbole. But the underlying premise is that even in advanced years, hijinks, humor, and adventure are still part of the spice of life.

For boomers, a flashback from many decades ago recalls Reader's Digest magazine, filled with funny sections of jokes, stories, and anecdotes that always brought a smile to one's face before being largely shunted aside by the advent of the Internet and Facebook. And if you found something that really struck your funny bone, you were anxious to share it with someone else and laugh with them all over again. It did a heart good.

So, this chapter is devoted to a number of eclectic jokes and stories told and retold in various renditions over many decades. The whole purpose is to bring a chuckle or a good-humored laugh that you can carry with you throughout the day. So what does this have to do with fourth-quarter people? Plenty! It is imperative that you set aside a little time to laugh each day. It is as necessary as food, water, and exercise.

While humor is varied and personal, and not everyone will warm to every joke or even find some funny at all, there is a guarantee that you will find at least one or two nuggets of humor here (ignore the rest) that you will be anxious to share with someone else that you know will also get a kick out of them. The goal is a reminder to realize the importance of finding humor in your life wherever you can. For many, Facebook threads or You Tube posts of funny, touching, or simply amazing clips from friends and relatives is a form of therapy that releases good vibes. It is always a mood enhancer and sets a tone of inner joy about your day when you find a great joke or a website you can't wait to share with a friend. Make your own file folder of favorites as we often forget over time and you can share the best with new friends. So here are a number of diverse jokes to pick and choose from. Some you may not care for, but that's OK. If you only like a handful of them, that is still a decent batting average. So enjoy! Smile! Laugh! Share! Often, your attitude in life determines your altitude in life. Here we go:

Be careful what you wish for. A husband and wife, both sixty years of age, are walking along the beach when the husband picks up a bottle and is startled to see a genie pop out. The genie turns to the husband and tells him he can grant him one wish. The husband nods toward his wife with a boyish grin and a wry smile and sheepishly tells the genie, "I would kinda like to be married to a woman thirty years younger. Poof, he is now ninety!

A young man, Jack falls for a beautiful twenty-five-year-old nurse named Jennifer and wants to marry her. He also tells her his widowed father is sick and has only a few months to live and he stands to inherit twenty million dollars. A week later, Jack visits his father, who introduces him to his new nurse Jennifer... and his new stepmother!

A gentleman who had a number of serious physical health issues was told by his doctor to wait in the waiting room while he spoke privately to the man's wife. The doctor explained to the wife her husband's very delicate and fragile medical situation and instructed her that she should never argue with him, always agree to sex when approached, always be pleasant, fix his favorite foods, and generally try to wait on him hand and foot for his well-being. The wife returned to the waiting room and looked at her husband and said, "Bad news– you're going to die."

The best proof that there is intelligent life in the universe is that no one has contacted us!

Winston Churchill, on being asked by a lady if he was flattered that he drew such large crowds to his political speeches, replied, "Yes, but whenever I feel this way, I am reminded that if I were being hanged, the crowd would be twice as big."

A man on his deathbed, knowing this is the end, whispers to his wife, "You know what? You have been with me through all the bad times. When I got fired, when my business failed, when the house burned down, when I got shot, when my dog ran away, when my health began to fail, you were always there." As the wife's heart begins to glow, he says, "I think you're bad luck!"

Ships at sea have protocols to avoid collisions. An officer on deck on a dark night saw a light in the far distance and signaled, "Move two degrees to your portside." Back flashed the reply, "You move two degrees to starboard." Incensed, the officer of the deck flashed back, "I am an admiral, who are you? I insist you move two degrees to portside." Back came the reply," I am Seaman Jack Miller. You move two degrees starboard." The admiral became flustered and angry and flashed back, "Move as I demand. I am an aircraft carrier." The response came back quickly, "Sir, move two degrees starboard. I am a lighthouse."

A ninety-year-old man married a twenty-five-year-old woman. In the hotel for the honeymoon the next day, the wiped-out twenty-five-year-old bride stumbled downstairs to the coffee shop. The waiter said, "You look terrible. What happened?" "Well," she replied, "he told me he had been saving it his whole life, but I thought he meant his money!"

If a man speaks in the woods and a woman does not hear him, is he still wrong?

Las Vegas is the only town where you can arrive in a $25,000 car and leave on a $250,000 bus!

A very old gentleman named Joe from a small town won millions in the lottery. Joe, not being notified as yet, caused some concern among some of the townspeople because of the old man's two previous heart attacks and how he might react to such news. So they agreed among themselves to have the local priest break the news gently. When the priest met with old Joe, he tried to sound out Joe in a light and jesting tone. "Joe, what would you ever do with millions of dollars if you won the lottery?" Joe replied, "I'm old, Father. I'd probably give it to you." The priest had a heart attack!

A man walking on the beach found a bottle, and out popped a genie, who granted him only one wish. The man said he had a fear of flying but that he had always wanted to visit Hawaii and would like a bridge built for him over the Pacific Ocean so he could drive there. The genie did not look happy. He complained, "That's over two thousand miles away. Do you know how hard that is? Do you know how much steel, cement, and labor is involved? Do you know that in places, the ocean is two miles deep? Don't you have something easier?" The man thought and said, "You know, I have always had trouble understanding women. Do you think you could help me out with that?" The genie replied, "Would that be a two-lane or four-lane highway?"

Behind every successful man is a shocked mother-in-law.

An older gentleman is driving home from work when his wife rings him on his hands-free car phone. "Honey," she says in a worried voice, "be careful. There was a bulletin on the news just now; some lunatic is driving the wrong way down the freeway." "It's worse than that," he replies. "There are hundreds of them!"

In a small town, after a routine checkup, the local doctor escorted the always complaining Ms. Parker out of his office while rolling his eyes. Ms. Parker was the local town's spinster, well-known chief gossiper, meddler, troublemaker, and all-around pain in the neck. The doctor's next patient was widower Sam, and the doctor sadly gave him the bad news about his latest test results and told Sam that he had only six months to live. Sam was crestfallen and said, "Doc, what should I do?" "Hmm," the doctor calmly said and thought for a minute. "Well, I suggest you marry Ms. Parker. It will be the longest six months of your life."

Top ten signs of fourth-quarter people:

1. In a hostage situation, you are likely to be released first.
2. No one expects you to run–anywhere.
3. People no longer think you're a hypochondriac.
4. When your ten-year-old granddaughter is a better techie than you are.
5. People call at nine p.m. and ask, "Did I wake you up?"
6. When you think an Instagram is a telegram and you

answer the front door.

7. When you do a Google search to locate where you left your glasses.
8. When your "get up and go" sends you a text message to locate you.
9. There is nothing left to learn the hard way.
10. Your secrets are safe with your friends because they can't remember them either.

An older couple, who were both widowed, had been dating for a long time. Encouraged by their friends, they decided it was finally time to get married.

The couple went out to dinner and talked over how their marriage might work regarding finances, living arrangements, and so on. Finally, the old gentleman decided it was time to broach the subject of their physical relationship. "How do you feel about sex?" he asked rather sheepishly.

"I would like it infrequently," she replied.

The old gentleman sat quietly for a moment in deep thought, then leaned over toward her and whispered, "Is that one word or two?"

A concerned senior citizen called the doctor. "Is it true that the medication you prescribed for me has to be taken for the rest of my life? The doctor stammered, hesitated, and replied, "I'm afraid so." "Well, just how serious is my condition? The bottle is marked No Refills."

Jack was at a party, listening to a group of guests who were trying to impress each other by touting their past accomplishments in high school. When it was his turn, he humbly declined to say anything but, when pushed, he modestly and reluctantly told them that he had been senior class president, valedictorian, voted most popular, most likely to succeed, best athlete, and was even the teacher's pet. Later in the evening, one of the men remarked to Jack's wife about how proud she must have been by her husband's high-school achievements. Puzzled, she said, "You do know Jack was home schooled!"

A missing poster sign was nailed to a tree. "Missing: husband and dog. Reward for dog."

Many years ago, an Amish boy and his middle-aged mother are in a department store for the first time and are mesmerized by their first encounter with an elevator. The walls open and close, with seemingly different people entering and exiting from the elevator. They notice an old gentleman with a cane walk into the tiny enclosed space, and the doors close. A minute later, they open back up, and a handsome young man steps out of the elevator. Intrigued and mystified, the mother tells her young son, "Go get your father."

Aging is when you hear snap, crackle, and pop before you go to have breakfast.

A politician locked in a tight re-election fight included a campaign stop at a local Indian reservation. He promised them he would fix the pot-holed road leading into the reservation. The response was electric as the Indians shouted Uuumm phahhh! Uuumm phahhh! Encouraged by the response the politician also pledged a new roof for the grade school and more funding for the health clinic. Each promise elicited more excitement, the stomping of feet, and many cries of Uuumm phahhh! Uuumm phahhh!

The tribal chief then thanked the politician for coming and asked him if he would like to see their prize winning dairy cow. Showing respect, the smug politician readily agreed. As they walked across the field for a closer look at the cow, the chief warned the politician to be careful not to step in the Uuumm phahhh!

The four stages of life: You believe in Santa Claus. You don't believe in Santa Claus. You are Santa Claus. You look like Santa Claus.

Okay, admit it. There was at least one or two that you liked, right? Well then, share them with several others, and laugh again with them. Find some more on your own that bring you a smile and a chuckle. The bottom line about "yukking it up" is that whatever tickles your funny bone in life, a goal should be to laugh often, laugh hard, share it, and do it again. And if you have a couple ol' sourpusses in your inner circle, it is time to find some new friends who appreciate the "endorphin" highs of good laughter.

21

MOVIN' ON FAST–THE BIG SIX-FIVE

65! "You gotta be kidding me"

Why do I feel more and more like Bill Murray in *Groundhog Day*? you exclaim to yourself. "Sixty-five!!! Wow, I just had my sixtieth birthday! Honey, wasn't that last year? Or certainly it was the year before that. Did we skip a few? What did we do for my sixty-second, sixty-third, and sixty-fourth birthdays, anything special? I can't remember. How did this take me by surprise yet again? I was just trying to get used to the number sixty. What's with all these ads in the mailbox for Medicare advantage plans? Don't they have the wrong address?"

It's so surreal. It feels like an imagined out-of-body experience. It seems that the superhighway of life has been traded in for a bullet train and that the scenery out the window is whizzing by faster than ever.

So what is the big deal about sixty-five? After all, it is just a number that comes after sixty-four. (Can't you hear Paul McCartney singing in your head, "...when I'm sixty-four"?)

Well, numbers have power all their own. No one aspires to amass a wealth of $990,000. A millionaire sounds so much cooler and has a nice ring to it. No man aspires to be five feet eleven when an even "six footer" makes a psychological difference. No one does nine push-ups when exercising, runs nine kilometers, or wants to drop nine pounds. We like meaningful numbers.

Similarly, but in a different context, the same is true about significant life numbers that mark milestones on our journey: Six is the number for entering first grade; sixteen, driver's license; eighteen, high-school graduation; twenty-one, the legal age for alcohol; twenty-two, the ideal time for college graduation. Different personal numbers will follow for everyone's first full-time job, marriage, and birth of one's children. While the age for taking Social Security benefits may vary for boomers, age sixty-five is the last universal milestone and is linked by everyone to Medicare and general retirement.

The number sixty-five can be blamed on or attributed with thanks to the Germans. Back in the nineteenth century under the "Iron Chancellor," Otto von Bismarck,[22] Germany was instrumental in setting up one of the first large-scale modern-day pension schemes for the elderly of that era. In 1889, the age of seventy was initially chosen and later reduced to sixty-five in 1916 as the age for qualification. Subsequently, in 1935 when the American Social Security program came into being, sixty-five was also chosen as the age of retirement, based on actuarial tables at the time. Then in 1965, President Lyndon Johnson's Medicare program was enacted and sixty-five was selected again as the age for receiving benefits. Due to longer lifespans, Social Security is being phased in to age sixty-seven for full benefits while Medicare still remains at sixty-five.

While turning sixty puts you in the "senior" category, sixty-five is different in that it starts leaning one into the "old" category whether one likes it or not. It is a mental calculation made by those of all ages on both sides of this line marker. Resistance is futile. Yet there can still be a wide divergence in this regard, depending on an individual's health, energy, engagement, enthusiasm, and attitude towards life. Millions in the sixty-five-year-plus group are still working and are vital, vibrant, and plugged in. Millions of others exhibit these same dynamic qualities but have simply shifted gears to other pursuits in retirement. Sadly, those who have been unlucky by genetics or misfortune are living a compromised life along with those who have trashed their health by self-infliction of bad lifestyle choices. These individuals often stand out by looking much older than their chronological age. Of course, the clock keeps ticking for everyone.

W. Clement Stone, a businessman (who lived to be a hundred) and motivational speaker, years ago exhorted audiences that the most important words that should be taken to heart are "do it now,"[23] which in the current generation parallels the Nike shoe "swoosh" logo with its famous admonition of "just do it." Both of these phrases proclaim that procrastination is the enemy of any endeavor we wish to achieve. A mañana, mañana approach has ruined more lives perhaps than anything else. Fear of doing, sloth, or lack of discipline has robbed many a life from being fulfilled.

So what should be said about sixty-five that would be much different from turning sixty? The answer is very little except added emphasis since one-fourth of the fourth quarter is now over. (Note: a stunning illustration for motivation is to get out a tape measure and place one thumb on sixty-five inches and your other thumb on your hoped-for life span (say eighty-five or more) and compare the visual to the first sixty-five inches. It is dramatic.) However, with each passing year, the qualitative differences in our lives become more pronounced. What does this mean? Simply put, it means the beginning of the law of diminishing returns.

When it comes to aging, the difference between eighteen and nineteen is basically zero. Turning from twenty-nine to thirty, one notices practically nothing physically. But you can already see where this is headed. Imperceptibly, as we get into bigger numbers, there is a separation factor that begins to take place. Arbitrarily, changes in our early forties are not a big deal, but it is different from when we were younger. It is subtle but undeniable that around this age we are annoyed that for the first time most of us need glasses for reading since the print looks smaller. We can't eat the way we did when we were younger and still defy the scale. At the gym, playing with young kids, or working around the house or yard all afternoon, we take mental note of our stretched muscles and affected agility being different than when we were in our invincible twenties. For professional athletes, their career is over.

By fast forwarding to a present age of sixty-five or more we need to consider the yearly separation factor of one year at a time. We notice that when sitting on a plane or in a car for a long stretch of time, we tend to stiffen up and need to walk around to loosen up. Some friends make jokes about getting a can of oil of WD-40. Seniors are annoyed when they begin to miss a word or phrase here and there in conversation and have to ask, "What did you say?"

Back to our football game analogy and playing in the fourth quarter of our life. Most "seniors" have been giving it their all through the first three quarters and are starting to show some fatigue as the fourth quarter begins. They are a little banged up with minor aches, sprains, and cuts, but they shake them off as just part of the game. True grit is required here, and playing slightly hurt is just part of the game. They may not be as fresh as a daisy like in the first and second quarters, but veteran players make adjustments to conserve their strength and energy to play smarter. They still have some gas left in their tank, and the game is still close, exciting, and on the line.

Indeed, the focus is so much on the game, the crowd, the score, and the strategy that players often just block out any minor pain that can slow them down. They are "in the zone"[24] and nothing else matters but the game. However, they may not realize they have a lost a step or two until a fresh substitute player comes in for the other team. So it is with the game of life.

Turning sixty-five, which is still early in the fourth quarter, may reveal to us some small physical setbacks, yet most of us can continue to play the fourth-quarter game of life with enthusiasm. But this may not apply to teammates. You may be in fine health, but if your spouse or best friend is ill or in distress, the trip, the project, the big plans may all fall apart because your partner has been carried off the field either in death or chronic illness. It is almost like a war zone where two soldiers are on the front line, and suddenly one is struck down while his buddy does not have a scratch on him. It is just an unknown in life.

Turning sixty-five should be a reminder to implement those plans, wishes, and desires right away even if you are on your way to being a hale and hearty one hundred because the roller coaster ride is so much more exciting to share with special people you like and love. So at sixty-five, the "do it now" words of wisdom are even more urgent. Often, who is on the trip with you is much more important than the trip itself.

22

WISDOM: I DON'T GET NO RESPECT

We drink at the fountain of knowledge but gargle at the fount of wisdom.

Wisdom gets short shrift. Like the late comedian Rodney Dangerfield, it gets no respect. Knowledge is the great quest today. Being smart is an attribute everyone likes having ascribed to them. Techies, nerds, and geeks are all greatly admired for their skills and abilities even if most young and old do not want to be them due to perceived social deficits. However, the revealing joke for the twenty-first century is this: "What do you call a nerd ten years out of high school? Answer: Boss." Strikingly, there is a growing cadre of a Silicon Valley "high-priest class" of "technocrats" that are becoming the twenty-first-century equivalent of the nineteenth-and-twentieth-century captains of industry and the seventeenth-and eighteenth-century land barons of the past. They are lauded for their creativity, ingenuity, and being producers of great wealth.

Tellingly, for people in all walks of life, with a hundred things to preoccupy their attention and "to do" list, the acquisition or even appreciation of wisdom seldom cracks this list.

For fourth-quarter people (or any life quarter) with lots of life experiences, these brief paragraphs on wisdom should not be taken lightly. Properly understood, wisdom should be considered as a blueprint for a proposed magnificent monument to a well-lived-life constructed out of the highest values that will stand the test of time. The same is true for a life of meaning. It is never too late to "wise up." Nor is it ever too late to pass on life's lessons to following generations.

Wisdom sits at the apex of all the virtues, not knowledge. This is one of the fundamental problems of mankind. We associate knowledge with power and the quest for success that will bring us money, influence, sex, love, fame, and material gain, but it is only a means to an end whereas wisdom teaches us how to live and what is truly important. It teaches moderation, introspection, and deeper insight. Knowledge only teaches us how to get or discover something. There is a world of difference in the two concepts that is lost on most people.

In some Asian societies, elders are much more respected than in Western cultures. Part of this is tradition and custom but also the idea that older people have made more mistakes, have more experience, and see more clearly the pitfalls and hubris of youth. Elders grasp how much trouble and heartbreak can be avoided rather than the myopic view often displayed by the impetuousness nature of youth. Asian youth, in many cases, are therefore taught to venerate their elders with more respect.

The columnist David Brooks in his book *The Road to Character*[25] adroitly differentiates between résumé virtues and eulogy virtues. In essence, our lives are consumed by our résumés: our academic degrees, titles, awards, position, and accomplishments. In stark contrast are the "eulogy virtues" of what will be said about you at the end of your life. These virtues cluster around loyalty, compassion, caring, purpose, family, and enduring friendships.

A good life is all about making good choices and remembering that there can be more than one "right" choice available. It is worth contemplating what success really means to you in its broadest meaning.

Wisdom needs to be restored to its rightful pedestal at the entrance door of the pantheon for all virtues that informs a meaningful and fulfilling life. Unfortunately, in today's age, it is often relegated to the basement to sit in a dusty little corner of a forgotten room. It is also a biblical admonition: "So teach us to number our days, that we may apply our hearts to wisdom."[26]

Wisdom should define purpose in life and how a life should be conducted. The insightful words of Albert Einstein are also instructive: "Try not to become a [person] of success, but rather try to become a [person] of value."

23

SERVICE WITH A HEART

"A society grows when old men plant trees whose shade they will never sit under."

Greek proverb

It can break you just watching the news. War, hunger, terrorism, disease, injustice–the list is very long. The needs of the world are so enormous and crushing. We often respond with a self-defense mechanism of a shrug and looking the other way, along with rationalizing that "it's not my problem; I've got enough of my own problems to keep me busy, thank you very much."

The good news is that you are not responsible to solve the problems of the world. That is above your pay grade. You are hereby absolved of any guilt-trip feelings and off the hook. But this does not mean doing nothing. The other side of this coin is you are responsible to do your bit in proportion to your talents and resources. If there is a small hole in the dam and you have a small plug, you are to use it, not just stand back and say, "It's only a tiny leak." You simply do what you can, more if possible, but certainly not less. If you are amazingly blessed, it may be your assignment to build an entire dam rather than plug a small leak. Make a difference.

A man was walking along a mostly deserted beach one morning after a fearsome storm the night before. The heavy tide had washed up thousands of starfish onto the beach and left them stranded in the warm morning sun. Many were writhing and twitching in an obvious death spiral and unable to reach their home in the comfort of the ocean just a hundred feet away. Life was ebbing fast, and soon this stretch of beach would become a mass funeral ground for them all. The man walking the beach between the surf and the warming sand would stop every ten or twenty paces and pick up a struggling starfish and fling it back into the ocean almost as if he were trying to skip a stone. A lady walking in the opposite direction observed this and approached the man and scolded, "You are wasting your time, sir. There are thousands of them all dying on the beach, and you can't save them all." The man looked at the lady while holding up a starfish in his hand and replied, "That may be true, ma'am, but try telling it to this one!"[27]

Tragedy and unfairness afflict humanity everywhere, but good Samaritans are a special breed, and everyone should strive to become one in their own way. Rising above one's own self-interest to help someone in distress is not only charitable but noble. It is the glue that keeps a society sustainable through thick and thin.

Everyone likes a payday, but there is more to income than just dollars and cents. There is also such a thing as "psychic income" that affects our mood, spirit, and a sense of unselfishness. At its core, it is practicing a hundred random acts of micro-kindnesses each year and expecting no quid pro quo in return. It can take form in hundreds of ways–simple things like taking the extra five minutes to praise a store employee for good service (and doing it in front of a supervisor that you have requested to see) rather than just complaining when something goes wrong. Waving a car ahead in traffic or someone in line at the grocery store who is in a hurry or with fussy kids shows consideration. Taking the time to listen to a child or to help someone in need displays a spirit of generosity. The psychic income from doing these small acts rebound to our benefit much more than most people realize. The attitude of gratitude to brighten another's day can be exhibited to others and often costs nothing but our attention.

Public service, however, requires a little more effort to aid a community—from cleaning up a blighted empty lot to coaching Little League or leading a fund drive for some worthy purpose. Talents may differ, but those who help others often get just as much of a blessing in return as those helped. What is public service? When it is not about you, but others, it is public service. Your reward is the quiet satisfaction that comes from knowing you did a good thing. It is as simple as that.

It is impossible to calculate the end result of helping one individual. Much like the starfish thrown back into the sea, a person helped may go on to school and through their efforts help thousands of others, which would not have occurred without your assistance and intervention at the right time in the first place. Perhaps this individual that you have helped is of modest means but may have a son or daughter or grandchild who decades later makes astonishing advances in some scientific field or cutting-edge technology. One never knows. If there is a shipwreck and we can help save one life, would we not throw them a life preserver? Many will be lost, but some will be saved, and for them, like for the starfish, it means everything. Perhaps one day after a run of bad luck, you may be a starfish yourself, praying for a kind stranger to pass by.

So contribute something. Whatever your ability level is,

determine to make a difference. Impacting a life can carry on for generations after you are gone, spreading far and wide, creating an effect you could scarcely imagine that you can be genuinely proud of, even if you are never around to know it. It is astonishing to hear in thousands of interviews of successful people over and over again how many honor and give credit to their parents, a special teacher, coach, friend, or other mentor for their success. Equally noted by these movers and shakers is the often expressed lament that so many of these life changers did not live long enough to see the fruits of their investment and its resulting success. Again, you just never know.

In the Navy, sailors are organized around a hundred different functions required to maintain the ship. From the captain to the cook and from the engineer to the deck hand, everyone has a role to play. If the gong goes off and the public address system barks out the order calling urgently for "battle stations, battle stations, all hands report to battle stations," all the sailors know their places and what is expected of them. Each life is dependent on the expertise of fellow crew members to fulfill their duties as part of a team effort.

Like a sailor in the Navy, everyone should find their "station" in life beyond their vocation, where they can make their own meaningful contribution to society. Sometimes, what you add to another life does not equal two plus two but a sum of five or a thousand (or even an exponential factor) for that extra intangibility of caring by going the extra mile.

Many people today confuse citizenship with public service. Citizenship is all too often defined narrowly. Some will claim that they have fulfilled their role as a good citizen by voting, paying their taxes, and obeying the law. Done! But this is a minimalist view that fails to strengthen society in a number of ways. Public service requires a commitment to sometimes "go above and beyond" what is merely required. In essence, it is like a camper's creed when hiking in the wilderness to leave your campsite better than you found it. When looking at the marvels of the modern world and all the new inventions and discoveries that are made each year, it is easy to forget that we stand on the shoulders of giants who came before us. Their hard work and dedication laid the foundation for succeeding generations to build upon. They passed the torch, and it is the purpose of public service to keep the torch shining brightly and passing it on once again to those who follow behind. The concept of "pay it forward," whereby our good deed for another is to be repaid in kind to still others, has a multiplying effect.

Interestingly, it may not be your calling to be the next Mother Teresa or volunteering your weekends once a month to feed the homeless. People who do these acts of charity are to be admired and appreciated, but it is not everyone's role.

A businessperson who is highly successful and efficient in what they do may be wasting their talents at a food kitchen although there are personal and psychic benefits for being on the ground to see where the rubber meets the road for the underclass. Instead, perhaps the greatest public service such a businessperson could perform is in spending their time in the comfort of their fancy air-conditioned office with their feet up on their desk making phone call after phone call to contact and prod other people of wealth and means to fund another shelter, to build another school, or to open a number of health clinics to serve the needy. Such a businessperson may personally have had rare contact with a person of need on a human-to-human level but through their efforts may have helped hundreds or thousands of people in need. Their involvement has provided the needed outreach funding to establish hundreds of Mother Teresa's to carry on. Their noble public service has enormous value as well as the individual on the front line.

Likewise, public service is a physician or a scientist who donates their personal time in a lab doing research work for no compensation to work on a cure for an obscure disease that pharmaceutical companies ignore as not cost effective, but that still afflicts and destroys thousands of lives. Even if the doctor never meets one of these patients, the work of public service in this context speaks for itself. The lawyer who works pro bono to right a wrong in the justice system is a hero on a white horse with a pen in one hand and a law book in the other. A tradesman who helps build a house for a veteran who is disabled is a saint in their own way. Even those with more modest backgrounds can change the world. Helping a child to read or merely being a cheerleader for a discouraged child or adult can leave a lasting impression. A parent can impact the world, for "the hand that rocks the cradle is the hand that rules the world."[28] Find your niche beyond your family unit and fill it.

24

MARRIAGE:
THE SECOND TIME AROUND

"Life is like a box of chocolates;
you never know what you're gonna get."

Forrest Gump

Getting married again as a senior is a different proposition
from the first time around the wedding cake. When you were
young, you were often clueless and pretty much broke as you
started out on the hoped-for road to marital bliss. Being "in
love" was all that was needed, and somehow the future would
take care of itself. Rose-colored glasses and naiveté
completed the scene of a beautiful wedding. The only thing
missing from the fantasy wedding was the slow walk into a
gorgeous sunset on the beach with swelling music and a fade-
out shot with a voice-over wedding planner intoning, "And they
lived happily ever after." This is where all fairy tales end and
the movie credits roll. Unfortunately, in too many relationships

courtship ends in the glow of the sunset and marriage begins at dawn.

All the old rules of getting married again still apply. But now the rules are magnified by experience. When you were young, both you and your new partner made mistakes, plenty of them. From these mistakes you learned, adjusted, negotiated, and moved on or hit the rocks and split up. However, at sixty plus, it is a different world. You are, for better or worse, a stick-in-the-mud in your own ways no matter how much you try to convince friends and the world how flexible you are.

Some may be offended by such a description, yet it is nevertheless true in the sense of likes and dislikes. One claims to like this food and hate that food. One likes casual, the color blue, antiques, getting up early, shopping, hobbies, gardening, the beach, etc. The next person in line has a completely different set of preferences. The point is that in the fourth-quarter people are who they are. Yes, they may be a little more forgiving and tolerant in some ways than in younger years and make a meaningful attempt to go more with the flow. But real change? It ain't happening. Fundamentally, what you see is what you get. An old dog can sometimes learn new tricks but quite prefers its own routine.

The fourth-quarter subset of the group who remain single, due to a divorce or the passing of a spouse, comprise two camps. The first is an emphatic, "Nope, I have no interested in getting married again. I like things my way, and I don't want to cater to anyone." The second group would like someone special if they could find the "right one." Companionship, shared memories, and a special intimacy on all levels–emotionally, intellectually, physically, and spiritually–is a desired attraction. The reason why finding someone like this is so difficult to achieve is because each person in this age group wants to find someone special that fits into their life, not to fit into another's life. There's the rub.

All adults can be placed into one of five categories in a hierarchy of desirability. In first place is a great marriage whereby two partners share a full life and a love with one another that is truly special. This is not easy to find or achieve without effort. In second place is a single person who is happy with who he or she is and with life in general. It may be sweet to find a soul mate, but life is still pretty good and they have few complaints. In third place is a marriage that is neither fair nor foul. The romance is gone, and this is more a marriage of room-mates. It is rather blasé and leaves much to be desired, but it is like a comfortable old pair of shoes one is reticent to throw out. In fourth place is a single person that is miserable with their current situation in life along with their single marital status. They daydream and would like to be rescued, but no one is showing up, which adds to their gloomy outlook. In fifth place is a marriage that is a complete disaster. A divorce is often threatened but stops just short of the brink. This desperate marriage is only hanging by a thread because of family, finances, social status, religion, or the real fear of being lonely with no one to fight with. It is sad. So be aware that while the ideal is to strive for a number-one slot and a hoped-for great marriage, it is often the exception when reaching for the brass ring.

Fast forward now to the fourth quarter of your life. You and your new squeeze may or may not be wiser, but you do come to any new relationship with baggage. Some bring a suitcase or two; others bring a rusty old dump truck piled high with issues and complications. If the latter is the case, be smart and run like hell–salvage jobs never work out. When it comes to marriage at any age, the best advice is to go into it with both eyes wide open and afterwards with one eye shut. It helps to overlook the faults, shortcomings, and annoying habits of the one closest to you during the marriage journey together.

Another important consideration is whether a previous

marriage ended by death or divorce. If you are marrying one who has lost their spouse in death, it can be difficult to compete with an idealized version (a ghost?) of one's first love that may come from a highly selective memory. You may have trouble measuring up. Decades of history, memories, children, and life challenges are not just suddenly wiped away and never will be. The past gives frame and reference to an individual's previous life. It does hurt to play second fiddle, but it may still be okay if you learn to play, so to speak, a different instrument in the orchestra. You bring your own music and arrangements. On the other hand, a bitter former divorce can bring resentment and suspicion into a new marriage that hurts both partners. Fear of getting hurt again, a suspicious nature, or the pain of the past can result in such a cautious spirit as to set up a troubled and doomed relationship from the start.

Seniors are often a little arrogant in thinking that a lifetime of experience qualifies them on almost any subject that comes along, especially when dealing in relationships both personal and observed over many decades. Both men and women think they have a handle on it. Both are eager to shoehorn someone into their life rather than the other way around. But it bears keeping in mind that it is absolutely preferable to have no one than the wrong one.

Seniors who are getting remarried can benefit from a pre-marriage seminar, just as much as young newlyweds. Community organizations, churches, and family counselors all put on pre-marriage seminars with the end goal of helping couples make sure they start off on the right foot with no misconceptions. The greatest pitfall is unrealistic expectations by one or both parties involved, regardless of age. Love is blind is more than just a wise saying and is not restricted to just the young. In addition, fourth-quarter people's lives are just more complicated than twentysomethings starting out. The biggies of work/retirement, lifestyle, sex, money, stepchildren of any age, health, religion, and personality all deserve an in-depth review. There should be no sudden surprises later on. After all, the best time to split up is before the wedding.

An excellent shorthand list that each partner (of any age) should bring to the table is the seven H's, to see if they match up with one another. They are Head (common thinking), Heart (love for each other), Hormones (mutual sexual attraction), Honesty (without it... forget it), Humor (laughter, the glue that does a heart good), Honor (loyalty and respect), and Humility (not taking one's self too seriously). That pretty much wraps it all up. If you can both pass this simple test, you are good to go. If yes, you may get the eighth H, which can be a slice of Heaven. If not, you may end up with the ninth H, which is a taste of hell.

Even chronological age is a topic of concern if, say, a man is a number of years older than his spouse-to-be. A spry sixty-five-year-old woman of means who is marrying a seventy-five-year-old man of modest means and just average health needs to consider whether she is getting into a situation to be the "nurse with the purse." Similarly, a seventy-year-old man of some means, betrothed to a woman of sixty with modest means, needs to make sure he does not merely represent "the man on the white horse" come to rescue fair lady in financial distress. Gold diggers of both genders come in all ages and packages. Caveat emptor is in order.

Of course, being older does have its merits in that individuals know what they want. The downside is what they can realistically get or even what may be good for them. Finding a "babe" or a "hunk" may be easier to find than to keep. Settling for an ice-cream cone when you crave a banana split can be hard even if the split will give you an upset stomach and make you sick. However, seniors who feel this new person in their life "clicks" with them may be anxious to move on to the next step in the relationship.

Naturally, some adult children are uncomfortable with the idea of some stranger taking the place of Mom or Dad because things will seem different and awkward whether because of death or divorce while other children may be delighted a parent found love again. Some children are concerned about inheritance arrangements and how this will affect them. A few offspring genuinely take on the role of parent, counseling "don't rush into anything" primarily out of concern that a parent does not get hurt emotionally or make a big mistake. Broken hearts have no age limits. One humorous aside is of the eighty-four-year-old professional gentleman who had lost his wife two years earlier and was seeing a new lady. When he spoke with his daughter in her fifties (of his plans to get remarried right away), she cautioned him to "take some time to think this over." His reply was swift: "How much time do you think I have left?"

The most farsighted plan is the one that faces facts openly and transparently. The issues of money, inheritance, and family-budget contributions on the part of both spouses should be acknowledged, legalized, and finalized before there are any "I do's." If one or both parties bring meaningful assets to the marriage table, a prenup agreement is just common sense. It can always be changed later by the consent of both parties, but it establishes a baseline for expectations. If this is a financial marriage of equals, there should be accounts of his, hers, and ours, and they should be clearly kept separate. Only the "ours" account should show comingling (mixed-up-together) while all other assets, pension, real estate, and bank accounts are kept separate in the name of the ownership spouse. Legal counsel should definitely be sought.

Second marriages have a higher divorce rate than first marriages, and third marriages an even higher rate than second marriages. One good feedback loop to use as a sounding board is trusted friends or family that have your best interests at heart. Ask them sincerely for their unvarnished analysis of your "intended" to round out a more complete picture of what you are getting into. They are not heavily invested and can often see things that you may have missed, ignored, or dismissed as inconsequential. In effect, they act as a third and fourth eye for you. In addition, another telltale sign is how your intended partner gets along with your long-time friends and you with theirs. Pets are no small issue either and can often take priority over you. So if you don't like his/her friends and even more so his/her family, there will be trouble in paradise. Count on it. Think twice.

The good news is that if you find someone you love and who loves you, what a blessing. In the fourth quarter of life, this is just icing on the cake. Pinch yourself and go for it if you both feel it is right for you after having done your "due diligence" on each other to ensure compatibility and understanding. Those people who were lucky enough to have one good or great marriage are fortunate, but to luck out twice is like winning the lottery twice. The marriage contract is just that, a contract with serious obligations for both parties. But be mindful that the real tests of a marriage almost always center on family, finances, health, loyalty, interests, quirks, and personality. A loving heart can go a long way and trump almost all adversity. It does not guarantee smooth sailing, but it does mean you will enjoy the trip more whether in calm or stormy seas.

25

MONEY

"Money should be treated like manure...
You need to spread it around."

Thornton Wilder, paraphrased

Since the dawn of time, when it comes to feelings about love, men and women have long felt the same conflicted outlook about relationships best summed up in the expression, "Ya can't live with 'em, and ya can't live without 'em." But that sentiment is not shared about money. We know we can't live without it. Ya just gotta have some. And more money is always thought to be better than less money. But it is in the details where things can get sticky.

A young child on the verge of tears may ask his or her Mommy or Daddy, "Why do you have to leave me and go to work?" If the answer that comes back is, "Honey, we work so we can pay the bills," it may be factual and true, but it also leaves an awful lot out. And there is a world of difference between a mere job for sustenance as opposed to engaging and meaningful work. Certainly, the obvious reason is that we need money so that we can provide for the absolute essentials of life like food, shelter, clothing, iPods, smart phones, tablets, cable TV, laptops, Netflix, Disney World, a fancier house, a second home, a big RV, a lakeside mountain cabin, a beach house, a cool speedboat, and a driveway full of hot cars. Okay, that's a little tongue-in-cheek humor after the food, shelter, and clothing bit, but not by much when talking about the American dream.

Our modern lifestyles have turned materialism in to an ever-increasing demand for more "goodies" to keep us entertained and satiated. Amazon and the Home Shopping Network are a click away and often a day or two away from showing up at our front door. Already in some larger cities, they are shrinking the window of delivery down to mere hours, giving instant gratification a whole new meaning straight from our smartphones while we sit on the living-room couch. Some writers joke that with a big enough database on your entire life, stuff could show up at your doorstep before you even think to order it! Already plans are being implemented to link sensor bar codes to your refrigerator to an Internet account to self-order items that are running low.

Many years back, when Madonna sang about being just a "Material Girl" for her legion of fans, she wasn't kidding around. When paired with Cyndi Lauper's old anthem, "Girls Just Wanna Have Fun," this frame of mind kind of rounds out the American credo of more of everything is always better. It is deeply rooted in our consumer culture. Indeed, one of the most chronic diseases any young man, or older man for that matter, can have in the romance department is "no money, no honey." The blinding "bling culture" is not lost on men and puts a lot of stress on them. Just buying tickets to a game or concert these days almost requires a down-payment plan.

Switching for a moment to baseball metaphors, seniors are

rounding third base and want to make sure they have enough speed (health) and power (money) to carry them through to home plate in the ninth inning. So let's be clear about retiring when the day comes that there are only a dozen big concerns you should worry about. Health, which covers numbers one through ten (health is everything); finances, which is number eleven (you gotta have some money); and number twelve is what you will do with your remaining clock time with some proper planning. Failure to take care of your health makes numbers eleven and twelve moot, which is why health is repeated ten times as over-the-top hyperbole to get the point across that this should always be your top priority (i.e., put down that soda and fries, get up, and leave for the gym now!). Correspondingly, if you have neglected to take care of your finances (number eleven), your future plans regarding your remaining "clock time" may be problematic and greatly curtailed.

But let's talk turkey about money. Despite preachers who rail against the "love of money," philosophers who can wax eloquent about a simpler life, and wise old family sages (which soon may or may not include you) who caution about the curse of "filthy lucre," money in and of itself is neutral, and there is nothing intrinsically wrong with it. Indeed, many confuse the concept of money as a convenient means of exchange for ordinary daily transactions and the "love" of money, for which some people will lie and cheat or do and say anything. For it is not the possession of money in any sum, large or small, that is potentially negative, per se, but how it was gained and to what purpose its use is employed. A poor man who takes his paycheck to the bar at the expense of his children has done great and lasting harm. The rich heir who squanders the family fortune on an ego trip as a compulsive spendthrift brings no honor to the family name.

Money in its proper context, after food and shelter, should

be valued as opportunity. It opens doors and fosters possibilities. Certainly, there is a place in life for nice things, and no one who has worked hard and fairly should be made to feel guilty about it for a second. They should justly reap the rewards of their hard work and enterprise. But if one's overriding focus is just for the trappings of wealth, it is a shallow pursuit indeed. The crucial test is this: If one wants lots of money in order to buy, to get, to control, to obtain power for its own sake, then some reflection over priorities is in order. But if one says, "I would like money to do, see, learn, discover, explore, grow, fix, help, or become someone of value in addition to feathering my own nest," it is on a different plane of virtue. The former is mere ego and vanity for vanity's sake, and the latter is all about opportunity and making a mark, not a stain. Money has the power to destroy or be frittered away and also the power to transform.

Fourth-quarter people have more than a forty-year relationship with money, bills, and savings. And the results of these decisions put the boomers all over the map in preparation for the "last quarter" of their life along with any potential of "overtime." Since one size does not fit all, we will have to divide this group up into several categories. See which group describes you.

The Squirrels: These are the planners and savers for the coming winter. They are busy "squirreling" away enough nuts and acorns away in a safe place in order to bear the brunt of the winter months that will soon arrive after autumn. They are an industrious lot and are preplanners, making sure their fridge is full and that all contingencies of their plan are carefully considered. Their motto is "better safe than sorry."

The Piggies: These are the carefree little piggies who are much more attuned to the epicurean view that life is to be lived for today and to worry about tomorrow—well, tomorrow. Their motto is "eat, drink, and be merry." Delayed gratification is a scorned concept. You only go around once in life, and life is just one big party that allows them to live in the moment. The result is that all these piggies have built themselves a financial house of straw. It will not stand when the winds blow or the wolf shows up at the door. They have nothing to show for their profligacy, and they cry and moan that the squirrels who have stored plenty should be forced to share with them. They have planned poorly or not at all.

The Birds: They have worked hard all season long to build a little nest that will be modest but comfortable. They didn't have much and were limited as to what they could do. Unfortunately, unexpected winds, rain, and the storms of life tore at their little nest, leaving it in tatters. Misfortune, most often not of their own making, has become their reality. Sadly, they neither have the time or stamina left to restore it. They make feeble attempts to patch things up the best they can, but it is a far cry from their modest hopes and dreams. Those storms seemed so unfair, and they have so little to fall back upon.

The Ostriches: The head-in-the-sand approach to financial planning is the defining characteristic of this group. But it can take different forms of short-term thinking. The most common refrain is to ignore it and avoid feeling overwhelmed and depressed about it. "We just don't have enough money, so why beat ourselves up over it?" Others fear self-loathing because they know they are chronic spenders and are poorly self-disciplined with their money. The "I'll get to it soon" crowd genuinely knows this issue needs to be addressed but procrastinates with a hundred other priorities or excuses. A few lucky ones will take the attitude of "I don't need to do anything because I stand to (hopefully) inherit money from my folks when they pass on." Excuses all–there is no time like the present to be the adult in the room and make the firm commitment of a detailed written plan before the month is out and then to actually follow through and implement it.

Financial planning for most families is an ad hoc affair at best. Watching a two-hour movie on TV with the family always beats sitting down at the kitchen table agonizing over a long-term financial plan. For many families, they will joke that they don't need to do this at all since their plan is to survive the month by paying the rent or mortgage, buy some food, put gas in the car, try to pay some money on the outstanding credit cards, and repeat it monthly. Then die. That is their financial plan.

There is much discussion regarding income inequality in America, but the divide in wealth and assets is a much greater divide. Bridging the triple gap of inheritance, higher education, and two-income stable marriages that make up the main factors for the overwhelming lion's share of wealth disparity, inequality will be a growing societal challenge in the twenty-first century.

A significant number of boomers have been blessed to be the heirs of "The Greatest Generation," who are passing on several trillion dollars as they are fading fast into history. Within just a few short years, this greatest generation will all be gone. Conservative by nature, in having experienced the Great Depression and World War II, they knew the value of a dollar. They were careful to pay off the house and keep some money for a rainy day because in their life experience, life was uncertain.

As the boomers step up as the next generation to fade off the world stage over the next forty years, they will also leave behind an even bigger stash of money, with estimates ranging from ten to forty trillion dollars. Plus, it will be even a greater bonanza for the "haves" as the boomers were the first widespread birth-control generation and for the most part hewed to the informal two-child policy. This means the money "split" between siblings is greater than previous generations that may have been split up between four or five brothers and sisters. Just the proceeds from an inheritance to pay off a house mortgage "free and clear" is a huge deal or having available a pot of money to educate grandchildren or to help secure a retirement for the next generation is a tremendous stress reliever. Some lucky couples will make out like lottery winners by getting a double windfall, collecting from both sides of the family.

Of course, the one true fact of life is that no one has a crystal ball for the future. The only certainty is that there are "black swan" events that no one can predict that will happen in the future. Trying to ensure a secure financial future for our families is not a slam dunk. People who try to hit a home run every time they come up to bat strike out the most. So perhaps the best path one can follow is the KISS principle: Keep It Simple, Stupid.

People in the financial world ascribe the terms "smart money" and "dumb money" to how it is invested and managed, either wisely or foolishly. But remember that ninety-nine percent of the smartest people from the best schools with stellar resumes and golden reputations did not see the 2008 crash coming. So smart and dumb are relative terms. Derivatives, collateralized debt obligations (CDOs), recklessly leveraged deals, margin lending, and liar loans in the subprime housing market hyped by hubris and greed nearly collapsed the entire world financial system. Any investment that sounds too good to be true is ninety-nine per cent of the time one to avoid.

Having an updated trust or will, investments in low-cost diversified no-brainer index funds, adequate life insurance, and (in some limited circumstances) annuities, if appropriate, can take most of the financial mystery away by making things simple, simple, simple.

26

SHOW ME THE MONEY!

Those who do not know where they are headed will end up there.

For the minority of readers who are reading this section that have all their financial affairs tied up with a nice ribbon and bow, congratulations. This is not for you, and you get a free pass to the next chapter of this book. But for those who cannot financially locate where you are or even which direction to go since you see no road or familiar landmarks, well, is this not the definition of being lost? It may be small consolation, but you are not alone in the financial wilderness as millions of others are also floundering about.

Seniors who have not already planned a long time ago to put money aside are at a distinct disadvantage since they do not have the benefit of time and the magic of compounding money. Many have hit the panic button, causing stress and depression as they survey their future. And for those who have tried to plan but whose nest egg was devastated by divorce, illness, recession, job loss, or a bad investment, they will also have to make adjustments. Perhaps the greatest lesson of all is for you to help the next generation see the light, avoid pitfalls, and get on a more sustainable financial path with the lessons you have learned, for better or worse, even if a little late in life.

It is important that we take a small break here to clarify that any and all discussion of finances and legal questions throughout this book should not be construed as legal or financial advice but only used as a general guide for your consideration. Every situation is unique, states' laws are different, and changes need to be updated as conditions, age, and resources change. Professional assistance should be sought, depending on your level of knowledge and expertise. One word of caution here and that is to stick to a "fee only" advisor who gets no kickbacks from putting your money into certain stocks or other types of investments. You can get robbed paying excessive fees from such conflicts of interest.

Ignorance is not bliss when it comes to money management. Therefore, your first priority about money is to become well informed. For those who want good, down-to-earth, practical information, I recommend buying books by Susie Orman or Dave Ramsey. These financial writers can also be followed on TV and radio. They speak plain English to everyone and don't get you lost in the weeds with obtuse economics. (One of the best jokes about economists is that if you put three of them in a room, the only thing any two of them will agree upon is that the third guy is an idiot.) Their easy-to-understand writing and conversational styles explaining what you should be doing with your budget, savings, and hoped-for investments is a wise expenditure of your time.

Next, it is important to track where your money is going. This can be a real eye-opener for some. It can be helpful to keep a daily journal or spreadsheet for a couple months. Some people track their spending with precision, but the vast majority of us do not. Still, most people do have a general sense of their spending, but not really a tight system of accounting. It is surprising how money can tend to drip away like a leaky faucet. People of all ages who experience an increase in their finances from whatever source discover that their spending levels usually rise in tandem. It always amazes people that there does not seem to be any more money left at the end of the month than there was before. Lifestyle expenditures just creep up, but not so much in the savings department. This speaks volumes about human nature, not money management.

One of the most effective money-saving techniques is the pay-yourself-first plan. Just like the idea that you won't eat the donut or cookie you don't see, this idea is that money you don't see is money you won't spend. Having ten percent of your paycheck or pension check automatically deducted into a 401K plan is a must-do strategy. For seniors who are very near retirement, this amount needs to be "maxed out" to the limit of what is allowable under the tax code and then additional funds saved on top of it in another investment.

For seniors who are already retired, living expenses need to be budgeted at no more than eighty to ninety percent of your income if possible, depending on your situation. Human nature is such that our appetite tends to adjust to the size of the pie available on the kitchen counter. Inflation and price increases will rise over time, and therefore you will have a built-in cushion to meet extra expenses. Not everyone can do this, but for those who are able, living beneath one's means is wise and makes for a more peaceful sleep at night.

The most important rule about money is that when employers are handing out free money, take it! This is a no-brainer. Imagine you are at any store or bank and they tell you for every dollar you put aside for a rainy day, they would do the same (free money). What a deal since everyone knows it will rain someday. Likewise, all people know that, barring tragedy, they will be old someday.

In financial planning terms, you take every single dime your company offers in matching 401K programs. Money placed in a bank certificate of deposit these days is lucky to yield two per cent. To double your money (compounded) would take you thirty-four years. Simple interest would be fifty years. And you are most likely to have a negative return when considering inflation. So you are actually losing money every year in purchasing power. However, matching funds through work means doubling your money (100%) in one year. Hmmm? Let's think this one through together. Thirty-four years compared to one year? Duh! Even a two-to-one company match is a fifty percent return. Never turn down deals like these. And make sure your kids and friends are doing this as well since it is never too early to start. Over time, they will be grateful.

The next free-money plan to jump at is to max out an IRA if your employee plan does not do so already. Imagine putting money aside and not paying any taxes on it. Yeah! Then you get to let it compound and grow for many years while not paying any taxes. Yeah again! Then when you do take it out in retirement, you will get to pay fewer taxes by being in a lower tax bracket. Yeah, for the third time!

On the expense side of the ledger, credit cards deserve special attention. For ninety percent of people there is rarely a good reason to have more than two or maybe three cards, maximum. If possible, try to carry just one since it is so much easier to track all your charges. The allure of credit card offers and a thousand offers of reward programs from airlines, gas companies, etc. is a daily onslaught. Be tough and reject them all, except the one or perhaps two you use all the time. Keep things simple, and don't stress out over trying to keep track of a dozen cards, which is a fool's errand and not in your interest.

A credit card should be used simply for convenience and safety and paid off at the end of the month without fail, no exceptions. The rule is if you can't pay something off at the end of the month, don't buy it in the first place, period. A surprise bill for a car repair or a plumber problem should come out of separate savings, never "carried over" on the credit card.

It has been said that if you love gambling, don't go to a casino, own one. Similarly, credit card companies love charging "outstanding balances" twelve to eighteen percent in interest, which is much like owning your own money-printing press. To put this in perspective, if you could get an eighteen-percent return on your money with little risk, you would double your money in four years. If investors could get an eighteen-percent return on a top-rated bond, the stock market in equities would crash overnight in the stampede to move money. So, would you like to make eighteen percent on your money? No problem, just never carry a credit card balance, and you just saved eighteen percent. Wow.

Credit-card companies have the audacity to charge customers a yearly "maintenance" fee as well as high-interest charges to swell their coffers. These fees alone usually amount to just under a hundred dollars a year so as not to scare members away. However, one ten-minute phone call can usually save you this yearly fee by simply asking it to be "waived," or you threaten to leave by closing your account. Customer service for billing will hem and haw and talk about everything else under the sun to keep you on the hook. Some may put you on hold to check with a supervisor (all part of the game) to see what can be done for you. But in the end, if you are persistent, most (not all) will cave and waive the fee, and you will save eighty-five or ninety-five bucks, all in a ten-minute call. If they say no, don't pay the yearly fee, cancel the card and switch to another company, which will be anxious to give you free incentives to boot. The card companies count on people's laziness or ignorance to just pay the yearly charge. Try getting it waived. It's your money.

If you struggle with controlling your spending, try putting all your credit cards in a bottom sock drawer and leave them there. Pay everything you can in cash. Studies show people spend less if they have to fork over cash. Also, a credit card is instant gratification (a borrowed loan for thirty days) that many tell themselves they will pay off by the end of the month– "I promise myself," but not all promises are kept when there is some emergency or other "pop-up" bill needing to be paid.

Plastic does not feel like "real" money. In a different form, but with the same result, this is the great secret of Las Vegas casinos. It is why they all use "casino chips" for gambling. People are much freer with little round chips than with real money. Just this one psychological trick earns collective billions for casinos the world over. Along with some free alcohol to cloud one's judgment, the winning combination goal is to separate an individual and their money as quickly as possible. Even the exciting ding, ding, ding of slot machines is designed to fool you. Half the time, people are "cashing out" their own money rather than "winnings" from the slots. Many slot machines don't even dispense cash anymore but give out paper slips, which is more efficient for them. They don't even want you to get tuckered out from pulling the handle on the "one-arm-bandit anymore. It is too time-consuming. A push button is so much easier and quicker and allows for more "spins." These "improvements" mean more money for the house. You lose.

One of the best paths to wealth-building is taking every extra dime you have and paying off the mortgage if it is not free and clear already. This is psychic freedom. It gives you a psychological lift that is hard to duplicate. Yes, your brother-in-law and TV financial gurus will tell you to keep the mortgage tax deduction and invest excess funds in stocks or real estate to get a higher return. They are mostly right in theory, but absolutely dead wrong about human nature. While this is good advice, only a small handful of people follow up with implementing such a plan since they find other places to spend their money rather than to invest it. For the other ninety percent of us, a conscious plan to have this monthly mortgage burden gone from our lives is liberating. People just sleep better at night. A large weight is lifted from their shoulders. Besides, you can't live inside a bond or a stock certificate when it is raining and you need a roof over your head.

For the great majority of Americans, their home is their biggest asset. Therefore, it should command one's greatest attention. If approached properly, it is one of the fastest and surest ways to build wealth over time. Unfortunately, too many Americans of all ages and income levels, when purchasing a home, get stars in their eyes and buy more house than can be justified by their wallet, which puts them in a very stressful situation from the get-go. They ignore everything except what is the lowest monthly payment they can get from a lender. (Indeed, "teaser" rates were also a factor contributing to the 2008 crash.) Instead, this should be turned upside-down and considered from building equity as fast as possible. Fourth-quarter seniors who feel unprepared for retirement especially need to view their home as a sound investment.

There are several approaches to consider. The first is to move and downsize your home if the kids are gone and you and a spouse are rattling around, using only half the house. Selling and getting a smaller but cozier place can mean that you are now free of mortgage debt in your new pad. The second plan of attack is to call your lender and ask if any prepayment penalties can be waived and put more money each month (or a lump sum) to the principal to pay it off much quicker. The third approach is to refinance your home to a ten-year or fifteen-year loan with no prepayment penalties, and you get a slightly better interest rate. Yes, you can have about a thirty-five percent higher monthly mortgage payment (or much less, depending on the current equity in your home) that some will cry is completely impossible to achieve. But for many it is not impossible and simply requires awareness and re-ordered priorities. With some analytical budgeting, they will be surprised at how quickly they adjust. Furthermore, if this is looked upon as "forced savings" to build a nest egg, it makes even more sense. But the best surprise is that nearly all this extra money goes to paying principal, so it is like paying yourself first with real savings in the bank. How wonderful.

Human nature is such that most people will not save the additional funds when taking out a thirty-year loan as opposed to a fifteen-year loan by investing the left over balance in stocks, bonds, or real estate. The reality is they will spend these funds on other things like a new car payment. But a car, whether new or used, is a depreciating asset that loses money every year, whereas a house over time is an appreciating asset. Even the terrible collapse of housing prices from the 2008 recession has seen most of them recover and in some hot markets even move beyond their previous highs. As Mark Twain advised, "Buy land. They're not making it anymore."

I cannot urge you more strongly to spend half an hour on the Internet to see the difference between a fifteen-and a thirty-year amortized loan. You will be stunned at first and then flabbergasted. (Note: there are many sites; an easy one to try is bretwhissel.net/cgi-bin/amortize).[29] For example, the break-even point whereby the majority of your monthly payment is going to principle rather than interest is as follows: For a $150,000 traditional loan at six percent for thirty years, the break-even point comes at eighteen and a half years. For a $150,000 loan at five and a half percent (you get a better rate with a shorter loan term) for fifteen years, the break-even point occurs in just two and a half years. Yes, that's right; on a thirty-year loan, you get to pay for an additional sixteen more years (mostly interest) to get to your halfway point. The best part of all with a fifteen-year loan is watching the equity in your home rise quickly, which is real money, your money, not the bank's money! It may be hard to juggle at first, but a fifteen-year-loan is the way to go for most everyone who thinks things through. It is as much, if not more so, a mental mindset adjustment as a financial one. Equally important is to share this insight with your kids and grandkids. While the Federal Reserve has kept rates very low following the 2008 crash, they are anxious to slowly raise them back up to historical norms. Making this change while rates are low is a smart move.

Another great way to save money is to become (if you're not already) a savvy shopper. In order to make your money go further, it is important to resist the false siren call of Madison Avenue with its lure of brand names, pricey labels, high margins, and sucker "sales" come-ons. Ben Franklin said it best, as we all learned in grade school, even if we do not always take it to heart: "A penny saved is a penny earned." Saving money on the things we buy at the store is just as valuable as having an extra check in next month's deposit account.

By being a wise shopper, a dollar can be stretched another fifteen to thirty percent further with little trouble at all. That is a fabulous return. What many shoppers, even smart ones, often do not realize is that a manufacturer of food or clothing can sometimes make a product by the millions in the same factory and just slap on different labels for its varied distributors, who then market them differently.[30] It is the exact same item, but the price differential margins can soar to as much as one hundred percent or more on some items. The customer is paying a huge premium just for the label and perhaps also for the high-fashion store it is displayed in.

Too many shoppers get sucked into thinking price and value are the same thing. They are not. There are a lot of upper-middle-class and wealthy shoppers at Wal-Mart because they know how to save a buck. The same can be said for those buying in bulk like an army Quartermaster General at Costco, which can yield significant savings. A savvy shopper can save a ton of money.

Our last consideration is the stock market. Scary! Rigged? Confusing? Risky! All kinds of emotions come into play when talking about the stock market. For every friend or acquaintance who claims to have made a "killing" in the market, you know others who have taken huge hits. Others are embarrassed and just keep mum. Plus, there are over seven thousand mutual funds out there and enough "market noise" with a financial guru on every other cable station hawking their product to give one a headache. What is the average guy or gal supposed to do with any extra funds (after the house is paid off first) to put to work? And the plea is not to make this complicated as no one has got the time or interest to obtain an MBA in finance.

Everyone is different, but here are some general rules to consider with your financial advisor.

A) Savings vs Investment: There is an important distinction between these two concepts that is lost on many people, especially the young. Savings for an unexpected emergency or a big purchase is always a good idea. However, it is not an investment, rather delayed spending. Saving for a car, furniture, or a vacation is just money set aside to be spent later. An investment is different in which its purpose is to produce income and increase wealth. Stocks, bonds, real estate, IRA's, a business, and especially an education are designed to throw off more cash.

Educating following generations about these differences is an important responsibility for all "seniors."

B) When talking about money and retirement, opposing forces of reality and expectations collide in the present to divine the future. In any discussion with a financial planner, both sides come to the table with different questions. A prospective retiree on the verge of retirement wants to know one thing: Will he or she have enough money to last longer than they do? Alternately, the financial planner wants to know what level of lifestyle a retiree wants or can afford to live with before they even tackle the retiree's original question. What lifestyle is an individual or couple going to be content with, to live up to, or adjust downward. That is the primary question.

C) If you can't stay in the stock market for a minimum of five years, you should not be in it at all. A good strategy is dollar-cost-averaging putting in money every month or quarter on a regular basis and not trying to divine the market.

D) More people have made money in the market by being patient and rational, rather than by their sheer brilliance. Otherwise, just buy a lottery ticket. You can't time the market highs and lows. When the great tycoon J.P. Morgan was asked what the market would do, he replied, "It will fluctuate." Remember, no one has a crystal ball. NO ONE. Stuff happens both on the upside and the downside.

E) The market is controlled in a death grip between greed and fear, with fear always having the edge. Loss hurts proportionally more than the joy from gain.

F) Never put all your eggs in one basket. (e.g., see Bernie Madoff, Enron's employee pension fund)

G) Asset allocation: This depends on your age, risk tolerance, the number of assets involved, and goals (for example: retirement expenses or grandchild's education inheritance). The less you have, the less you should put at risk. There is little time to make up losses.

H) Good strategy: Diversify by buying index funds like the S+P 500 or the Russell 2000. Keep it simple. By doing this, you do not need a financial planner of any kind and can save a lot in fees. This is the advice of famed investor Warren Buffett and Jack Bogle of the Vanguard fund, two of the smartest investors ever. Do not pay over .02 percent in fees for these funds. Avoid any purchase of any fund that charges over .05 percent in fees for anything and be even skeptical about that. Fees are for them, not you. They can hurt.

For fourth-quarter people with the clock ticking, you do not want to spend all your time worrying about the next buck. Some will unfortunately fall into this category of perpetual worry because of a small income, but many can make a concerted effort to make the mental adjustments if they are willing to enjoy the simple and good things of life rather than be mired in an endless loop-cycle of what can, may, or might happen. Life is too short for that. The trick is to pay attention and do some research; do the best you can with your investments and then call some friends and go out for dinner.

27

LITTLE MONEY?

Living and surviving on a shoestring...

Millions of Americans enter the fourth quarter of their lives completely unprepared financially for their future. The reasons for this state of affairs are all too familiar. Many were held back by simple bad luck due to poor health, inadequate education, investments going sour, job loss, or bailing out family members, much of it out of their control. Others faithfully and diligently worked all their lives in tough, demanding, low-wage jobs as they struggled just to keep body and soul together and did the best they could. Millions of others just made terrible decisions decade after decade and could never seem to get a firm grip on life. Personality defects, stubbornness, and a lazy or rebellious streak sometimes compounded by alcohol and drugs all resulted in a stunted life. For all of these groups, it is not an auspicious place to be this late in the game of life. For most of these who rely solely on Social Security or some form of public assistance, living on the edge is always a precarious balancing act with no margin for error. What to do? How to cope?

Unfortunately, there will be no silver bullets offered here. We are talking about reality where the rubber meets the road. Yet there is still a big difference between things looking bleak and looking hopeless. Like most of life, our outlook on the world around us is critical in dealing with one's circumstances. So the first thing to do is to adjust one's attitude to look at one's personal situation through a fresh pair of eyes.

Consider for a moment, in what country in the world would you most prefer being poor or struggling? Perhaps with the exception of a few generous European countries, the United States still ranks very high. When considering the world as a whole, the poorest Americans still live immeasurably better than the vast numbers of people living beyond our shores. This is not meant to be construed that the poor in America should be content with their lot—not at all—but simply as a useful point of reference. Money is nice to have to smooth one's path, and there is no denying that. But perspective can also be found in the story of the man who cried out to God because he had no shoes until he met a man with no feet.

The richest people in the world have more in common with the poor than many realize. The main difference is they have much nicer stuff, lots more stuff, and more options in life. But they can only eat one meal at a time, drive one car at a time, wear one set of clothes at a time, occupy one house at a time, and get the same twenty-four hours in a day. The downside for many wealthy people is that they spend a lot of time worrying about losing their money, managing it, investing it, maintaining it, or growing it. It is often more than a full-time job dealing with a business, the stock market, accountants, and tax attorneys. In addition, they are often conflicted in dealing with the drama of family, friends, and a hundred charities who all want a piece of it, if not the whole enchilada. Money is mostly a blessing, but can also be problematic as well. Much time and energy is drained away from life by not taking the time to stop and smell the roses. So even for the rich, everything that glitters is not gold. Many of them are on a merry-go-round that they find very hard to get off.

Not to be foolishly naïve, but one starting point is to look at the cup of life that is half (or even less than half) full and to not dwell on what is missing since this does not accomplish anything helpful. On the most basic level, if one has food and shelter, one can get by, but these days, rental housing and even food are not cheap when tied to a limited, fixed budget. Solutions to these problems may require doubling up with a family member or a friend to reduce expenses. Moving to a cheaper side of the city or farther out in the country can also make a dollar go much further.

Next, one needs to check around to see what public services are being offered for any particular situation. Often, there are thousands of people who go without available assistance simply because they are uninformed of the programs and opportunities around them. Many communities offer free educational classes or activities in a number of areas. In addition, public libraries and public parks are free to enjoy. There are also many other civic, sports, and church events that are free to attend if one seeks them out. It is a great way to get out and about. Generally, the more people you talk to, the more one can find out what is happening in the local area. Also, it helps to focus on other people's lives since no one really wants to hear about your latest aches and pains or how difficult your life has been. Empathy quickly wears pretty thin, and people avoid those they perceive who are whining all the time. The idea is to attract people, not push them away.

Technology is moving forward at a dizzying pace, and in one

sense anyone can travel the globe without leaving home. Visual tours of all the great sites of the world are–and will become even more so–common without the hassle of flying, passports, and being herded like cattle from place to place. Virtual reality and holograms in high definition will assure us all of an experience free from bad weather, madding crowds, and foreign foods that may not agree with us. On one level, it may actually beat being there. One can become a jet setter without leaving home. Our personal avatars can meet up with others in cyberspace that will alter our view of the world in ways we can't fully appreciate presently.

It is very important to recognize that even though an individual may be a fourth-quarter person, they can still improve themselves as a human being in many ways. Personal growth should be a goal. Learning new things, becoming a better human being, or helping someone else should be an important priority. A rolling stone gathers no moss. Don't vegetate but keep moving forward.

Finally, do not let anyone steal your joy in life, which includes yourself. No rich person owns laughter or has a corner on good times. Indeed, many of them are overstressed. Work on a cheerful disposition, a grateful heart, and a sunny outlook. Strive to have many friends and more possibilities in life. Keep in mind that nobody likes a grumpy sad sack. Remember to take every occasion to laugh, smile, share, and sing. Money has its place and is important, but it is not everything.

Money can't buy character, wisdom, integrity, love, morals, manners, faith, grit, compassion, curiosity, humor, reverence, class, respect, persistence, loyalty, true friendship, or common sense. There is great value beyond dollars and cents. True wealth is often relative.

28

WHERE THERE'S A WILL…
THERE'S A RELATIVE

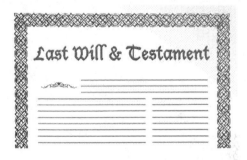

An elderly gentleman had very serious hearing problems for a number of years. He went to the doctor and was able to be fitted for a set of hearing aids that restored his hearing completely. The elderly gentleman went back to the doctor a month later for a checkup. The doctor remarked, "Your hearing is excellent. Your family must be really pleased that you can hear again." The gentleman replied, "Oh, I haven't told my family yet. I just sit around and listen to their conversations. I've changed my will three times!"

Parents have always tried to encourage their children to be persistent with the old adage that "where there's a will, there's a way." However, when it comes to money and property, a will of another sort to divide up the goodies often brings out an entirely different side of the human animal. The knives come out, and there can often be lots of bad blood left on the floor.

Classic movie scenes of a recently departed one depict family members and interested parties sitting around a lawyer's wood-paneled office in rich leather chairs for the reading of the will. The lawyer pontificates in a low, monotone voice, reading point by point the details of who gets what, according to the wishes of the deceased. The movie scene is generally one of civility and solemnity. After all, this is really the final word as all the eulogies have been given; the funeral is over, the burial completed, the tombstone set in place, the epitaph displayed, and the friends have all scattered to once again pick up their daily lives.

All participants in this small movie drama do their best to show respect while at the same time trying to hide any outward show of being greedy or having an outsized sense of entitlement. Even though all present affect a pose of studied decorum, an air of expectancy hangs in the air. There is a quiet nervousness about whether unexpected surprises lurk in the shadows both on the upside and the downside for each hopeful beneficiary.

Relationships are often complicated among siblings and doubly so when there are in-law spouses and grandchildren involved for consideration. In-laws often see a honey pot and attempt to wield undue influence behind the scenes to stir the pot with whispers to their spouse of "Don't let your brother or sister run the show or get more." And so it begins! Outstanding debts, trusts, life insurance, life estates, heirlooms, property, stocks, cash, and philanthropic considerations can all come into play. Inevitably, in the movies, no sooner has the will been read than conflict arises quickly, and the deceased, who is not even cold in the grave, has set off a chain reaction of intrigue, suspicion, and dashed expectations for some. Indeed, the movie plot itself shifts quickly to issues of jealousy, conniving, dark secrets, and the settling of old scores that take center stage. Issues of control from the grave as outlined in the will with conditions, caveats, and stipulations further stir the pot. But the reading of the will is revealing; the shocked look, the raised eyebrow, the furtive glance, the disappointed tear, the big smile, the shaking of the head in approval or disapproval are all on display in this drama. But such a scenario is not reserved for the elites and the upper crust as depicted in the movies.

Even in the most modest of inheritances, the scramble can be just as ferocious, if not more so, since there is less to fight over. In the real world, nearly everyone knows of someone whose family relationships were severely damaged or ripped apart in some way over an estate, whether large or small.

Even ostensible fairness by the departed of equal-share splits can cause acrimony and shatter families. A parent decides to just divide the pie in equal portions, and that is it, simple and fair. Not so fast. An adult child may feel that a sibling in the past got extra help with schooling expenses, a new business venture, a home loan, etc., and thus evenhandedness has not been balanced out and achieved. Another may feel slighted and used for several years of devoted care and help to an aging parent who lived nearby, in contrast to a distant sibling who contributed nothing in time, expense, or nursing care for the dying parent.

An adult child who is single without children (or fewer children) may feel slighted as another sibling's children are generously provided for at the expense of their perceived fair portion. In other cases, hard feelings are reinforced against the sibling who is the perennial screw-up (the prodigal son or daughter) who has made bad choices in life and can't seem to get their act together. Rewarding such irresponsible behavior with an equal share seems to be outright folly to the "good kids," much as a slap in the face. If there is a surviving stepmom or stepdad who is left with the lion's share of an estate, relationships can turn nasty. Indeed, a bad will can engender great resentment of the dead (even beloved) who has caused these conflicts to fracture families and cause grief among the living. It is important to remember that while most people think it is about the money (and it most often is), it is equally about "perceived" fairness. Who was loved more, who manipulated whom, all compounded by attitudes, arrogance, squabbles, and past family history. In these cases, money is just the means to keep score. It is very personal. Beware.

First things first: If you do not have a will (or trust) or have not updated it in the past three to five years, do not let the sun go down today without making an appointment in order to make or review your will. This is the easiest thing in the world to put off, and procrastination slowly turns into months and years with a self-delusional "I'll get to it later" attitude.

Of course, If you are one of those very few people who are superstitious and think the very act of making a will may shorten your life in some cosmic, supernatural way, let's be clear: you are nuts. Or if you are one of those few who are in denial about your own mortality ("I will live to be a hundred") and just find it "uncomfortable" thinking about getting hit by a bus or dealing with "the great beyond," it is way past time to get a grip, be a mature adult, and take care of this business right away. It is that important. If you love your family and would like to have your say should misfortune occur, this needs to be done and not put off any longer. Go ahead, make the call; I will patiently wait for you and will still be here upon your return.

Okay, are you back from making the phone call? Good! Remember, it is not just old age or some affliction that may finally catch up with you way down the road but a fall, a traffic accident, a sudden heart attack or perhaps even falling out of bed tomorrow morning that will make it too late. Stuff happens.

So what are the many considerations and pitfalls people

make with their wills? They can be legion, depending on the size of the estate and, more importantly, the tricky permutations of family structure that one leaves behind. Also, family dynamics have a way of changing and morphing over the years, whether they are spouses, children, grandchildren, or extended family. Your will should change accordingly by being updated regularly. But remember, it should not be used to punish or be vindictive to those left behind unless, of course, they really, really, truly deserve it. Don't feel guilty cutting someone off for outrageously bad behavior. Do not be a sucker. You are not to support a local drug dealer for an abusive offspring, which is what you would be doing, playing middleman–"bagman"–between a junkie and a pusher. Neither should you fund a foolish and unwise spendthrift relative. You know the saying by heart: "A fool and his money are soon parted," but it should never be with your money.

One should not overlook sentimental items (heirlooms) that may be a source of contention. Some may have monetary value such as a car, painting, musical instrument, jewelry, etc., that one child may look upon as "cash" while another may look at it as a "keepsake" memory and not for sale. Even items of little monetary value such as dolls, dishes, furniture, or "memory" items from one's childhood may take on special meaning.

So how do you play the role of Solomon to ensure you can truly rest in peace when your time has come? Besides praying that your progeny will behave respectfully and with grace towards one another, here are a number of ideas. First, plan ahead and talk openly and get feedback from your intended beneficiaries. A child who you thought may want a particular item may express ambivalence and not really care. Second, compensate by giving something else to another that "balances out" if you can. Third, give it away early so it is not even in your estate. Fourth, have your executor hold a lottery, and whoever wins gets it with each having an equal chance. Fifth, have it sold and divide the assets avoiding any sense of favoritism. And lastly, plan to live past one hundred and fifty by outliving all your children and friends to avoid any issues! Good luck with that plan.

Regardless of the many different situations fourth-quarter women face, they need to be proactive and claim their best possible future in the fourth quarters of their lives. Those who solely trust others, even family, and the winds of fate sell themselves short and make a big mistake. A wise woman is a prepared woman as best as her circumstances allow.

Fourth-quarter women who are married to men who like to maintain control of the finances and who are reluctant to share details or information need to have their husbands read the following paragraph to encourage them to make changes in their mindset since they think they will outlive Methuselah,[31] which ain't gonna happen.

If men truly love their wives, they need to face the fact that the odds heavily favor their wives outliving them. Furthermore, the odds of both spouses making it into overtime (past eighty) together are less than fifty percent.[32] Therefore, a man needs to show respect that his wife is provided for to the best of his ability if he is the first to go. Marriage is a team sport, and men need to think of it in terms like passing the baton in a relay race. If the wife is not intimately involved in the family finances, both spouses need to sit down together to review in detail their own personal situation.

For very traditional marriages, it is a good time to start jointly paying the bills, reviewing accounts, and examining all holdings as a couple. Men should look upon this as a form of "love" insurance—just in case. If a husband is suddenly taken, a wife will be very grateful that she is in the loop. In some cases, in which the wife "takes care of everything," the reverse pattern should also be followed. In some old-time stuffy retro-marriages, it would also be good for the wife to give the husband a home-economics crash course in Laundry, Food Management, and Vacuuming 101. Of course, the best practice is for both spouses to be involved together in all aspects of their financial well-being and sharing in all the family chores.

One truth in life is that a majority of currently married women turning sixty-ish will sooner or later find themselves single again, facing life without a partner to lean on. In their eighties and nineties, this disparity increases very sharply. These realistic facts should be a clarion call to quality women to be proactive in planning their fourth quarter and beyond and to begin reviewing this process promptly and not putting it off further.

29

PRIORITY CHECKLIST

"Before anything else, preparation is the key to success."

For people with organized or semi-organized lives, lists are essential to keep everything straight and one's life on track. We lead hectic lives, trying to multitask and satisfy hundreds of demands on our time, crammed into a twenty-four-hour day. There is the shopping list, the "to do" list, the monthly bills list, along with lists for birthdays and special occasions. We make "playlists" on our iPods and organize pictures in lists of "albums," while occasionally making a note to add to our "bucket lists." Throughout our day, we are constantly making mental lists in our own heads on a variety of subjects. And we have not even mentioned the many lists needed to do our jobs at work or for family and social events.

Well, here is one more list for you to consider. This critically important list should have a file-folder name with the title, The Final Checklist. It is your life list.

#1   First thing on your life checklist should be a will or a trust. Wills can be simple and should be made that way as much as possible. Clear, unambiguous, straightforward, and complete should be your goal. Of course, everyone's financial situation and family dynamics will be different and can sometimes be convoluted. Small estates or even large ones can be structured in such a manner that complexity is kept to a minimum. Remember that different states have different rules for wills and that if you move your domicile (i.e. your home residence) to another state, it may affect your will and how a court probates it. Also, out-of-state property may mean different rules might be applicable.

While some states allow you to do a holographic will (generally one in your own handwriting, dated, declaring it is your final will and expressly revoking all previous ones, and signed) there are pitfalls for the average person that they may not appreciate or understand. For simple wills with a small estate, there are some good Internet forms and questionnaires that may suffice and are relatively inexpensive. However, for anything more detailed, a competent lawyer should be consulted to cover all contingencies. Nothing here is intended as legal advice per se but food for thought as you work your way through your own unique situation.

#2   What if I die with no will? Each state has their own rules of "intestate succession," which means your assets will be distributed to your family members according to each state's "formula" for distribution. This could mean that if you had no immediate family left, a long-lost uncle or cousin way off in never-never land would get whatever you left behind. It also means if you have a family member you wanted to make sure "got nothing" for whatever reason, they still collect because you had no will. (Important: with a will, make sure someone trustworthy knows where it is kept.) If you have no family but dear friends, they will get nothing, and your possibly deadbeat distant relative could cash in.

#3   Trusts: Many people prefer to set up a trust instead of a will. Trusts and wills have much in common but have differences that are important for estate planning. A will is a public document that is published and is overseen by the court and goes through probate, following established court procedures. A trust is a legal construct that takes effect immediately whereby assets are placed in the "trust" and beneficiaries receive funds under the terms outlined in the trust under the guidance of the named "trustee" that you have selected. Trust documents stay private and are not published like a will, where everyone has access to it. Again, you should consult an attorney if you wish to go this route, which many find to be advantageous over a will.

#4   Overlooked scenarios: People have a preset imagination of the world without them. They rarely take into consideration common accidents that could take their lives along with one or more loved ones and therefore don't often have a "backup plan" of how things should be arranged under this new set of facts. Also, one should contemplate an alternate executor trustee of a trust–if your first choice dies or is incapacitated–to fulfill your wishes. Trustees can also steal from the trust (or deviate from it) unless they are trustworthy. Be extremely wise and choose carefully someone who will scrupulously follow your wishes.

#5   Children, grandchildren, and pets: Everyone wants the very best for their offspring. Hopes, dreams, and aspirations are boundless when you have young grandchildren. Yet cute and well-behaved small kids may not always turn out the way we expect as teenagers and young adults. Life happens, and you are not around to assess the situation. Tragically, many "good kids" can be lured off track by alcohol, drugs, or other addictions. Some become allergic to work or schooling and would be delighted to sit around and do nothing or just party (drinking and smoking pot) with your pot of money. You cannot control everything from the grave, but this is sometimes where a trust and specific instructions to a "trustee" are very helpful. Instructions for some trusts do not pay out until a beneficiary is thirty or thirty-five years old, with the idea that age and maturity (hopefully) will inform wiser choices.

Instead of a lump sum going to a young person (which many times can do more harm than good) a monthly stipend can be granted, pending approval of the trustee's discretion that there is no addiction or behavioral issues and that other conditions are met. The last thing any parent or grandparent wants to see is for their progeny to go on "welfare" not from the government, but using Grandpa and Grandma's money to fund their expenses. That is a tragedy of the first rank. In addition, there may be grandchildren born after you are gone, and you will never know how they were raised (divorce or death of a parent) or the choices these children will make. A good attorney can help you sort out the options and pitfalls you may wish to consider or avoid.

Contingencies should also be planned as to what would become of your beloved pets (many of whom are more loyal and loving than family members) if you were no longer in the picture. The tragedy of beloved creatures that have no one to love or care for them is heartbreaking. When there is no plan in place, all too often, a traumatic animal-shelter experience and death await. There can be a world of difference between a mere "pet owner" and a "pet guardian." An appreciation for God's creatures in our care should be held in high regard and consideration for their future well-being should be planned for. Pets deserve our respect for they have no voice and no choice. Compassion is in order and demonstrated by pre-planning.

#6   The in-laws conundrum: Can you imagine giving half or even all of your estate to a complete stranger? Your life's savings? That can't happen, can it? It is unlikely, but it most certainly can with a few unlucky breaks here and there with decisions made by other people, not you. Yes, you will turn over in your grave.

In this scenario, you leave a sizable nest egg to your married son or daughter. They comingle these funds (mix them all up with their family finances rather than keeping these funds separate and distinct as separate property) with their spouse. A few years after you are gone, their spouse leaves your child and takes up with some loser. In the ensuing divorce, your ex son/daughter-in-law gets half the money, a large chunk of which is your money that you left to them. These funds are now often at the disposal of the new boyfriend or girlfriend. So your hard-earned money is going to the upkeep of some complete stranger (and possibly their kids) you never knew or heard about. Yes, it is outrageous, but it can happen.

#7   The spouse consideration: Every marriage is unique to that couple. No one else on the planet quite understands the dynamics between two people in a marriage. Legal rules by statute protect a spouse and are established by law, but separate property (may vary by state jurisdictions) of premarriage funds, inheritance, prenup or postnup arrangements that are maintained in separate accounts, are generally the provenance of the deceased spouse, to dispose of in any manner of their choosing. Without proper planning, a surviving spouse could remarry and then shortly thereafter die. Then all the family funds accumulated over a lifetime could quickly evaporate and be passed over to a stranger (and their lineage), unknown just a couple of years earlier. Also, a subsequent divorce could also mean a loss of assets transferred over to a smart and conniving new partner. There can be landmines everywhere.

#8   Conditions: Yes, you can set up a trust for your grandchildren and make it conditional. They get x number of dollars each month they are in school in pursuit of a college degree (within an allotted time frame of, say, six years) supervised by the trustee you have selected and a defined bonus amount at graduation. This can be a strong incentive for any young person to make sure they stay focused on getting a solid education.

#9   The big unknown: Nothing can blow a hole in an estate faster than a serious extended health crisis. Many people are under the illusion that Social Security will pick up the tab for long-term nursing care. News flash–nope, you are on your own. The stories are legion where a lifetime of savings went not to the kids, grandchildren, philanthropy, or a dreamt-about world cruise on the high seas but instead went to enrich a nursing home.

From Alzheimer's disease, stroke, or a debilitating accident to a very advanced old age, this is a personal and financial disaster for all concerned. The very rich can write a check, the very poor will be placed in government care, though often in substandard conditions, but the vast middle class is stuck unless they had the foresight and smarts to purchase long-term health-care insurance coverage, which too few do. And the premiums are not cheap since you are more likely to become disabled than to die.

Depending on your home state that you live in, the type of facility, and the level of care, a nursing home can cost from forty-thousand to one-hundred-thousand-dollars a year. One should also check policy provision as some policies may give back your premiums to your estate if you pass on and have never used the benefits. Over a decade or two, this can be a substantial sum for the surviving spouse or beneficiaries. The proper view of insurance is that you pay your premiums and hope you *never* have a claim. You are a winner.

#10 Health directive: Along with a will or a trust, this is a MUST DO critical document that needs to be placed among your important papers in case of your mental incapacity. It states what you want done and not done by medical personnel should you be in this position. In no uncertain terms, you are telling a loved one—along with the doctors—exactly what to do. Believe it or not, this is an act of love for loved ones. By knowing in advance that this is what you want, much of the agony and indecision is taken out of their hands, and they do not have to play God, wondering what to do under stressful circumstances.

For some family members, they want every medical intervention done for their loved one, no matter how lousy the outcome may be for you. These are the one-in-a-million "hopers" that want to be part of a medical marvel. However, most people take a straightforward mathematical approach when considering the outcomes along with the pain and often totally compromised quality of life that is not worth living. They want family members to love them enough to "pull the plug" and to do this for them. There is no dignity or point to needless suffering. These discussions with family members should be made in advance so that everyone knows the score.

11 Philanthropy: This should not be overlooked whether you have a large or a small estate. Those blessed with sizable means should leave the lion's share of their wealth to the causes of their choice. Even though every parent wants to make life easier for their children, large sums of money has cursed and ruined a lot of young people just as much as it has helped and blessed others to achieve greater heights. It is very difficult to tell which will be which and what the effects will be on the following generation as well. A sense of entitlement does little for character development.

Every parent in their private moments marvels in one way or another about how different their kids have turned out from each other despite the tight familial bonds of the same parents, home, expectations, culture, values, religion, and outlook. As for philanthropy, your blessings, hard work, and good fortune need to be shared with others who did not have the same opportunities, privileges, education, or just dumb luck that came your way or that of your children. Have a generous spirit.

Philanthropy should never be considered as only a dead person's game. There is no rule saying you can't start parceling out some of your money while you are still alive.

Those who are very fortunate to have their personal financial needs met should be actively giving away their assets as they move deeper into the fourth quarter of life. However, many are leery of doing this because they are afraid of losing control or not having enough to meet their lifestyle. It is that haunting voice in their head of "What if this or that unexpected thing happens? I may be vulnerable." So paralysis takes over as a default response. It is difficult but noble to fight against this natural human impulse.

#12 A supplemental plan is one of planned giving while you are still alive. There is joy in being a giver and bringing happiness to family, friends, or chosen charities when appropriate. As you age past sixty-five, seventy-five, eighty-five, or beyond, you should be downsizing along your life journey. The challenge here is to follow the advice of the billionaire and former New York mayor Michael Bloomberg, who advises that great financial planning is that the last check you ever write is to the undertaker and it bounces! Andrew Carnegie, the great industrialist proclaimed that "the man who dies rich, dies disgraced."

Money is to be enjoyed, but ultimately to benefit others after your needs are met. Naturally, all older people are very afraid of not having enough in their old age and fear healthcare costs more than anything. All of this is understandable and part of human nature, but as the clock of life rolls on, consideration should be given to lighten the load of your bank accounts and possessions. It is true that you can't take it with you, but how much more wonderful is it for you to give it away while you are still here and to see a smile and some hoped-for gratitude than for some "trustee," who may do things differently, doling things out after you are gone.

One other advantage to this idea is that one can prevent many misunderstandings from the grave that cannot be rectified or explained. When it comes to family, you may have certain reasons (hopefully justified) for helping out some more than others, and while you are still in control, you can manage these assets as you see fit. But a lawyer-accountant just reads the dry words of a will/trust without any context unless you decide to leave a detailed explanation for what you want done. However, if you have given nearly all of it away, there is much less to fight over when you are gone.

You should also be very careful not to penalize success.

Just because a child has done well through their education or business with lots of hard work and devotion is no reason to consider them "less" in the context that they "really don't need it" just because another sibling took another route in life and due to different choices or perhaps some bad choices is in a different place. Favoritism, fairness, bias, guilt, and family history are stormy seas to navigate. Just keep an open mind and heart.

As difficult as these discussions can be about your life list, it is sometimes very appropriate (and often revealing in reactions) to discuss issues openly with all family members the provisions that are in your will. This way, there will be few surprises and no false expectations.

30

YOUR HEALTH IS YOUR WEALTH

Never count your wealth only in money.

The sentence above is well worth reading again several times over. These are seven words everyone should tack on their refrigerator as a daily reminder. Of course, money is important to pay for the basics of life. But it is not the be-all and end-all. Yeah, right! Blah, blah, blah! People who say money isn't everything are mostly the people who have money. Coming from them, it sounds disingenuous and more than a little glib.

In a materialistic world, worth is too often attributable to one's net worth. But consider for a moment what real wealth is as it relates to human joy to put things in perspective. Quick–you have five seconds to decide each of the following questions. Ready? Go! Would you choose a million or even a billion dollars if it meant you had to be blind? Never again to see the face of a loved one, never drive again, never see a sunset, read a book, or watch television or a movie. Quick, your five seconds are up. Next, would you choose to give up your hearing, never to hear a child's delight or a loved one's voice again or to use a phone; never to hear another note of music in your life or to hear the roar of the ocean or a crowd—ever? Quickly, your answer needs to be immediate. Or, for this pile of money, would you choose to give up your education and all that flowed from it, including becoming illiterate, never to write or read anything ever again, not even a street sign or a billboard, or even this book? Or would you choose to give up your faith, your morals, your principles, or sell your soul for mere money? How about choosing to give up all your family and friends you have ever known in your entire life and moving far away from everything familiar, never seeing or speaking with any of them ever again? Just having your five senses intact means you are rich.

Perspective is everything. Contemplate the meaning of "real" poverty: no friends, no hope, no future, no joy, no passion, no interests, and no curiosity—nothing to look forward to. Not once was money mentioned.

Of course, money has its place in life. Business tycoons and sports and entertainment stars use money as a way to keep score as in a game of Monopoly for who is top dog. It bestows bragging rights. The bumper sticker slogan "He who dies with the most toys, wins" is emblematic of a culture that worships at the high altar of the bottom line. And make no mistake; money and financial wealth are a blessing if used wisely and judiciously for personal, family, and community well-being.

It is laudable that many of the brightest and most innovative entrepreneurs of our age are not just taking their billions and sitting idly on a Pacific island beach somewhere sipping piña coladas but rather investing huge sums of their companies and personal fortunes (and their own time and prodigious effort) into all manner of new inventions, research, and inquiry into pushing the frontiers of knowledge into the realm of reality. Furthermore, many are making a pledge to give away the lion's share of their fortune to charity.

So let's come full circle and simply state the obvious that real wealth is being an active, thinking, mobile, healthy individual. Everything else in life we strive for is a bonus. Of course, there are millions of individuals who cope with physical and mental challenges of one kind or another who have shown amazing grit and determination to lead meaningful lives in spite of their circumstances. But these have done so by adjusting to their limitations and moving forward to compensate as best they can. These special people may be held back, but they are determined not to be held down by their physical conditions.

Perhaps no more amazing person has ever lived (and contributed by her own example) than Helen Keller, who had everything against her and still managed to wow the world with her indomitable human spirit. She was a marvel and inspiration to all, both the physically challenged and the able-bodied. Sadly, millions of others are crushed by their disabilities, sinking into depression, isolation, and despair. It is very understandable, but still sad.

Yet what would millions of people today give to be able to shed a wheelchair in order to walk; or to see again, hear again, or to get out of bed and not to be tethered to machines, doctors, nurses, or pills? What would one give to be free of constant headaches, hurt, pain, drug addiction, nausea, conditions, syndromes, diseases, disorders, or afflictions? The answer is they would give almost anything they possess because material things literally pale in comparison. So your health is your wealth. The two words even rhyme. Perhaps they rhyme to show the linkage for what is of true value in life. True wealth is good health. You won't find it locked up in a bank vault.

Unfortunately, we do not have control over our genetics, nor can we predict some diseases or anticipate accidents causing us injury. But the good news is we can tip the rest of the odds greatly in our favor by following a sensible lifestyle. And it is all found in the Big Four–nutrition, exercise, lowered stress, and sleep. Within these four pillars lie the secret that holds up the temple to good health.

Nutrition: Little will be said here since everyone KNOWS what must be done. Eat much less, skip the junk food, and eat more vegetables and fruit. Not carrying extra weight is critical as it lets us move better and gives us a psychological lift much more than many realize. Doing it is the hard part, but it is priority number one.

Exercise: Forget this idea to lose weight if eating habits are not changed. You are defeated before you even start. It won't work. Simple as that! Exercise, however, is helpful to maintain proper weight and is critically important for vitality. It gives you energy; it throws off endorphins that elevate your mood and keeps your heart, muscles, and blood pressure running smoothly. Humans, like the animals we are, are designed to move, not just sit and slowly fade away. Studies show that exercise is often superior in many medical situations than any drug. And it is free!

Stress: Some stress is good for us. It makes us pay attention; buckle down, and up our game. It can make us stronger. But being overwhelmed with too many demands and being anxious or insecure all the time can lead to trouble. Some stress, like family and work, may be beyond our control, but much of it is not. Generally, the heart of the matter is composed of anxiety and procrastination that make up almost all of the stress in our lives.

Some anxiety over children, money, health, and relationships just come with breathing. And some short term anxiety is not always bad if it does not paralyze us but forces us to make good changes. The bad part is worrying over those things we have no control over and not doing anything about the things we do have control over. Additionally, stress relievers like taking a mellow walk, yoga, meditation, soft music, a good book, or just a quiet place to unplug from our wired world can help restore the soul.

Along with anxiety is its twin of procrastination: being unorganized and unfocused and always leaving things for "later." It is that queasy sick-to the-stomach-feeling, much like a teen-ager who failed to do their homework or is unprepared for a pop quiz. The same is true for life in general. Indeed, the difference between a child and a mature adult is the mature adult does what needs to be done when they "don't feel like it."

Huge amounts of stress can be relieved by just taking care of business in a timely fashion because then there is so much less to worry about. Those who complain they do not have time rarely factor in the twenty minutes every hour wasted watching commercials on TV or even the whole two hours of wasted time watching what turns out to be a crummy movie. Somehow, there is always time for whatever we really choose to do.

Sleep: The elixir of the gods for the renewal of the body and mind is sleep. Yet most Americans are sleep deprived and cheat the clock at both ends of the day. Everyone talks about how busy they are and that there are just not enough hours in the day. This is true for some but nonsense for most of us. If one handicaps time schedules for the amount of time spent on the Internet surfing, texting, Facebooking, or tweeting along with TV binging and many other "non-essential!" activities, it is quite clear this is about personal choices and time management and has little to do with getting enough sleep. Most of us come up short.

While there is great obsession over diets to lose weight and admonitions everywhere to get out and walk or go to the gym, sleep is often overlooked. Yet sleep greatly helps to regulate our metabolism, makes us more alert and less cranky (exhibit A: any child who has not had enough sleep–look out, for there is hell to pay). Sleep allows us to perform better at work, lowers our stress, and helps us become more pleasant and patient people.

The human body works best on rhythm. Having a standard bedtime and a time to rise makes our human machine run at an optimum level (Ben Franklin's wisdom: "Early to bed and early to rise makes a man healthy, wealthy and wise.") and helps greatly with self-discipline. Millions of people claim they are "not morning people," which for a very small group may be true, but for the vast majority it is all about ingrained habits as "night owls."

While millions moan about insomnia, visit doctors, pop pills, and drink coffee all morning, most of this can be attributed to a lack of proper sleep. In addition, a poor diet, lack of exercise, and stress, which are the other three pillars of our four-pillared temple, makes for some very cranky people. Each pillar affects the others in profound ways. When observing the animal kingdom, it is noteworthy that sleep (and a cat nap) is an integral part of their daily ritual to preserve their strength and stamina for survival.

Some secrets to naturally falling asleep at an appointed time are self-evident. News Flash: A phone has no constitutional right to be answered. There are no phone police requiring anyone to jump at the very first ring. Let it go to voice mail. Sleep ritual is important to try to avoid unwarranted stimulation. TV, computers, cell phones, and tablets are all bad ideas and don't let the brain and body relax. Consciously turning off your mental track of things to do or problems to solve is important. They can wait for the morning.

Good strategies to follow are to ensure a very quiet and dark room, perhaps with some very soft music and a book with some uplifting message. A scary movie or intense book is not a good idea. The goal is to mellow out.

Another precaution about sleep is not to eat anything after suppertime. Loading up on munchies before bedtime means your digestive system has to work all night. It is like leaving your car in the garage with its engine idling all night with the wipers, radio, and the lights still on. It is not good for your battery! Check out the endnote at the end of this sentence for one website suggestion you may want to check out if you are having sleep issues.[33]

Finally, for caffeine addicts, stop or cut way down. For those who find this impossible, try at least to avoid the caffeine fix of coffee or soda past lunchtime. For aging "Boomers" it can mess with your sleep cycle much more than many appreciate from when they were younger. It can have the same effect on your body as a musician who is off-key and out of tune with the band.

Boomers believe they are all the children of Lake Wobegon: above average for sure, maybe not a star, but above average, they have no doubt. Yet lives are cut short because many did not take care of the four pillars of their temple.

Some of the greatest ideas and plans in the world are in the cemetery simply because people ran out of time prematurely. Yes, we know we are not immortal, but most of us have this personal plan to be a vibrant, independent, mobile, together person until about ninety-five when we are peacefully taken in our sleep one night. That's the plan. This idea of poor health and slow dying before then is for the birds. Not for us. But we are issued with only one birthday suit and need to take care of it. Better late than never for a tune-up or makeover. So promise yourself you will turn over a new leaf in your life starting tomorrow morning bright and early!

31

SHAPE UP OR PLAN TO SHIP OUT–
EARLY

*"If I knew I was going to live this long,
I would have taken better care of myself."*
Baseball Great, Mickey Mantle (passed at 63)

This is a tale of two different world dimensions that share the same planet. In the first dimension, you see them everywhere: seniors walking and jogging in the early morning sun with their iPods, lifting weights at the gym, doing laps in the pool, performing aerobics, practicing graceful tai chi in the park, or doing the Wii at home. They are plugged into the belief that if they do these things, they will look better, feel better, and live longer in good health.

In the second dimension, you see them everywhere: seniors who take every opportunity to miss an opportunity if it involves any physical effort. They are the first to look for a chair to sit on and will ride in anything with four wheels in order to avoid walking. Their idea of an invigorating hike is a slow stroll to the kitchen, and they do not need to be called twice to come to dinner unless it can be brought to them. This group is fundamentally comprised of fatalists resigned to "what will be will be." They promise themselves they will make changes sometime in the future (i.e. the far-distant future that requires little effort and that never arrives). Lots of denial and mind games are in play. Their lame "excuses" would fill a book. There are seven days of the week with each one having a name. "Someday" is not one of them.

Fourth-quarter people begin to see physical signs with increasing frequency that they often ignored before. Health issues that they would address later have all of a sudden become now. Some signs are subtle: an ache here, a pain there. With a little aspirin, it goes away. Others are far more serious signs, the flab, the bathroom scale, the tape measure, shortness of breath, back pain, and noticeable fatigue. It is no fun when your get-up-and-go got up and left you while you were still sitting on the couch.

Being fit and trim is the goal at any age for optimum health. Many people of proper weight and appearance from the outside can still be far from fit as they have little endurance and suffer from a variety of ailments. Good cardiovascular health is not accomplished by sitting all day in an office or at home. The excuse that "I just don't have the time in a busy schedule" is the biggest lie in the world. It is about choices. It is so much easier to preserve health than restore health.

Unexpected events can occur at any time. Earthquakes, hurricanes, tsunamis, or a streaking meteor out of the sky can catch the unsuspecting off guard. Call it fate, bad luck, or bad karma. Going to work in a skyscraper on 9/11, parking on a rainy day under the old oak tree that decides to give way at that very moment, the gas stove left on by accident in the kitchen, and the mentally ill guy at the mall with a gun can all lead to unexpected random events. There is often nothing we can do to save ourselves or those we love. These indiscriminate events are unexplainable.

However, when it comes to your personal health, there are many things you can do to not only lengthen your life but to give it vitality. Age will in the end take its toll on everyone, but the analogy to a car engine is apt. Those in the sixty to one hundred age category may no longer have a body like a V-8 three-hundred-horsepower muscle car of the past. But with care in changing the oil, new spark plugs, a change of tires, and a few cosmetic upgrades, you are still good to go to get anywhere you want.

A car driven correctly with only a one-hundred-fifty-horsepower engine today will work just fine for nearly all your needs. And to complete the analogy, the cars of today are so much better made than in the days of your parents and grandparents. You get better mileage, wear, tear, and longevity than ever. The same is true of modern medicine when compared to that of our grandparent's generation. So be assured that if you take care of your body, it should take care of you and provide you with lots of quality miles on the ol' odometer of life. But like a child's toy that has been misused, abused, and "run through the wringer," it is tough to repair. Even the best doctors and surgeons complain that they can only work with what they are given. They can pull off the occasional miracle, but it hardly ever happens –that's why it's called a miracle. The inspirational words of the English poet William Ernest Henley are worth considering.

Invictus

Out of the night that covers me,
Black as the Pit from pole to pole
I thank whatever gods may be
For my unconquerable soul

In the fell clutch of circumstance
I have not winced nor cried aloud
Under the bludgeoning of chance
My head is bloody, but unbowed.

Beyond this place of wrath and tears
Looms but the Horror of the shade,
And yet the menace of the years
Finds, and shall find, me unafraid

It matters not how strait the gate,
How charged with punishments the scroll,
I AM THE MASTER OF MY FATE:
I AM THE CAPTAIN OF MY SOUL.

Ask yourself if you are the captain of your own ship. Being in charge of your life and responsible for your own health in order to get the most out of your life is essential. It is what "true grit" is all about. If you have been putting this off, NOW is the time to give it your full attention.

32

A HEAVY SUBJECT

There are old people, and there are fat people,
but there are no old, fat people!

Have you ever noticed the phrase "the little old man" or "the little ol' lady" in conversation, observation, or in story form? Bluntly stated, with no politically correct sugar coating, the reason for this is that all the fat ones are dead. Think for a minute: how many obese one-hundred-year-olds have you seen in your lifetime? The answer is probably zero. How about ninety-five-year-olds or even ninety-year-olds? Maybe an odd one here or there, but they may be as rare as a four-leaf clover out in the pasture. The wake-up call is pretty clear. Excess weight and shortened life spans for seniors go hand in hand. It is an inescapable fact of life and aging. The hard truth is if one is heavy and has made it into one's sixties but fails to address this issue head on, the odds of seeing the end of a fourth quarter are very slim (pun intended), much less seeing a lot of overtime. The referee in the game of life will call time out as they bring out the stretcher to carry you off the field of life.

Obesity is a peculiar affliction of plenty in our cushy, modern way of life. We simply love food. We reward children with it for being good and ourselves with it as well. We eat when we are nervous, excited, bored, lonely, tired, depressed, happy, or bummed out. It is comfort food that stands in as lover, best friend, and therapist. Food is celebrated as "dinner on the town," having a picnic at the park, firing up the barbecue in the backyard, a potluck with good friends, or a hit-and-run fast food pickup. Food is central to a celebration or special occasion of any kind and the first thing that is offered to guests. Snacks and goodies are everywhere. Yum, yum!

Historically, mankind's daily concern was having enough to eat and surviving till next week or through the winter. Food security was a family's number-one concern. Amazingly, around the world today, emerging developing countries are now experiencing in just one or two generations a seismic shift in health concern from malnourishment to upward-trending obesity rates.

In the United States, food as a percentage of our income is cheap, cheap, cheap. The dinner-plate size at many restaurants has steadily grown into the main serving platter plate of yesteryear. Portion sizes have ballooned, and expectations have followed close behind. And in America, the word more is always equated with better. "Supersize," Big Gulp's, and Whoppers' were unfamiliar terms a couple generations ago and in more recent years have been under attack. Buffets of "all you can eat" are competitions between patrons who want to see where gluttony can end by trying to get more than their money's worth. It is treated almost as a sports competition. Thousands of venues sell large thirty-two-ounce sodas along with free refills approaching that of a six-pack to complement double-sized burgers and extra-large fries. With so much sugar and caffeine is it any wonder why kids today are so wired and are often mis-diagnosed with A.D.D. At the movies, an entire day's caloric intake can easily be surpassed by a bucket of popcorn, assorted candy, and monster sodas. It is so easy to do.

The "couch potato" crowd's concept of exercise is standing up to curse while looking for the lost TV remote in the seat cushions before settling back down. Later, during commercials or when they grab the remote to put the show on pause, they will struggle in their attempt to do a "full lap" to and from the kitchen for more goodies before resuming their near-horizontal exercise program in their comfy recliner.

When it comes to being overweight or obese, there is a multibillion dollar industry devoted to books, magazines, seminars, and a thousand programs and "secret" formulas to lose unwanted pounds. Rarely, if ever, does an issue of popular women's magazines fail to carry an article on losing weight. For millions of food junkies, the battle of the "bulge" is not even a battle anymore as they have thrown in the towel and willingly run up the white flag of surrender without much of a fight. Lip service and self-deception are on full display citing well-rehearsed chapter-and-verse of every obstacle in the world that prevents them from taking action. "I'm gonna, gonna, gonna, start next month to make some changes" which everyone knows is mostly chatter and a wish rather than a serious and committed plan.

Make no mistake. This is a very tough battle to fight. It is constant warfare. But like generals at war, no one wins every battle. The same is true for sports stars and even gamblers. Yet, they all get back in the game. They do not give up because the stakes are so high. The same is true of your health.

A world-class athlete laid up, immobile in bed for several months, would struggle to walk to the bathroom without assistance. Muscle atrophy, particularly of the legs, happens quickly and is even compounded as we get older. In the animal world, if predators or prey cannot run or move, they die. If humans cannot walk, their world continues to shrink, and they die earlier than others. But this goes beyond the issue of just fat. It goes quickly to the whole idea of quality of life. Those who would like to travel find it difficult since lots of walking is often required to see and do things. Others are not keen to travel with them because they slow them down. It can hurt.

Diabetes, shortness of breath, joint pain, fatigue, balance issues, and an assortment of other health problems rob many of the full joy of life. Throw in overt and covert snide comments, stranger stares, and embarrassment over seating from airplanes to movie theater seats along with an obvious bias from a potential employer, and you often have a recipe for depression and unhappiness. Euphemisms and political correctness abound to avoid the f word that comes with only three letters. Heavy, plump, portly, full figured, extra-large, and plus-sized words do not make the issue of compromised health go away. For women, average weight has gone from 140 pounds in 1960 to a current average weight of 168 pounds.[34] Clothing retailers have responded by just changing numbers and going to "vanity" dress sizes to make everyone feel better psychologically. The end result is illusion and delusion. Men are not any better and have packed on the pounds over the decades as well.

Still, it should be clear that everyone needs to be careful in making blanket moral judgments about other people, even fat people. There are a select few in this category who do have genetic, hormonal, or glandular issues that create special challenges in trying to maintain a healthy weight. These people deserve some empathy just as much as one that has a chronic disease. But people who truly fall into this category represent a tiny fraction of the universe of obese and overweight people and need to be under a doctor's care. Ninety-five percent or more just eat way too much and compound it by eating the wrong kind of foods and exercise far too little or none at all. There is no excuse for this group. There is no place to hide.

The computer-industry adage of "garbage in, garbage out" illustrates the fact that if bad code or poor data entry takes place, the resulting output is already headed to the garbage can. The same phrasing said about computers can be applied to food although kinder souls stick to the more benign, neutral phrasing of calories in (food intake), calories out (burned off by moving or exercise). While exercise is important for vitality, what one puts in one's mouth is a hundred times more important to control weight. (Note: one donut–just one–requires an hour of exercise to burn off–groan! A tasty restaurant muffin can require about a three-hour walk, and our meal has not even arrived yet! Bummer!)

Of course, losing weight is easier said than done, right? Absolutely, since food temptation is everywhere. Some vices like smoking or drinking can be avoided, but everyone has to eat in order to live. The brutal truth is a diet by itself will not work. It implies a strategy to lose weight, which millions have done successfully, but they have not kept it off because it does not change lifestyle or one's mental psychology. Jokes about being on a see-food diet (I see it, I eat it) show how difficult this can be.

Stress eating is also a huge problem as we try to compensate for demanding lives and schedules. Because we are stressed, we trick ourselves into believing we need to be "good to ourselves" to compensate, and our default option is yummy food and more of it. "Where's the ice cream, chips, and candy? I deserve it." Seconds, anyone?

The American westernized diet, which is heavy on meats,

sugar, salt, and oil in large quantities, heavily impacts a health-care system that is the most expensive in the world by far. Most types of chronic health problems are self-inflicted. A stunning and most revealing documentary that is eminently worth one's time is Forks over Knives (search on Netflix), which illustrates vividly the advantages of a simpler diet that dramatically lowers one's risk of disease, disability, and death. For fourth-quarter people looking to live healthy lives deep into overtime, watching this enlightening documentary should definitely be penciled in for one's weekend TV program viewing.

A government heavily influenced by the meat, sugar, and food industry by lobbyists, biased regulators, and favor seeking politicians rather than nutritionists and doctors with no agenda's does not have the American consumer's best interest at heart. It is about dollars and cents, not your health or well-being.

Unmindfulness eating, wherein you are not even aware you've drained the bowl of M&Ms or a bag of chips ("Betcha can't eat just one") while in deep conversation with someone or watching the tube makes it really tough. There is also the Catch-22 problem of "I am depressed because I am fat, and I am fat because I am depressed," making one feel overwhelmed. Most often, people who are able to control their appetites are also much more successful in controlling other parts of their life.

The total misuse of the word diet has caused suffering for tens of millions of people. It fails because there has not been a permanent revolution in an individual's relationship to food, exercise, and daily social habits. The problem with a diet is that people want to lose weight so they can go back to eating the way they did before. It never works. It just leads to a yo-yo weight gain and loss, makes one feel deprived, and makes life miserable. Dieters quickly feel cheated and defeated. But to be truly successful may require one's taste buds to be re-programmed. Comfort food, happy food, and reward food all beckon us with temptation. It is not about raw willpower alone, but it is most certainly about habits and psychological games played in one's head. And the first step for those who are challenged in this area is to become hyperaware of what goes in your mouth every minute of the day. Every morsel! Yes, 24/7/365.

Everyone is looking for a shortcut to weight loss. There is the hope for a magic solution, a magic pill, or some new spectacular product or some revolutionary exercise regimen that does not require too much effort. But now we come to the cruel truth. No exercise program in the world means much for weight loss unless one eats less and eats better. If one desires to lose weight, one has to eat fewer calories, simple as that. The greatest deception in the diet industry is that an individual can finesse their diet without any substantial changes and suddenly somehow, someway, become thin and fit. This is not the real world but the world of hype, hope, and expert salesmanship.

There has been much written about the human emotions of love and hate, often seen as the opposite sides to a coin. The literature of the world is replete with the noble lengths people will go for love and the ordeals they will bear for revenge and payback. Likewise, in order to achieve sustainable weight loss, a mental shift must take place whereby one hates the fat more in a visceral, fierce, passionate, and angry manner than they love and crave the food, causing a revolutionary change in behavior.

For those who are challenged in this area it helps to take an inventory of their fat and verbalize contempt for it. One needs to work themselves into a self-righteous frenzy of hate and disgust in order to encourage resolve to change one's ways. Is this a mind game? Sure. But one must internalize these angry emotions, not in a negative self-hatred way that is destructive and leads to further depression, but rather in the motivating spirit idea of taking the bull by the horns and deciding this will be dealt with "by all means necessary."

No one should trash their self-esteem, which is already at low ebb. Think about it as more directed anger at your conduct, not yourself. You are declaring war on the fat, not yourself. It should be viewed along the lines of a caring parent who punishes their child's bad behavior, not the child. This is all about behavior and bad habits, not personal self-worth. Otherwise, if one is not fully committed and "all in," it is just wishful daydreaming for an end result rather than a well-reasoned plan of attack for getting–and the Holy Grail of staying–healthy. Massive action is called for to make a permanent change in one's thinking and habits. And the battle needs to be waged constantly in the brain, where the outcome will be preordained before any changes in the body can take place.

It is often interesting to observe overweight people just talking about their favorite restaurants or favorite dishes and scrumptious desserts. They begin to swoon. Without their realizing it, their voices are more animated, and their eyes light up as if they are in love. They describe the food in rapturous terms and begin to salivate just thinking about it. They speak passionately about it, seemingly akin to a sexual experience–but even better, for their appetites can be satiated over a couple of hours at their own leisure and do not even require a partner. If this is you, become self-aware and take back control of your life. If this does not apply to you but to someone you care about, encourage them to seek help.

When it comes to physical fitness for seniors, even for those who are not overweight, here is the easy three-pronged test to assess one's condition. The first is when huffing up the stairs, do you grab the railing not for balance but to pull and drag yourself up the steps? The second is when getting in and out of a car, do you "plop" getting in and require a can-opener to get out? The third test is being able to balance yourself standing up without leaning on anything while putting on your underwear and socks. Of course, those past the fourth-quarter of life and into overtime may need some assistance, but those just entering the fourth quarter of life who find these tests challenging need to get serious about their physical shape.

Procrastination means that you may run out of tomorrows before you get around to doing something about your physical fitness. Exercise is like a continual tune-up maintenance program for your car, to keep it running efficiently and in good order. Or it could be considered like putting money in the bank and the interest you earn is better health with a more positive outlook. Positive exercise can lift your mood, attitude, focus, discipline, outlook, and energy in so many ways.

For those who are in denial about their weight, they should try the following eye-opening experiment with their doctor's permission. One weekend, get a backpack and load it up with twenty or twenty-five pounds of potatoes from the grocery store (or rocks in the backyard) and wear the backpack all day. Remember, no cheating by not moving around. Try to get in somewhere between six and ten thousand steps during the day on your pedometer. You cannot take the backpack off for one second, even when sitting, till bedtime. Then, in the evening when you do finally take it off, it will give you a shocking sense of what it is like carrying that much extra weight around all the time! No wonder you're tired. Hopefully, this little self-demonstration trick will be self-motivating.

A telling vignette of the "sedentary set" is to witness their actions upon arriving at a shopping center. They will circle the parking lot several times around and around in search of a close-in parking spot and burn up extra gasoline and an additional five to ten minutes of time just to avoid walking an extra fifty feet. You can even spot people doing the "parking lot dance," by trying to waltz into a prime spot–at the gym!

The key thing to remember about extra pounds is that not only do you have an ever-escalating mortality risk in the fourth quarter, but that it is crunch-time to do something about it. When someone is younger and abuses their body with bad food choices and bad health habits, the very fact of being young allows one to get away with murder. But as time marches on, the odds rapidly start to shift against you. The expression "It's the lean horse for the long race" is true. Fat horses all break down in the stretch. Even being slightly overweight by fifteen to twenty pounds can be a real concern that needs to be addressed. Lugging this extra sack or two of potatoes (or a 16-pound bowling ball) around 24/7 can be a real drag and take its toll on your heart.

The real reason why proper weight is so important is one's quality of life. Forget about cashing in your chips early–it is about dying slowly and miserably from a host of weight-related issues. It is true that if you feel crappy all the time, your life will be crappy most of the time. No one wants to be that person whose life revolves around doctor's appointments, hospital visits, the pharmacy, and struggling mightily to get into their fat jeans. It slowly constricts life options.

There are some things we have no control over in our medical genetic code. But many choices we make can greatly push the odds back in our favor. Of course, the biggest one is to stop smoking. However, we will not dwell on this since you would have to be living under a rock not to know how detrimental this vice is to your well-being. The same is true with alcohol or drugs. But food abuse is also a most vexing addiction and, like these other vices, shortens one's life.

Habit, habit, habit is the biggest blessing or curse in our lives. Good habits bring good things; bad habits interfere with our lives in many negative ways. So here are the ten rules of good health that can also save you a ton of money on diet and nutrition books. Post them on the fridge. This is all you need to know.

Rule #1   Eat less–portion control. Repeat: eat less–portion control! This is nearly the whole ballgame. If you eat with your eyes, keep one eye closed and eat only half as much. You will not die. Also, only shop at the grocery store with a "hard" list of items (no impulse buying) and never go there if you are hungry. Ban all junk food from the house. Yes, all of it. There will come a time when you will vandalize your entire kitchen by turning it upside down looking for your hidden "stash." Some find success by making their salad plate their main dinner plate. They pile it high, but there are no seconds.

Rule #2   Try to eat like a wolf at breakfast, a cat at lunch, and a rabbit at suppertime.

Note: Mom told us how important a good breakfast was, but who has the time? Yet we know it is not good to start the day on an empty tank with two cups of coffee and toast or a bagel as millions do. Our body machinery is not working most advantageously on that kind of diet. For those feeling rushed in the morning, it is almost exclusively because of a lack of sleep by not going to bed earlier the night before and not getting up early enough. For those who claim they are not hungry in the morning, this is usually from years of bad habits by eating later at night, cheating their sleep clock, or both. Their cycle is off. Habits are super-hard to change, but it can be done. It requires a new mindset.

Rule #3   Eat less meat, which is harder to digest. Eat more vegetarian meals. It's better for you.

Rule #4   Secret weapon: Drink water all day long, as much as you can, which cuts down hunger. Hydrate! Hydrate! Six to eight glasses a day exclusively of only water will impact your appetite.

Rule #5   Key! Get eight hours of sleep on a routine schedule. If you want to soar with the eagles in the morning, you can't hoot with the owls all night.

Rule #6   Dessert should rarely follow a meal–only on holidays and special occasions. Enjoy it slowly. No seconds.

Rule #7   Try to eat nothing after seven in the evening. Your digestive system needs rest and you need good, restful sleep. It will thank you.

Rule #8   Try not to be a snacker, but if you are, make your snacks only fruits and veggies.

Rule #9   If food came from a plant, eat it. If it was made in a plant, try harder to avoid it. Try to stick more closely to greens, grains, vegetables, fruits, and nuts.

Rule #10 Get a pedometer. Use it every day and take ten thousand steps. Even better are "smart watches" made by several companies, which can track many of your vital signs. So walk or jog your fanny off! Park far away, take the stairs, take a hike, and move! Without exercise, it is like having a car and putting it up on blocks in the garage. Over time, the car will rust, engine parts will degrade, the tires go flat, and the interior fades and cracks. It is soon on its way to the junkyard. Use it or lose it. You get the picture and know what needs to be done. Decide to do it.

Just like some nutty get-rich scheme cooked up by your brother-in-law or crazy friend, the snake-oil salesmen of weight loss are everywhere. They all promise pie in the sky with a thousand come-ons of "miracle" diets, pills, and tricks to lose weight, usually offering quick results with little effort. Ignore them all since they do not change habit. Expectations are also seriously out of whack. Weight that took years to put on (one or two pounds a year for forty years) will not disappear in a few weeks or even months. Anyone who claims differently is a quack. Even if you do everything right, without cheating, realistic weight loss is about one or two pounds a week.

Permanent weight loss comes from a process, not from a genie popping out of a bottle granting wishes. It also sets up a wildly false narrative that can be discouraging for both men and women focusing on belly fat and seeing little progress. They forget that much of their weight is unseen, hiding in their butt, masquerading as "junk in the trunk" plus heavy "thunder thighs" so that even if there is a decrease in weight, they may not see the results where they want for a long while and give up too easily.

Maintaining a healthy weight is really about becoming a kid again and learning how to spend your allowance. Generally, for men, they are allowed to spend 14,000 calories a week, and for women, 12,600. If this were real money, people would be a hundred times more careful where and on what they spent it on. Every bite that is consumed should cause your cash register to ring and require your brain to record it.

The next step is to recognize that a pound of fat equals 3,500 calories. Now we are just into a matter of simple arithmetic. If one wishes to lose two pounds a week, they must reduce their weekly (food intake) allowance by 3,500 calories and combine it with an hour and a half of physical activity of any kind (even shopping and errands count) during the day, and the loss of two pounds a week can be achieved.

Many dieters go crazy because they feel deprived and in a straitjacket. The cookie monster comes out, and they ransack the house for some stashed goodies close by that sets them back to zero or worse. Remember that there is not one solution for everybody and what works for one may not work for another. If one method does not work for you, try another, and another. Don't give up. But all "successful" programs for the long-term must change habits, or it is a futile quest.

One reason why fat people can eat so much is because they claim they do not feel full. This can be partly attributable to weak abdominal muscles that do not contract properly and send the wrong signals to the stomach. It is like "pushing on an open door," whereby the stomach is stretched to accommodate a large amount of food versus the "closed door" concept, where a smaller, toned, and tighter stomach gets the message that it is full.

Exercise tightens and strengthens the body core of stomach muscles. Also, many yummy foods are often empty calories and so do not cause a feeling of fullness to signal the brain that the stomach is full. Others eat so fast (big mistake) by shoveling their food that by the time the "full" signal is sent out from their brain they have consumed far more than needed. Slowing way down (count to ten between bites) and putting only half as much food on a fork is advantageous. Ab muscles need exercise or they will just expand and sag.

There is one additional change that needs to be made but is hard for many people to accept, and that is to fall in love with water, the essence of life, since more than half our body is made up of the stuff. Despite plastic water bottles being everywhere, most people do not drink enough water. So take an empty gallon milk jug, fill it half full with water at the beginning of each day and drain it by the end of the day. Some will grumble and whine in protest. Water is tasteless, and I don't like it much. I much prefer coffee, tea, energy drinks, soda, juice, or beer, which are all mostly water anyway, so that should count instead of water, right?

The problem is that most of these beverages have drawbacks. The first three have caffeine, which can make you a little edgy and, perhaps out of a nervous high, tempt you to stress-eat more. They can also cheat you out of restful sleep. Furthermore, they are diuretics, which can cause loss of hydration. The last three are loaded with empty calories that defeat you before you start.

Just drinking water exclusively can cause the average person to drop ten to fifteen pounds in a year without making one other single change in their diet.[35] And consider the financial cost! Add up what you and your spouse or family spend on coffee, soda, juice, and booze in a month and then multiply that number by 480 (months = 40 years) and many are shocked to see a $50,000 to $100,000 bill or even more. That's a lot of dough.

The secret power of water (and lots of it) is that it can work as a hunger killer. Many people fail to realize that many hunger pains are really a mask for thirst pains. The body is signaling water, not food, and so we often misinterpret the signal. Often when we eat, then we drink as well. And if we get into a salt-sugar dynamic loop cycle with our meals, our weight plan is shot to hell. We are toast.

Conquering the evening munchies sometimes only requires a big glass or two of water to kill it off. Or if you need to have something, reach for a juicy apple or a bunch of grapes or baby carrots. Adopting a water regimen alone can help in the battle of the bulge. Much of this is habit and a mental calculation since we associate a "beverage" of any kind as a treat, and we love nothing better than to treat ourselves all day long. Coffee in the morning, tea at a midmorning break, a soda with fast food at lunch, an energy drink in the mid-afternoon, juice with dinner at home, a glass of wine or a can of beer in the evening to unwind. Water? Oh yeah, I swallow a little with all the pills I have to take because I am out of shape.

One way to do a reliable review on good water consumption is the bathroom checkup. A very pale, very light shade of urine yellow is preferred. The darker it is generally suggests being under-hydrated and you should increase your water in-take. Water can also aid in alleviating constipation. It is a win-win plan.

Everyone is familiar with looking in the mirror in the morning and not being pleased with looking "haggard" whenever we fail to get enough sleep. Indeed, among the top beauty secrets of models and actresses is getting enough sleep. To help us look our best and function better, sleep is critical. It can also be instrumental in cutting down on our caffeine fix of coffee and soda addiction.

If we get a good night's sleep, we are less likely to need a caffeine "fix" to jump start us from our morning stupor. We don't need to be jerked wide awake because our bodies are signaling that we are cheating it on sleep from the night before. It is no fun dealing with cranky and grumpy people at home or at work who are in bad moods all the time because of a lack of sleep on their part. Furthermore, contrary to some beliefs, one can get more done working fully engaged by getting a good night's sleep than another person working in a hazy fog of sleep-deprived semiconfusion.

For those who have honestly tried everything to control their eating by giving it their best shot but are still coming up short, bariatric bypass surgery of some sort should be considered in consultation with their doctor. For some there is fear of going under the knife while others may worry about cost and insurance issues. But lay these concerns aside. What this is really about is being able to enjoy a vital fourth quarter of your life and not be worried about early death, disability, or a compromised life. This may be in your life interest and should be considered seriously. Do some serious research and talk with many who have had the procedure and can speak to the ups and downsides of the surgery.

The bonus payoff to proper weight management is that not only will you live years longer, but the best part is your years will be healthier, happier, and more vital. Indeed, many seniors bemoan the fact of how tired they are all the time. Well, carrying a fifty-pound barbell around all day while not getting any exercise could be reason number one. People who make the transition to eat less and smarter and exercise more feel it is a life-changing experience for them. Furthermore, it goes far beyond just their weight issues because mentally, they feel in control of their lives again. Besides, if you don't have your health, nothing else matters much anyway. Quality of life nearly always trumps quantity of life. In the words of Abraham Lincoln, "In the end it is not the years in your life that count. It's the life in your years."

33

INNER SPACE

The greatest mystery in the universe is between your ears.

"Space, the final frontier," fires the imagination of mankind. What is "out there" in the seemingly infinite universe defies our comprehension. The space program excites millions who dream of mankind's potential to one day explore vast new worlds and to discover the mysteries they may hold. Yet it is the human mind, made up of a few pounds of spongy gray matter divided into two hemispheres, that is the most complex and fascinating object to be contemplated in the universe. And controlling such a powerful force for good or ill has been the story of mankind's history and existence.

Control is a mighty word. Indeed, its twin is the word power. The world has been consumed from its earliest days by power. Kings, czars, potentates, popes, dictators, and generals have all spent their time and efforts getting it, guarding it, keeping it, flaunting it, or if lost, trying to get it back. Untold millions of innocents have been enlisted, co-opted, coerced, lied to, or manipulated into serving as soldiers to get or to maintain power and have died accordingly. Only a very small minority of causes for a call-to-arms have been for noble causes. Throughout the past, the family, clan, tribe, religion, or nation has always been about the rules of social and political organization. In the end, who is going to make the rules and call the shots? Will it be the individual, the clan, the community, or some specially designated individual or group that will hold the power of carrots and sticks to assure compliance with whatever individual or entity has decided upon on any given matter?

Business leaders also crave power that lets them act as "captains of industry," which worked for them in the industrial age. But today's tycoons, who rule over empires of employees, suppliers, and consumers, aspire to even greater heights. They wish to become members of the rarified "masters of the universe" circle whereby they can bend markets, politicians, bankers, and others to their will and for their profit, which will further their power and influence to even loftier heights. In the words of the former baseball star, Reggie Jackson, the aspiration is to be "the straw that stirs the drink." They strive to be a mover and a shaker, a maker and a doer, a star and a legend all wrapped up into one.

However, now we come to the pièce de résistance. The real struggle of mankind is the titanic quest to get power over one's self. It is the struggle over the human condition in all its frailties of personality, wants, needs, contradictions, aspirations, and attempts to understand the meaning of life itself. Socrates said, "Know thyself," along with his twin gem of insight proclaiming that the "unexamined life is not worth living." Socrates, born nearly five centuries before the birth of Christ, recognized even then that the internal world of what essentially was going on between our ears through our mental capacities reflected by a moral code was the template necessary to live a life of meaning and purpose beyond mere survival and acquisition.

Today, we would consider a holistic view of an individual. The quest should be to develop "inner powers" of self-discipline, honor, restraint, courage, judgment, self-awareness, nobility, and above all, wisdom. These traits require a great deal of introspection and self-control, which is the beginning of real personal power. Of course, like any tough battle, these are the most difficult fights of all.

Conquering "inner space" on many levels means fighting the age-old battle between good and evil, mind versus reckless emotion, hormones versus impulse control, and compassion over selfishness. Cultivating the capacity of delayed gratification and valuing the centrality of wisdom by placing it on a higher plane over knowledge itself are lofty goals. For far too many people it is much easier to badger, manipulate, control, bully, or dominate others than themselves. So even as we engage with the world around us, a realization that "inner space" of mind, heart, and soul is what truly defines us should be our primary guiding light.

There are five parts to the whole concept of aspiration. They need to be imparted to the next generation as well as taken personally. The first is "thinking better" which means being self-aware that what we occupy our minds with largely defines who we are, hopefully for the better. The second part is "speaking better" which means being civil and respectful towards others in word and speech. (i.e. no foul language) The third part is "behaving better" which is reflected in manners, decorum, and deportment. The fourth part is in "doing better" that is demonstrated by our best efforts at any given task. The last part is "becoming better" that is revealed by yearly self-improvement as a human being.

34

VANITY, VANITY, ALL IS VANITY

*When I get up in the morning and look in the mirror,
I can see that God has a sense of humor.*

"You're So Vain" was a hit song by Carly Simon in the early 1970s about a lover who was self-absorbed. Things may have gotten worse with the current generation with a seemingly unquenchable obsession over media and a fixation with fame. Many young people crave the attention to become famous simply for being famous, no accomplishments required. The appealing job description is to become a celebrity that does not require any talent except self-promotion by using the press, along with viral social media acting as their agent to further their own "brand." That is a pretty good gig, many wannabe's conclude. And this requires full-time attention to clothes, body image, and drama, real and faked, in order to project a version of their fabulous, yet shallow, selves.

Interestingly, the fourth-quarter group these days has their own take on vanity. Everyone knows they can't stop Father

Time, but there is a fight to at least slow him down a bit for as long as possible. And just about everyone has a friend or someone they know that gets talked about behind their back. See if you recognize any of the whispers. "She had a lot of work done." "He got a hair transplant, I'm sure." "Those boobs are not real." "She's popping diet pills like candy." And so it goes. The hidden message is often mixed, part gossip, part huffiness, and perhaps a touch of envy.

The fourth-quarter boomer crowd has always been self-centered and flashy in many ways but was a little more reticent to be so public about it, with the exception of some outliers. But boomers are now just as eager to embrace a new generation's sea-change in attitudes. Any false modesty is out. If you've got it, flaunt it. Boomers want to defy aging, look their best, and simply say, "Why not, if it makes me feel better about myself?"

One view is that I may be older, but I do not have to look older. Wrinkles, gravity, hair loss, and weight issues are all enemies to be held at bay. The concern is that the body packaging is showing signs of wear and tear. Hollywood stars of stage and screen of a certain age have caused a new standard that is equally desired by the general public. But looking "fabulous" generally requires some extra help.

Hollywood stars who have had "nips and tucks" (they even made a TV show about it) to stay eternally young (and employed) in front of the cameras are in constant fear of "aging out" of roles and the industry. Rich socialites do the same to keep husbands, find new husbands, or simply keep up with the "scalpel race" among their social circles and to extend the mirror hype and hope of "Mirror, mirror, on the wall, who's the fairest of them all?"

Vanity is different from pride or self-worth. For the very young who view the world without filters, nuance, or a lifetime of experience, they can be caught up in the glitz, the preening, and the spectacle of a narcissistic show without substance. But for seasoned fourth-quarter people, vanity wears thin if the whole point is about ego, showing off, and me-ism. It is all Christmas packaging with no present inside. It is not attractive, and most discerning fourth-quarter people see through it for its superficial shallowness. Gaudy and garish vanity for its own sake loses its phony charm. Discerning people quickly move on.

In contrast to vanity, personal pride in one's appearance and manner as a complement to one's core essence should always be encouraged. Abraham Lincoln was once accused by a critic of being "two-faced" on a public issue, to which he replied, "If I were two-faced, do you think I would wear this one?" Even Lincoln in this humorous response recognized he was not going to win anything based on his looks. But having proper pride and putting your best foot forward in everything you do are wonderful traits to possess. Unfortunately, many today display far too much carelessness in dress, behavior, speech, and attitude. Sloppiness is far too accepted and prevalent in the public square today.

For seniors, many cannot sign up fast enough for physical improvements, for the latest cosmetic anything that is available. It could be likened to upgrading the living room with new rugs and drapes to freshen up the room. After many years, it is time for a makeover. For other seniors, they vacillate and are not sure, wondering if this is right for them. They want to justify the cost of going under the knife and need to talk themselves into self-permission for something that seems to them to be a vanity quest. After all, "What will others say, and how will it affect me and my relationships?" they ponder.

Well, time is a-wasting. Face lift, why not? If you can afford it, go for it. Nip and tuck? Just do it! Varicose veins? Make the appointment. And this is not just about women anymore since men are increasingly looking into all types of cosmetic procedures. They are feeling the heat at the office or in public to keep up with the competition. Get that hair transplant, color that hair, and look into electrolysis? Yes, go ahead. Life is short. Salute yourself in the mirror and be the best self you can be. Just remember that none of these procedures will substitute for flaws in one's personality, integrity, or likability. Those deficits require real work and sustainable strategies.

Some women, it has been noted, would choose beauty over brains because men can see better than they can think! But reflect upon other areas of our lives and how we primp and prepare. We landscape our front yards and mow the grass. We prepare the dining-room table with the very best we have when guests are invited. We make repairs to our cars, and we wash, wax, and clean them all for making a good impression. Is this vanity? No, it is pride, and that is a good thing. In a youth-oriented culture in which boomers have always fancied themselves the center of attention, there is no reason not to fight off Father Time if you can.

For men, a little hair coloring can take five years off one's countenance. Yes, there are a few older "silver foxes" out there that look great, but they are the exception to the rule. For balding men, a hair transplant can do wonders for one's self-image and confidence. For those men who have beards or mustaches, they gotta go, which can take another five years off your "face age." A rakish and trendy beard in a man's thirties can look cool and be a fashion statement, but in the fourth quarter, it adds to age rather than subtracts. Furthermore, a man should retain the habit of shaving seven days a week without fail (unless deep in the woods with the bears and deer) even if he's just going to Home Depot. Don't get lazy. Two or three days' stubble on a sixty-five-to-eighty-year-old just looks like an old "grizzled geezer" gold prospector looking for his mule.

Likewise, women need to pay attention to dress, hair, and make-up even when running errands. Unfortunately, the truth is that people who "look old" simply become invisible, and younger people, without even being aware of it, overlook them almost as if they are not there. Even many seniors do this unwittingly among their own cohort. In their own minds they perceive themselves as younger, but view their contemporaries as showing their age.

Equal time must also be given to a second group of boomers who may be (money aside) just a little less pretentious and more comfortable and accepting of themselves in their own skin. Despite the passage of time, their self-image is just different and oriented in other ways. Their answer to the question of "Why not?" is "Why?" "If my family and friends accept me for who I am, and I accept my older status, I don't feel a sense of urgency to go down the whole "makeover" road. Besides, I am a down-to-earth person, and it is just not me." There is nothing wrong with this view either except to look neat and put together. There is no definitive answer to these types of questions of what is right for each individual. But it is worth taking the time to parse out the lines between pride, self-worth, self-improvement, and vanity.

Two areas that do need special attention are losses in hearing and sight. Too often, for some, vanity is a factor in both cases. Hearing loss is tough for anyone. Speaking is how we communicate, and nothing promotes isolation and withdrawal from life faster than hearing loss. It is even more isolating than blindness. No one likes to be left out of the conversation, and it is like being thrown back to childhood when Mom and Dad spoke in code or with big words to keep you in the dark except now you have trouble hearing the words.

It is amazing the number of seniors who have some hearing

loss and refuse to get checked out by an audiologist, and if need be, show great reluctance to consider getting a hearing aid. When confronted with a compromised hearing condition, too many are resistant out of a false sense of shame or embarrassment. But let's call this what it is. This is just stubbornness, denial, and stupidity all rolled into one. It is a perfect example of "there's no fool like an old fool." For some, it is the last straw that they have finally crossed the Rubicon into old age. It is the big, flashing neon sign, saying you have arrived in the land of Geezerville. Baloney! Regardless of age, whether sixty or ninety, it is the wrong way to look at aging. If you have a flat tire, you change it; engine trouble, you fix it. The correct response is, "I don't want to miss out on anything."

The good news is that hearing devices (new terminology) are smaller and better than ever. Are they perfect? No, but they are getting closer all the time. Some are so small and transparent they are nearly invisible. Patience may be required to have them adjusted several times to fit your needs, but the same can be said for a lot of things. Roll with it; you will be glad you did.

Also, if you notice that the TV sound is not quite what it was or there is some wording you are missing, the best thing you can do for yourself is to buy yourself some good wireless (no cords) headphones that connect to the TV. It is among the best hundred bucks you will ever spend. First, you can hear and understand the TV with much better clarity, but the other blessing is for a wife who does not have to listen to "the game" all afternoon blaring away as constant background noise. The same is true for the husband who wants to take a weekend nap on the couch while the wife is watching some movie on Netflix he has no interest in. This is just common courtesy, and many will wish they had done this many years ago even before hearing issues became apparent. It is also great for young children who may be watching cartoons or video games while giving the rest of the house peace and quiet. You can purchase great headphones at Best Buy or order them on the Amazon website. You will not be sorry.

The rule about TV should always be that a television never holds a house hostage. A house should own a television, but a television should NEVER own a house. Being respectful to others is paramount. Sometimes, silence really is golden. Shut the TV off.

When eyesight begins to be more of a pressing issue, don't think twice about getting glasses. Many seniors don't wear glasses at all except for reading. Others need prescription glasses all the time but will complain that they "spoil their looks" and get frustrated always looking for them or losing them. Instead, they try to muddle about. (Note: for just reading glasses, order a dozen pair on Amazon for seventy-five bucks and scatter them around)

Glasses just come with being in the 4th quarter of life for nearly everyone. It is also a safety issue. No one wants to admit that vanity caused them to trip or fall on the stairs and end up in the hospital, regardless of age. Millions of others have opted for Lasik surgery or to have surgically inserted eye lenses to improve vision and avoid glasses altogether. For millions of others, contact lenses are a way of life. In life, as in driving a car, it is always good to see where you are going. Enjoy the view of life's parade.

When it comes to pride, stand tall, be bold, use common sense, and always try to be the best you can be.

35

GET ME A DOC

An elderly gentleman who had outlived several doctors was interviewing another one to see if he would be a good match. The old man asked the doctor how many years he had been a doctor. The doctor proudly responded that he had been practicing for over twenty-five years. The old man was not impressed. "Practicing," he huffed. "You would think, after twenty-five years, you would finally know what you were doing."

When someone is injured or suddenly collapses on the floor, people rush to their aid and immediately yell out to others within earshot the words, "Get a doctor," in a loud and pleading voice of great urgency. Time is of the essence, and breathing issues or blood loss must be attended to immediately to prevent a potential tragedy. Professional care can't arrive or be accessed quickly enough. In these situations, time seems to get warped when everything is happening rapidly and, at the same time, dragging as if in slow motion. When we or someone we love is at their most vulnerable, nothing matters more than a caring doctor and compassionate nurses. Our lives are in their hands.

Too many healthy people ignore taking the time to visit their doctor. They feel healthy, have no complaints, don't have the time, and don't want the hassle. Some don't want the lecture to lose weight, eat better, and exercise. Besides, they reason, doctors are only for when you are sick or injured. This is a mistake—first, because preventive checkups could save you a lot of grief later on or could even save your life. But the real reason to go is to establish a rapport with your doctor. If they never see you, you just become another patient chart among hundreds. So if crunch time ever comes, like a car crash, fall, or serious illness, you want a great doctor who will make you a priority and not phone it in by treating you as a generic patient.

Doctors are human beings who relate to people as we do. Someone we know just has priority over someone we don't in every walk of life. We want someone who will go the second mile for us. In a time of crisis, you want your doctor to know your name and to be able to attach your face and personality to the broken and forlorn figure lying in a hospital bed. So, if for no other reason, go and see your doctor twice a year if only to schmooze and share a good joke while having your vitals checked. It's good insurance.

In times of great need, we all want special treatment and special attention. Hopefully, we will be among the lucky ones who will never be put in this position, but if the need arises, the time to make the personal connection is long before a crisis occurs. A good personal relationship established with your doctor can make a difference. It is also wise not to make the mistake of confusing a good bedside manner, which we all value, with expertise, smarts, and dedication in his/her area of specialty. Ideally, we all want both, but smarts should come first when dealing with our precious health.

In medical school, which only takes the best and the brightest, the competition to get accepted is fierce. Many with less-than-stellar grades do not even apply, and of those who do, many are disappointed by not making the cut. It is often said that the hardest part of medical school is getting accepted. But once in the program, even though students are ranked in their class, as a practical matter this means little except internally for some highly sought after residency programs.

For the public at large, the joke goes like this: "What do you call a medical student who finished last in their class?" The answer is: "a doctor." First, last, or in the middle of the pack, they all get the same title. Think about it. Have you ever walked into any doctor's office and, while glancing at his diploma and board certifications hanging on the wall, ever asked the question, "Hey doc, where did you finish in your medical class?" It is never done or even thought about. We just assume the doctor is competent simply by becoming a doctor. Yet in sports, we know there are good players, and then there are star players. The same is true for mechanics, contractors, and teachers. But in the medical field, it is tough to figure out which is which, and the high priests of medicine try to protect their own turf. So what is the game plan to find, or to switch to, a doctor you have confidence in? While there is no tried-and-true way, here are a few guidelines that may help.

#1 No rookies: A newly-minted doctor, fresh from graduation, was just starting his first day of residency in the hospital and found himself starting his first rotation in the emergency department. Although twenty-six years of age, the doctor had a baby face and looked much younger. A burly, middle-aged construction worker had come in with a deep laceration on his hand. The newbie doctor commenced with the procedure to sew up the wound while trying to act as professional as possible. He did not want to let on that this was the first time he had ever sewn up a patient before. The construction worker looked the young doctor up and down a few times and gently commented that he looked awfully young and then just bluntly asked, "Hey doc, how many of these have you done before?" The young doc, with a wave of his hand, a heavy sigh, and an air of authority to deflect the question, replied, "Ah, you wouldn't believe it," leaving the sly and witty impression that he had done this procedure many times before and that this was just a matter of routine. Yes, everyone needs to start somewhere, but you do not want to be that guinea pig.

The sweet spot for your doctor should be in the thirty-five to fifty-five-year range—not too young and green but not too old to be out of touch and going through the motions with other things on his mind. Younger doctors in their thirties can be a good thing since they have the latest training, may be more on the cutting edge of new technology, and are energetic and eager to establish a good reputation. Still, a little seasoning is also a good thing. Is this age discrimination? Yes—so be it. It is your health and life you are entrusting to another person.

#2   Next, consider screening out anyone over the age of sixty. This has nothing to do with competence and has more to do with the fact that he or she is aging in the fourth quarter along with you. Despite having developed a rapport and comfortable relationship, they are likely to leave you soon, even if they work part-time to age seventy or more (and may prune you from their reduced patient load). They are slowing down, have already made a lot of money, and are probably taking more time off. Even if they are good, they may no longer be on the bleeding edge of medicine as keeping up with it all requires a lot of time. They may be in cruise mode.

Having said all this, there is one big caveat. A good older doc may be more understanding of your situation since they are tuned in to getting older themselves. A downside of younger doctors, no matter how bright and well intentioned, is that many have an unconscious bias against older folks and do not want to listen to their multiple health issues and can be rather dismissive. They can brush people off and chalk serious complaints up to aging, thereby missing things by not being as thorough as they would with their younger patients. You may want to stick with your older doctor if you feel he is still on top of things. You need to make good judgment calls.

#3   It sounds elitist–no, it is elitist–but check out what school your doctor graduated from. A top-name school is more selective of the cream of the crop, so this can only be in your favor. Foreign doctors need much more scrutiny as to where they trained and the quality of their medical training. Some are good, and some do not measure up.

#4   Reputation around town: Rely on referrals of people you trust and respect. If they are willing to vouch for a doctor based on their own experience, this is much better than going blind and taking potluck from some book directory. If you have some friends in the medical field who are doctors or nurses, they are generally in the know of who is good and whom to avoid. Ask them if they would be comfortable having this doctor treat them in an emergency. It can be telling.

#5   Personalities: This is often a very intimate relationship, and you need a certain comfort level if you are to be naked, poked, prodded, and probed. If it doesn't feel right, keep looking. Making this more complicated is the fact that a very good doctor may not be accepting new patients. And if you are lucky to be included, he or she may be very busy, which may make it harder getting a relatively quick appointment.

#6   Specialists: Even though they are a doctor, you would not be comfortable with a dermatologist fixing your broken arm or a proctologist doing brain surgery. Your homework is required. If a particular procedure is to be done, find out how many this doctor has performed over the years. Don't assume that an older doctor has done this procedure. They may be adding it to their repertoire with you being their first chance to "practice." Ask lots of questions.

#7   Finally, let your doctor know your thoughts and wishes regarding your care. Honesty and openness are critical between doctor and patient. Your doctor can't fix what he or she doesn't know. Pain, falls, concussions, alcohol abuse, drugs, a chocolate addict, or whatever, they need to be informed. You also need a frank discussion about your wishes regarding end-of-life care in case you have a severe accident or life-threatening illness.

#8   Follow-up: Lots of patients forget to thank their doctors. In a rushed setting, many doctors have lots of patients to see with busy schedules. But they are human also and like to hear that they have made a difference. It is one of the reasons why they went into medicine in the first place. Take the time to express gratitude at appropriate times with a card and sincere note. It will be much appreciated because it is so rare. You will stand out. And you will be remembered!

36

BOOZE

A drunk driver pulled over by the side of the road:
"Officer, sir, I swear to drunk, I am not God."

Jokes involving alcohol are often hilarious because they relate to stupid behavior unless someone gets hurt. Then it's not funny at all. Everyone then skulks away. And the casualty list is staggeringly high. When it comes to booze, Americans are schizophrenic. They give the problem lip service but at the same time are in denial and look the other way from the real damage booze leaves in its wake. A common feeling is "it's them" who may have a blind spot about booze, certainly not me. "Anyway, let's change the subject, please," many implore. People start to squirm.

So why bring this subject up at all since seniors drink less on average than other age groups in the general population? Because the abuse of alcohol negates everything else that is positive to live your best life with the precious time left in your fourth quarter. Abuse of alcohol can cause friends to drop away rapidly, and its negativity compounds all the other challenging issues facing members of the fourth-quarter club. It is like putting sand in your cars gas tank; it fouls everything up. Yet surely, some will argue, with an older and wiser age group, this is not as significant a problem as is teenage drinking or as it is for society in general. After all, no one in the media is talking about "seniors gone wild." The truth is this is a hidden problem among seniors.

According to studies under the auspices of the National Institutes of Health (NIH),[36] nine percent of Medicare beneficiaries have a serious alcohol issue. So if this does not impact your life, it most certainly does for a family member, relative, or a friend that you know and care about. And you need to "speak up" out of genuine concern and "call them out" to get help while at the same time dismissing the b.s. nonsense they use to defend, excuse, or dismiss their conduct. It will not be pretty, it never is, but friends who really care tell the truth as they see it. It is like collateral damage from a hand grenade. For every problem drinker a constellation of family members and friends around them are injured in one way or another as an innocent bystander.

NIH government studies point out that "among adults 60 and older, it [alcoholism] is one of the fastest growing health problems facing the country." Yet it warns "the situation remains underestimated, underidentified, underdiagnosed, and undertreated."[37] The website goes on to point out that as it relates to seniors, healthcare providers (generally younger professionals) tend to dismiss alcohol abuse by ascribing problems or symptoms instead to aging, dementia, or other related health problems. It flies below their medical radar. Adult children are frequently in denial about their parents, and seniors try to hide it. No one is a better liar than an abuser of alcohol.

Strangely, the media, along with most everyone else,

always talks about "alcohol and drugs" in tandem as if they were two separate categories. But alcohol is a drug and America's favorite one at that, no less. It just happens to be legal and socially acceptable. It is also mentally set apart from other drugs because it is taken in liquid form. It is not smoked, inhaled, snorted, injected, or popped as a pill. Because it is consumed as a beverage, often in social settings, people just categorize it in their head differently, but it is still a potent drug. And it causes more damage than all the other drugs combined, by far.

One of the most important starting points when discussing alcohol issues with anyone is norm-referencing. This just means establishing what the "norm" is for people in general. Because birds of a feather flock together, it is easy to overlook that there may be hundreds of other flocks out there, independent of yours, who do things differently than the social circle that you fly with. What may seem normal to you may not always be true for the general population.

One "norm-referenced" reality check that may be incredibly hard to believe is that almost fifty percent of the population is either a non-drinker or what can be referred to as a "seldom drinker." This is an impression no one would ever draw from the media, the popular culture, or the zillion beer commercials for every sports program. Indeed, the general notion is that "everyone drinks."

Surprisingly however, about one-third of Americans do not drink at all. Most abstainers do so for religious reasons, like a Mitt Romney or the late Muhammad Ali. There is also a large contingent of former problem drinkers who are now abstainers, such as former President George W. Bush and David Letterman. Legions of high-profile celebrities have passed through the Betty Ford Clinic and many others like it in an attempt to regain control of their life. Millions of ordinary folk from all walks of life have attended AA (Alcoholics

Anonymous) or similar programs in a quest to maintain sobriety one day at a time since booze has had such a damaging effect on their lives. Some other reasons people do not drink can be for medical-health issues, financial costs for low-wage workers, or simply a dislike for the taste of alcohol. A few make a personal or professional choice to forego alcohol as a part of their lifestyle, like the real-estate mogul Donald Trump (now President Trump) who witnessed the toll upon a brother and friends.

Additionally, there is what can be called "seldom drinkers," who consume on average only one or two drinks a month. If asked, they do not consider themselves abstainers per se, but alcohol plays no important role in their lives. These are individuals who may have the rare glass of wine or beer at a celebratory occasion or nurse a solitary drink for the whole evening in some social settings. These seldom drinkers make up an estimated additional thirteen percent of the population[38] and, when combined with the non-drinkers, the numbers rise to approach nearly half the population with whom alcohol is a nonissue. Who knew?

The purpose of this discussion about booze is simply to raise awareness among seniors to be on guard if they find themselves, or people they care about, in danger of using it as a crutch or an escape and to seek help sooner rather than later. A timely "intervention" can literally save lives or a bundle of trouble.

Just to put the alcohol question in a larger societal context of how serious it is, the following is the most incredible statistic you never heard of before. It is so far-fetched and amazing that most people have a hard time wrapping their mind around it because it is so profound on so many levels. Here we go: More Americans have been killed by drunk drivers alone than ALL the American war dead in all of American History. "Incredible," everyone says, followed by a skeptical "Really?

That can't be true. I don't believe it." Sadly, it is. Here is the roll call: The Revolutionary War, The War of 1812, The Mexican-American War, The Bloody American Civil War, The Spanish-American War, World War I, World War II, The Korean War, The Vietnam War, Iraq 1, Iraq 2, and Afghanistan.[39] America has fought twelve major conflicts over a span of more than 240 years, yet drunk drivers have taken more lives than all these wars combined![40] A confounding statistic, isn't it? But it gets worse! Much worse! "You've got to be kidding," many will say. "How is that even possible?" Well… wait for it… wait for it… here it comes… for the first 120 years of America's history, there were NO CARS![41] Mind-boggling! Incomprehensible!

Another astounding comparison that the role of alcohol plays is that since the national tragedy of 9/11, in which we lost 2,977 victims, America has suffered well over fifty 9/11s at the hands of drunk drivers, one nearly every three and a half months. Yep, more than fifty! It is hard to believe, but over 171,000 dead (out of roughly 552,000 dead motor-vehicle victims) were alcohol related, and the numbers climb daily[42] (see endnote for calculations). Imagine if terrorists had staged over fifty more such attacks since the twin towers in New York came down. Wait, it gets worse. "Not possible," you say? These numbers mentioned would only count the dead. It would not count the over 2.3 million additional casualties (terror-related wounded equivalency!) caused by drunk drivers (out of over 7,695,000 vehicle injuries) since 9/11.[43] These casualties could fill all thirty-two professional football stadiums in the country on a Sunday afternoon.[44] Words are so inadequate to impart the turmoil and heartache that are inflicted upon millions of innocents.

America would be a far different country if it suffered similar kinds of numbers in deaths and injuries at the hands of Al Qaeda, ISIS, or similar groups as it does from drunk drivers alone. It rattles the brain. If attacked with results like these, rampant fear and security like we have never known in our nation's history would result. Active military soldiers along with the Reserves and the National Guard would be stationed everywhere. Civil liberties would be restricted and intrusive security measures would be demanded. News coverage 24/7 would barely absorb one blow and its aftermath before being dispatched to the next big one. It begs the question, "Who are the real terrorists?"

It should be noted that in the following fifteen years since the 9/11 attacks, the number of Americans killed by terrorists in the U.S. have totalled less than a hundred. That averages out to about seven, yes seven, deaths a year. Amazing!

The United States is still vulnerable to terrorists, and the numbers just cited could very well change in the future. However, any contest between deaths caused by booze and those at the hands of terrorists is really no contest at all. Even a string of tragic events on the scale of 9/11 would not change basic facts. Drunks will win this morbid contest every time— by a mile.

All these deaths impacted by alcohol are a national tragedy. The purpose of lingering on this subject is for you, or those you care about, to get a real feel for the stupendous magnitude of the alcohol problem, which most do not fully appreciate. They are wasted lives, having died for no country, no flag, no mission, no purpose, no meaning, no cause, no family, nor close friend. Even demented and evil suicide-bomber terrorists with twisted ideologies die to make a statement, but perpetrators and their victims of drunk driving die for nothing. No acknowledgments await them, no honor guards, no grateful nation, no monuments, no fund drives, no moment of silence, and no recognition. There is no Veteran's Day or Memorial Day parade for them, just stunned loved ones left weeping around a casket, asking why. It is hard to grasp because it is impossible to comprehend what is among the most useless of deaths.

Incredibly, the alcohol problem is even worse than what has been recounted so far. We have not even spoken of the many millions more who suffer physical disabilities, mental trauma, and emotional scars that last a lifetime. But it gets even worse again. These statistics just deal with drunk drivers. It does not deal with deaths due to alcohol from murders, falls, freak accidents, suicides, drowning, boating, domestic violence, or liver poisoning.

The center for disease control (CDC) in Atlanta, Georgia puts the combined yearly death toll from alcohol at 88,000 lives, much greater by far than the cost in lives of 58,000 soldiers over a time span of eight long years in Vietnam. But it does not even end there! It does not include the millions of divorces or millions of scarred and damaged children impacted by an alcoholic parent or other relative. It also does not include the zillions of arguments, fights, hospital visits, police encounters, lost jobs, ruined careers, or broken relationships among friends. The human carnage of death, injury, trauma, and suffering greatly exceeds any war zone.

The continuing outrage over sexual assaults on campus or on the street almost always involves booze. However, take away the booze equation and the problem nearly disappears. Students, faculty, and administrators rail against sexual assault and self-righteously deplore its fallout. But very few want to address a culture of drinking that, by and large, causes an environment where such tragic behavior takes place. Many, if not most, of these assaults and rapes are not even reported.

There is also established norm-referencing for what is acceptable drinking behavior. According to the National Institute of Alcohol Abuse and Alcoholism (NIAAA), risky behavior for seniors begins with more than three drinks in a day or seven drinks in a week. For any single-event occasion, the standard is no more than one drink for a woman and two for a man based on body weight. Those who binge drink by attacking a six-pack for an afternoon football game on TV or knock back several when getting together with the "girls" need to re-think their game plans and switch to something more benign. Booze may not be an issue with you, but for another it can ruin everyone's fourth-quarter life plans with bad judgment.

One should always strive not to be a stumbling block for others. It is always OK not to drink. Also, one needs to seriously consider changing one's social group if it just centers around a drinking culture of excess.

One of the greatest dangers for seniors comes from isolation and loneliness. The loss of a spouse or a health crisis can quickly lead many to withdraw into themselves. Even those who are fine physically can experience dislocation if they have moved to a new locality without any longtime friends or ties to an area. Even if family members are close by, they have full and busy lives with only so much time available. For those who do drink, increased drinking can "sneak up" on these seniors as a coping mechanism until they (or others) finally notice that it is interfering with one's life. Others self-medicate, often in concert with pills, to escape from or to deaden the pain or depression they feel.

The bottom line is that alcohol is legal, and society tolerates the enormous damage it causes. We are not talking at this juncture about a glass of wine or a cold beer, but the acceptability in many circles about getting drunk. In some circles binge drinking is even encouraged. The movie franchise series *The Hangover* goes even further and actually celebrates rude, boorish, and loutish behavior. The same was true for the movie *Animal House* back in the 70's. Without booze there are no movies. The false premise is that it is all hijinks and no one gets harmed. There are few, if any, serious consequences.

The purpose of this chapter is to impart a greater perspective (and soul-searching reflection) for the proportionality of the fallout from the abuse of alcohol that touches so many lives. Gigantic problems like this are unfortunately not solved, just poorly managed. There is not the political will or grassroots demand to change things significantly. People recoil in fear of being called a prude and often remain silent. Any reform at all is immediately attacked as a form of Prohibition and heaped with scorn. The best to be hoped for at present is for as many as possible to become a catalyst to "move the needle" on this subject in your own life and to nudge others in the proper direction to fully appreciate the challenges when it comes to alcohol practices. Of course, the tragedy you avert and the life you save may be closer to home than you may imagine.

Nothing can rob someone of a full life more than an addiction, and no one should want to live their fourth quarter of life in a foggy haze. One of the saddest and lamest jokes you will ever hear is when someone quips, "It's the most fun party you'll never remember having." Many people, sadly, adopt the false view that it is not possible to have a good time without getting "plastered" or at least a little "buzzed." It is such a false narrative. Being sober with one's full faculties is the natural state, not being "under the influence" or "hammered."

Even the word PAR-TEH is co-opted by many, both young and old, to mean it must include booze or it does not qualify as a "real" party. Even for those who are not classified in the full throes of alcoholic addiction but who on occasion binge drink by going too far, it only takes one screw-up to change lives forever and to cause a lifetime of regret. Like being a house roofer by trade, it only takes one false misstep to ruin a life even with a twenty-year safety record. Besides, this is not only about you or one individual. Multiply the number of family members and friends a problem drinker has, and the negative impact of booze escalates greatly in a ripple effect.

Too many people take a narrow view of the "alcohol" problem. They are quick to defend themselves that they never drink and drive and wish to leave things there. It is all about sociability, joviality, and good times. But it leaves out the obvious cases of bad behavior or bad judgment. In old TV Westerns the fight scenes often centered on the saloon, never the general store. Today, bouncers are on hand at the nightclub, not the shopping mall. While smoking or obesity can take decades to exact their revenge on bad habits, abusing booze can do so in a matter of hours. And it does not even have to be you. It can be someone else that causes you to be on the receiving end as a victim of bad conduct.

Many relationships can never be salvaged from hurtful words blurted out while under the influence, which would never have been uttered while sober. Hurt and anger can cut deep, whether between couples or good friends. Some relationships can end in a single evening. A good read on these situations is the legal concept of "proximate cause." Ask yourself, would a negative situation have occurred "but for" the use of alcohol? If it would not have happened without the booze, there's your answer. Another way to look at it is if X happens, would the end result of Z happen without the intervening booze of Y? Troubled relationships of all kinds are just a fact of life. But alcohol can often put things over the edge in a hurry by acting like an accelerant of gasoline on a fire. It can flare up out of control in minutes. Run for cover.

Country music has legions of fans singing about love and loss, hopes and dreams. But it also has a melancholy dark side singing about honky-tonks, drinkin', whiskey, beer, and the often inevitable troubles that follow close behind of shattered lives and dreams. However, the joke is that once a good ol' boy stops drinking, he gets his wife back, his job back, his repossessed truck back, and his runaway dog comes back home. In essence, he gets his life back.

For any social occasion it is appropriate to ask whether alcohol being present is even necessary. Its absence can often negate "issues" and in many settings it is inappropriate in any context. Regardless, a smart host or hostess will always set the right tone for any social gathering and should not feel pressured. If alcohol is present, the message should be crystal clear that it is completely unacceptable to get drunk. There should always be soda, juice, water, coffee, and nonalcoholic beers or cider so that all guests feel comfortable and have alternatives if they do not drink. Another trick is to always make sure there is plenty of food available, which can cut down on the amount some will drink. An open bar is always a terrible idea as it only takes two or three "lushes" to potentially cause a scene, not to mention potential legal liability for the host. People are less free when they have to spend their own money.

Some "seniors" continue on with bad habits from earlier years; others, not fully cognizant of the dangers, increase their alcohol intake by more socializing and buying into the false idea that this is part of the "good life" while some may drink out of isolation or depression. Others who have retired from work and follow no particular routine can find themselves drinking late into the night since they do not have a morning schedule that requires them to be up bright and early. Some seniors binge drink on weekends like younger counterparts, which results in a "lost weekend." For those who may not think they have a problem, the true test is to go without any alcohol for six months. If you can't do it, you have a problem and need to seek help fast.

In much the same vein as alcohol, the changing laws regarding marijuana use should be viewed with great caution.

For a very tiny minority of people with medical conditions, marijuana has been found to be helpful. It can be beneficial. But, notice the word "tiny." As for those just wanting to get high, many of their life problems are just compounded. THC, the psycho-addictive part of marijuana, is often triple or more the potency level in comparison to what it was a generation ago.[45] And getting stoned is really a coward's way out of dealing with real life. Being lost in a haze of never-never land is just checking out of life, not checking in. Apologists claim that concerns are minor and not a big deal. Irony of ironies they suggest it is no more dangerous than alcohol which as we have just discussed is a disaster in our society. But imagine in a humorous vein if your souped-up computer or Smartphone could smoke several joints (not so smart anymore). How well would they work? Aspire to a higher calling since those who get stoned regularly don't drive down the road of life as much as they park on the side of the road while spaced out.

While on the subject of addiction and abuse, it should be noted that very few seniors would readily admit to being drug users. But, as news and social media testify and academic research confirms, prescription drugs (the legal kind) are abused in stunning fashion. Americans take more drugs, legal and illegal, than the rest of the world put together.[46] Although Americans comprise less than five percent of the world's population, we largely fuel the illegal world drug trade that cartels are supplying. As to legal drugs, we often demand them of our doctors, or go doctor shopping, to get what we want. We take drugs to wake us up, put us to sleep, calm our anxiety, relieve pain, and improve our performance at sex, sports, and work. We are always looking for a shortcut.

Doctors can often overprescribe medications for a variety of reasons. Many doctors practice defensive medicine and lean toward the view they do not want to be sued in close cases if some complication was not addressed, however remote. Patients also pester doctors for drugs for all kinds of real and supposed medical conditions, perhaps that have been marketed to them by television commercials that all end with "Ask your doctor if ???? is right for you." Furthermore, multiple doctors may be prescribing drugs that are bad in combinations, and no one is reviewing the total health picture of a patient's care.

Seniors in particular do not want to think they are drug users but merely medication users. Over time, however, the lines can get blurred. It is a general truism today that more than half the medications in America could be dispensed with if people followed a common-sense diet and exercise routine. But many Americans are lazy, and it is "Doc, just give me some pills" instead of making the needed lifestyle changes to get healthy and off the drugs. Doctors are pressed for time, and many do not have the inclination or the stomach to argue with their patients. Doctors often take the path of least resistance to just sign the prescription form if they can and move on quickly to the next patient.

Whether it be booze, weed, illegal drugs, or prescription drugs, don't let them steal your joy or your life out from under you. Try to avoid them all. You only get one life. Be smart and wise. Aspire to be better and to encourage others you care about to do so as well. Become a role model. It may save a life dear to you and also a heap of trouble.

37

ADAPT OR BE RUN OVER

"Don't look over your shoulder; someone may be gaining on you."
Satchel Page

In the twenty-first century, CEO's of old-time businesses run scared. There is a kid in a garage or a basement who is looking for a brilliant idea in order to come and kill their company. Some CEOs believe that "only the paranoid survive" and that someone out there is really coming to get them. The trendy term is "disruptors" for nerdy geeks who are out to change the world.

The contemporary message is that those who fail to change their business models to fit the times of the new century may be doomed. Amazon basically killed the bookstore in just a decade. Apple iTunes upset the entire music industry. The cell phone (selfie-anyone?) helped cement the long slide of Kodak's business model by turning it upside down and inside out. Facebook brought half the world around the campfire. Airbnb is impacting the hotel industry while Uber is out to cannibalize the taxi industry. Drones may soon drop of your pizza on your doorstep and threaten the entire delivery business, and driverless cars are on their way to shake up the auto industry. Wow, what a fascinating time to be alive.

The world is changing so fast and will not stop or wait for anyone. Fourth-quarter people often marvel at the world today when compared to their youth for both bad and good. Globalization finds countries big and small scrambling to adapt to changing realities and often brutal competition. While the twentieth century belonged to the big and the strong, the twenty-first century will belong to the smart and the quick.

For seniors to stay in step does not mean one must take up computer-code programming or take a class in nanotechnology to stay current. What is important is to embrace life and all the marvels that science and technology bring our way. It means having a curious and inquiring mind. It suggests a mindset that is unafraid (and humble enough to ask) to try new things outside one's comfort zone. It also means to adopt the twenty-first-century admonition of lifelong learning. And nothing beats being around young people to keep up with the latest gadgetry and the next big thing. It is good to take a class in anything that interests you at the community college just to soak up the infectiousness of youth or from your grandkids while learning at the same time.

There tends to be two noticeable camps among the fourth-quarter contingent when it comes to technology and changing times. In the first camp are seniors who are fascinated by cutting-edge new inventions and ideas and are eager to embrace them. The second camp resists the future as if the earth is shifting beneath their very feet. These seniors recoil at the warp speed at which things seem to change, but this is more a reflection of not understanding, and stubbornness, than anything else. Learning how to Skype and making a new friend somewhere around the world can be thrilling. Making a three-minute movie you post on YouTube of your grandchild or your dog's antics can be great. It allows you to reach out and share with long-lost friends near and far away in miles or years. Young people are willing to help you although you may need to slow them down a little. There are three aspects to learning that are instructive.

1. Tell me, and I often forget.
2. Show me, and I am still somewhat confused.
3. Involve me, and I understand.

So the secret is to let a friend or a fifteen-year-old mentor you in action rather than watching them and both of you thinking you understand. It seldom works. Learning by doing is always the superior route to go. So take the attitude that the world can still be your oyster at any age. Don't wait for your ship to come in; row out to meet it. Adapt as circumstances arise and move forward. The secret sauce is in the doing.

How fast is the information age moving? Consider that the 18th century was like getting water from the creek, the 19th century from a garden hose, and the 20th century from a fire hydrant, but the 21st century is Niagara Falls.

However, a word of caution is to not get trapped by technology as so many younger people are today by being addicted to their devices. For many people, their cell phones and the Internet are their lives, and to detach from them, for even a short time, is like "withdrawal" pains that they have difficulty coping with. So do not let Facebook, Twitter, and a hundred favorite websites suck your life away. It requires balance, moderation, and time management to avoid being swallowed into a black hole. Incredibly, around the world, special camps are popping up to help addicts (mostly young males hooked on video gaming) overcome their nearly 24/7 "screen" obsession and recover a more balanced existence.

One must be able to detach oneself and live a normal life whereby technology enhances your life but does not creep up and take over your life. Staying off the Internet is just as important as being plugged into it and being smart enough to know the difference and keep it all in balance.

38

STUFF

You can't take it with you.

What do you think is America's favorite sport– baseball, football, basketball, soccer, or hockey? None. You are not even close. Shopping is America's favorite pastime, hands down. Gigantic, modern-day temples of worship called "malls" are everywhere, stuffed to the gills with stuff for every taste and imagination. It is an Olympic sport bordering on religion in which Americans strive to take home not only the gold but also as much silver and bronze as their maxed-out credit cards permit. Make no mistake, we are dead serious about the serious business of stuff. Big SUVs and bulked-up pickup trucks are in great demand in order to manage and haul all of our stuff. A little Smart car parked at Costco is an oxymoron and would be considered a joke by most shoppers and un-American.

The author John Gray postulates in his book *Men Are from Mars, Women Are from Venus* the idea that men are hunters and women are gatherers. Men hunt for stuff when they go shopping. If a tool, part, or gizmo is needed, they will hunt stuff down as if on a commando mission. Women, on the other hand, are gatherers and mostly enjoy the process of looking and checking out all the new stuff laid out before them in an endless variety of choices, styles, and options. They may leave the house with nothing particular in mind but know that somewhere out there, if they just look hard enough, something will call out their name to them, something will catch their eye, and they will then be able to "gather up" the stuff and bring it home to their nest. Of course, this is where the great conundrum of sorting out needs (Do I really need this stuff?) vs. wants (I impulsively like this stuff and have to have it) takes place. More men than ever are also susceptible to this siren call; the only distinction is in wanting different stuff.

Over the past thirty years, there has been an explosion of self-storage facilities because a lot of Americans discovered that their garages, attics, and basements were inadequate to the task of holding all their stuff. This is despite the fact that new homes have steadily increased in size, doubling over the past fifty years[47] while, at the same time, the size of families noticeably shrank. Still, over twenty-five million storage units were built during this time that comprise the equivalent of seventy-eight square miles (three times the size of Manhattan) of space dotting communities all across America.[48] Remarkably, most of the stuff's monetary value (and it is mostly stuff) would not cover much more than several months of storage rental costs. Even more astounding is that many rarely visit their stuff but psychologically can't part with any of their stuff. They just keep wasting money each month in storage fees. As the saying goes, "only in America."

Of course, those who can't afford storage or are too cheap to get one have a house filled to the rafters with stuff. A walk around the neighborhood of single-family homes will always reveal a number of garages that are so jam-packed full that people park their cars in the driveway because there is no room for them in the garage. Stuff has priority. Stuff breeds and multiplies. For those with basements, some are stacked up like a treasure hunt for Easter. Indeed, in the infrequent encounters in the darkness below, there are often brief exclamations of "I was wondering where that thing was" to even discoveries of things they had forgotten they'd had.

The obsession with stuff can be seen at almost all national landmark attractions where the gift shop reigns supreme, often over the time spent at the historical landmark itself. Cruise ships docking at a port disgorge thousands of hungry locusts armed with credit cards eager to strip store shelves bare and shop till they drop. Thanksgiving "Black Friday" opening stampedes can rival the running of the bulls in Spain.

America's obsession with stuff is an amazing commentary on American consumerism. The pursuit of stuff goes roughly like this. We work in order to buy stuff. We need to work even harder to get better stuff. We spend huge amounts of time shopping for stuff. We worry that maybe we have the wrong stuff. We then need a bigger house because there is not room for our stuff. We are bummed out if our stuff goes out of style. We don't like other family members messing with our stuff. We need more storage to keep our stuff. We promise ourselves to get rid of junky old stuff but rarely do. We sometimes take vacations at historical places to look at old stuff belonging to famous people. We lose our patience when we can't cram any more stuff into a drawer or closet. We get frustrated when we misplace our stuff or can't find our stuff among all of our other stuff. We troll the Internet looking for cool stuff, trendy stuff, rare stuff, or just the latest stuff. We need security systems to protect our stuff. Our kids need a college education in order to pay for their own stuff. What a merry-go-round! In addition, some people go to garage sales to get a "good deal" on somebody else's unwanted stuff that then becomes their stuff, which then gets stored as stuff in their garage. Simply amazing!

The American dream of nearly all citizens is the aspiration of home ownership and making a cozy nest for one's self and family. It is a worthy goal. But if people are not careful, they and millions of others can get swept away with the quest for more stuff, which is then a problem that can interfere with their lives and personal finances. After some point, what's the point?

When we are born into this world, we arrive only in our birthday suit. On the other end of life, we leave with just a simple suit or dress when we pass on. That's it! Indeed, at your passing, a will or trust is basically designed to do one thing: divide up your stuff as to who gets what stuff because you can't take any of your stuff with you. Interestingly, most beneficiaries don't want your stuff and so would prefer cash instead, to allow them to buy their own stuff to their own liking. After all, stuff is personal. This is most obvious at any estate sale where much of the stuff is sold for pennies on the dollar, sent to a charity, or trashed because they can't even give away the stuff.

So what should the relationship be with stuff for fourth-quarter people? After all, many will point out that they spent a lifetime acquiring their stuff; they like their own stuff, and besides, their stuff gives them comfort and significantly defines who they are. And they're not inclined to giving any of their stuff up willingly. Fair enough, no problem. However, also consider the upside to "downsizing" a portion of your stuff. For some, this is a wonderful opportunity to "unload" and simplify one's life, not to live as a Spartan but to make an attempt to live in a more clutter-free environment in one's own personal space. In the parlance of the trendy phrase today, the idea is to reduce your "footprint." Similar to an overloaded old wagon train in the 19th century going west, lightening the load makes your journey so much easier and smoother.

Many people find this to be a challenge. They just psychologically cannot part with so many items, as if it is giving away a piece of their identity, their memories, and their past. On another level, some feel subconsciously that this is the first step on the road to "passing away" and don't want to even go there. They cling to their stuff, which gives them a good psychic feeling, much like "comfort food." But this is more an emotional gut feeling than a rationalized consideration. Stuff has no soul.

While some will prefer to downsize their lives to make them more manageable, the most important thing when it comes to stuff is to be self-aware and less sentimental over it. Remember, ninety-nine percent of your stuff has meaning that is only personal to you. If it has no cash value, it means little or nothing to others, except a keepsake memory. A good rule of thumb is to institute a three-year rule that if you have stuff in storage or around the house that has not been utilized in that time, out it goes to charity where others can really make use of it. Delusional thinking that you will use or need this stuff sometime in the future is generally a bad idea. The three-year view is that I own stuff, and the stuff does not own me. Big difference!

For fourth-quarter people who have spent a lifetime acquiring things and trying to build a comfortable nest, the key is to avoid the trap of trappings as evidenced by too much stuff. The goal should be to consciously untangle one's mental self from the blinding "bling" of consumerism simply for its own sake. Moving through the fourth quarter of life is all about priorities. Mindfulness, the ability to stop and really be objective about the state of your stuff is important. So be tough and don't get in a huff about your stuff. Living a more meaningful and fulfilling life is much more important.

39

FRIENDS

"Remember, George, no one is a failure who has friends."
Clarence, Angel First Class, It's a Wonderful Life

Friends are like dessert at the kitchen table. While immediate family, and even an extended "work family," is like the main meal that is being served on a daily basis, personal friends are often the dessert. They add spice and round out our circle of significant people in our lives. Of course, over a lifetime, friends can come and go; they move, fade away, or there is a falling out while new friends can arrive on the scene.

So who are your friends? How would you rank them? Make a list and start with best friends, people you can count on no matter what. Next, casual friends like neighbors and colleagues (people you exchange pleasantries with and who you are involved with but who are in a different category). These people would not be in your social circle if it were not for the fact you were thrown together. If you changed jobs or moved away, these people would quickly drop off your radar

226

screen. It is interesting that some people you have developed very close working relationships over many years or even decades disappear in the ether once you quit work and are out of there. Then there are acquaintances: people whose lives intersect yours but only at a distance and on the periphery. These are the friendly and familiar faces at the supermarket, the favorite restaurant, the dry cleaners, or scores of other venues and "pit stops" that make up your world. You trade Hello, how you doin's and well-wishes for a good day, perhaps with a little banter about the weather, sports, or some local gossip.

Generally speaking, most people have only two or three "best friends" in their lives outside of family. Most have been close friends for years and go "way back," and know each other extremely well. There is shared history, and getting together is as comfortable as wearing an old shoe. No need to be pretentious or strive to impress. There is acceptance on both sides for one's habits and foibles. It is in some ways like a mini marriage. They are also sounding boards, pals/girlfriends, and confidants if needed.

There are gender differences. Guys can buddy up as friends from days gone by from high school or college. More often than not, these bonds were founded along the lines of shared activities. Sports, fishing, biking, cars, camping, etc. are more traditional, but they can also include geeks and nerds who find affinity with computers or technical and scientific interests. Others lean toward business, politics, or academics.

Women, on the other hand, bond on a more emotional and intimate level. They value their BFFs (best friends forever) as reflective mirrors on their lives. Women's friendships are based less on the physical doing of things together than men's are and rather on a more personal level. Work, children, spouses, friends, fashion, and the topic of the day are all shared in common and can be reviewed and chewed over in great detail with relish. These friendships are important as a source of validation. Rooted deeply is the yin-and-yang of juggling life-balance demands along with met and unmet expectations for themselves and that of others. These concerns can often carry over into spoken and unspoken issues of body weight, looks, presentation, and acceptance. Women, quite unfairly, are often judged by different standards, sometimes even more harshly among themselves.

Fourth-quarter people find it harder to develop meaningful new friends. And this is a concern when they take stock. Some close friends who were a little older may have died. Some are time constrained, having full schedules of travel, work, and community engagements of all kinds. Others are so tied up in the drama of their kids and grandkids that they have little time. Still others, who do not live close by, travel less frequently. A few are just more jealous of their time, schedules, and interests. As a result, the circle can shrink pretty fast.

How to get new friends? The old adage is true. You have to be a friend in order to have a friend, and among shy or insecure personality types, this will require even more effort. It requires work like an investment club in which money is deposited every week into an account. And you have to be careful to have a balanced friendship. While it is part of the friendship compact to be needed on occasion, few want to be trapped in a codependent relationship whereby one party takes advantage of the other, and it descends into a giver-taker situation, which becomes unhealthy. Such a new friendship will wither quickly and is most likely doomed unless one party is so desperate and insecure they end up playing the "doormat" role.

Remember elementary school science class and being fascinated by magnets? In science class, it was always a favorite since it was a hands-on experiment that was not some abstract, scientific book formula. Magnets were only half science and half playing around with them. To a young kid, it is novel and magical in its own way.

So the question for you is, do you have a magnetic personality? No, I do not mean the rare person who walks into a room and takes command of it but rather the person who is warm and friendly in the simple day-to-day routines of life. First of all, do people mostly like you? If so, why? If not, why? It is worth taking the time to analyze. Don't get your underwear in a knot just because some people do not reciprocate your outreach. At a lot of stages in life, there are many crosscurrents in people's lives pulling them one direction or the other, and sometimes it has absolutely nothing to do with you. Get over it. Of course, in some relationships, people just "click" while in others, they don't. Sometimes, for reasons that can't even be articulated, it is just a vibe or gut feeling. You have that feeling towards some, and others may display the same to you. Move on. Don't stew wondering about it.

The second way to find new friends is to be proactive. Get out of the house and attend more functions, particularly where there is room to mix and mingle with others. You do not gain much by going to a concert, a movie, or a play while sitting on your hands for two hours and then going home. There is very little time for interaction. Food, however, is a universal excuse for getting together. A dinner, buffet, or potluck can generally draw a crowd. Community events, fairs, church socials, hobbies, card games, or informal gathering places from craft fairs to playing in senior sports leagues, to book, movie, cooking, or gardening clubs offer social engagement. You cannot make friends sitting home alone watching TV. Move!

For married couples who may wish to get together from time to time, there is the delicate double dance of compatibility. It can sound sexist, but if the wives do not get along, that is usually the end of that. So it is generally up to the wife to find a friend that she has things in common with, and the men can usually, but not always, find some common ground. There is also nothing wrong with "just the guys" getting together to watch the game on a Sunday afternoon, or for the wife to get together with "just the girls" for brunch and a movie. Everyone needs their space.

Coming up is a shorthand list of people who are liked vs. those who are not. This may seem like an elementary discussion, but it has value in an increasingly fragmented society. It should be noted that a willing spirit to evaluate yourself honestly is a worthwhile endeavor. Everyone can benefit with a little sandpaper to round off some of the sharper edges of their personality.

1. The first guideline is that most people like to hang around people like themselves whom they can relate to. That means being similar or in the same league as others when it comes to incomes, education, habits, interests, looks, and similar background. Different classes and styles can often mix harmoniously, but some adjustments may be necessary. But do not be a snob. Including a diverse group of people adds spice and flavor to any gathering.

2. Attractive people in the true sense of the word are those who are cheerful, upbeat, accepting, and kind. They are a like a warm campfire. Bring the marshmallows.

3. Like a magnet when it repels, people who are just whiners and complainers wear thin on other people. Don't be one. Those who are harshly judgmental and selfish are the types of people most others try to flee from. Abraham Lincoln said, "…it is better to be silent and thought a fool than to open one's mouth and

remove all doubt."

4. Class means good manners. Also, don't be afraid to break the ice by introducing yourself to strangers.

5. Do your homework. Get the standard "how-to" Dale Carnegie book, "How to Win Friends and Influence People" or one of hundreds of other, similar books. They are highly instructive and doubly so if you do not have an outgoing personality. Follow these principles, and they can literally change your life. Buy several that appeal to you. Do not just read the books but do so with a yellow highlighter pen. Make notes in the margins. Then put them into practice.

When people are dying on their deathbeds, no one has ever uttered the words, "I wished I had spent more time at work," but at such a time, it is all about family and friends. Tellingly, if people were on their Smartphones and saw the latest "special news bulletin" that nuclear missiles were on their way and would rain down upon them within fifteen minutes or less with no escape possible, what would they do? After a minute of shock and panic, every cell phone would light up as people were saying good-bye to loved ones and how much they meant to them. Nothing else would matter. Nothing! Our last minutes would be shared minutes and everything reduced down to that greatest emotion of all, love. Such is the power of the human bond for family and friends and what is truly of value in the world.

40

LIFE: WHAT'S IT ALL ABOUT?

Which way should I go?

Death scares people to death. Funny, right? Yet it is so weird; television, books, movies, video-games, and the 24/7 news cycle are all obsessed with death. The local news always starts with the tried-and-true ratings grabber of "if it bleeds, it leads" as their opening feature story headline. Otherwise, people with hair-trigger twitchy fingers hit the TV remote in seconds. Crime, war, natural disaster, and tragedy lead the parade. In movies and TV, dying on the big and little screens has become an art form in its own right. From dramatic death scenes to merely inconsequential "expendable extra's," the body count is very high.

Depictions of death (mostly screen-fictionalized, but some real exposure on the news) run in the thousands for a child before the age of eighteen. For most sheltered Americans, old and young, it is unreal, surreal, and abstract. Indeed, a good primetime who-done-it crime story is entertainment. However, if death does intrude upon us too closely in real life, we want it sanitized and euphemized. The most common phrase, "they passed away," seems to imply a benign disappearance act of some kind into the ether. For some children directly exposed to death at an early age, it can leave serious lifelong psychological scars.

More and more people claim that they are spiritual but not necessarily religious. They are frustrated with the dos and do-nots of organized religion that put them in a straitjacket of doctrines, customs, and "teams," with each one claiming they have the "truth, the whole truth, and nothing but the truth." Many good people genuinely get confused and lost in the cacophony of claims, interpretations, and some old traditions that seem to have completely lost their relevance. Other individuals basically opt out by deciding not to decide and choose instead to organize their life around themselves and live by a shifting moral code they make up as they go along. Still others are turned off by a negative encounter with "the good people" who have certainly "sinned and fallen short" of their own standards.

It is easy to witness firsthand the hypocrisy and failings of "religious" people of any faith or persuasion. But it is also unfair to be critical of those who have fallen short of very high goals and standards. It is always easier to meet lower expectations.

Some parts of the faith community lament that it is falsely portrayed or often perceived as a country club for saints that turns people off for not being good enough to join rather than an accepting hospital for imperfect people trying to find a better path and a "higher calling." It is also dispiriting, not to mention scandalous, to find out that good and evil can also coexist in the clergy and membership. Things are never clear cut, and there is sometimes evil in good people and some good in bad people, yet we do not like nuance and uncertainty. Still, believers and nonbelievers alike expect and demand a higher standard from those who claim moral superiority, especially upon leadership.

Faith can be contradictory, yet it also can be comforting to many who strive for meaning and a longing to make some sort of sense about the unknown in a confusing world. Faith begins where our senses and empirical rationality ends. Does mankind have a soul? George Bush, Sr. often quoted a funny favorite maxim, "The more I think about heaven, the more I pray the hell I get there."

The four burning questions of mankind are profound. Where did we come from? Is our origin from God, aliens, or an amoeba out of the primordial slime? The second question is why is mankind on Earth and, more personally, why am I here? What is my purpose (if any) for being on planet Earth, taking up limited space and, most disturbingly, for such a short amount of time, no less? The third question is the biggie: What future (if any) is there past this mortal life? Is there more, or is this brief life the whole ballgame? Finally, the last question to add in our quest for understanding is why is there good and evil in the world? It is confounding.

These four questions pretty much sum up all the existential questions of mankind throughout history. And no one has a definitive answer, just different truths with a large dose of faith and hope that transcends our understanding, much as a medieval peasant from the distant past transported to today's technological world would marvel and think they landed on an alien planet. Each one of us must figure it all out the best we can, hopefully adopting the best virtues found in faith and mankind during our brief stay on Earth. Everyone should strive to be aspirational.

It has been said that before you can become old and wise, you must first be young and stupid. Of course, this is not an accurate statement since there are many wise young people. Unfortunately, we also personally know a number of stupid old people who never did learn to wise up over a lifetime of missed opportunities and constant screw-ups. Still, it behooves fourth-quarter people to contemplate the four big profound questions of life. Regardless of how you approach them or even what conclusions you make of it all, it is a wise person who ruminates over them to inform their own life, beliefs, and values. It is tough to sort it all out, and the answers will always be elusive and incomplete. But this does not negate the value in making the attempt. It can also have worth by eliciting some insights when discussing the big questions of life with younger generations as they grapple with them in their own lives.

Making mistakes in life is a given. We all mess up. However, there are degrees to messing up, both major and minor, that can vary significantly. Much of the time, our poor decisions boomerang back to us. We pay the price. But if one has severely harmed or damaged another life, amends need to be made as much as humanly possible. It is true that you cannot restore broken china back to its original state, but one should make their best effort to pick up the pieces with a bottle of glue and without excuses. It is the backbone of the Golden Rule in how we would like to be treated if positions were reversed. One should never put off in the fourth quarter, or any quarter for that matter, the opportunity to have a clear conscience, seek forgiveness, and make a positive difference for the better. Time is precious and we do not know the limitations to our time-clock.

Life defined in perhaps its simplest form may be attributed to the Scottish writer Alexander Chalmers, "Something to do, someone to love, and something to hope for."

41

IT'S ALL ABOUT THE DASH –

Born–Died

Of all of life's events that transpire in our given time on earth, there are only two events that we have no control over, our birth and, generally, our death. No one asked to be born. It is a miracle of creation that we are born as sentient human beings that can think, emote, love, build, and manipulate our environment through creativity and innovation. Each of us is a distinct one-of-a-kind-original. We are capable of insight, self-awareness, and abstract reasoning. We can make tools and design machines for thousands of utilitarian purposes. Yet, after a relatively short time, we will pass off the scene, our moment in the sun as brief as a sunbeam in the twilight of the day.

When looking at a newspaper obituary or walking through a cemetery, the departed are always marked by the dates of their birth and those of their death. When we are young, we hardly notice the dates and are generally oblivious, but as we age into the latter part of the third quarter of life, we begin for the first time to track the two numbers and calculate the age at passing. Those who have passed on in the first three quarters of life, or even early in the fourth quarter, we feel sorry for as they seemed to have been cheated out of a portion of their life inheritance. Those who get their full four quarters and then some extra overtime we reflect upon and generally think "good for them, they had a good run" while also wondering whether we will be as fortunate.

Yet everyone who looks at these dates misses the most important thing of all. The dash! For life is not about birth or death, it is all about the dash in between. Perhaps the dash is a fitting symbol since we all seem to "dash" through life impatient for the next chapter in our lives. Still, the lowly and overlooked in-between dash represents it all, a life. Was it well lived? Was joy and happiness found? Did they find meaning and purpose? Is the world better or worse for them having passed this way by their contribution, or did they screw things up for themselves, their families, and others? It is the most important question at the end. Inquiring minds want to know.

42

GOD:
DOES HE GRADE ON THE CURVE?

"Everybody wants to go to heaven,
but nobody wants to die to get there."

Joe Louis

This is a touchy subject for many. From true believers to atheists and agnostics, everyone has wrestled with the concept of God in some manner. The subject of God covers all the human emotions. God also represents a handful of major religious faiths in the world that try to claim divine exclusivity along with a thousand splinter groups that interpret and reinterpret their own parochial points of view. If there is a heaven, perhaps there are many paths that lead there rather than just one privately restricted, narrow highway guarded by a toll booth and watched over by self-righteous finger-wagging clerics. The story of Gabriel (God's head angel) may be instructive. Gabriel is showing a new tour group around heaven when all of a sudden he turns quickly towards them and ask them to immediately stop talking and to be very quiet. In a hushed whisper he explains. Do you see those people, way over there, in the far distance? They are _____ (insert your faith or denomination here). They think they are the only ones here!

Theologians, writers, and laymen alike over millennia have struggled to come to terms about mankind's existence and if there is a connection to a divine creator. The bottom-line question since mankind's earliest history is whether there is transcendence beyond our brief spell of mortal life here on earth. And the corollary question is whether the life we lead here demands certain requirements to be met in order to achieve such transcendence. We yearn for answers, one way or another.

Most nonbelievers are good people. Of the intellectual nonbelievers, there is a tendency among them to be rational empiricists, much like the state motto of the "show me" state of Missouri. Living in a modern age of science, they take the view of First Officer Spock from the starship Enterprise that "it's not logical" to make assumptions about God because God cannot be examined under a microscope or put in a test tube. Unbelievers suggest that one just has to look around the globe at the current state of affairs today and to study mankind's bloody and grossly unjust history steeped in horror and calamity to conclude that God has been doing a crappy job; therefore, he does not exist.

Many people feel the world is a mess, just waiting for the next shoe to drop from nuclear holocaust, germ warfare, terrorist atrocity, or climate meltdown to do us all in. What is worse, from their viewpoint, is that God is so mysterious and does such a poor job of communicating by showing his hand, his plan, and any specific details that it just doesn't make much sense to them. It is like God playing poker with his cards close to his vest, no peeking allowed. Reading from Holy texts and scripture as interpreted and re-interpreted by clerics and prophets is a sometimes inscrutable process that shifts over long periods of time. A military cemetery is striking in its symmetry with its neat rows of Christian crosses interspersed with the Star of David and the occasional crescent moon that signify the three great monotheistic faiths. But to an agnostic, the appropriate symbol may be a question mark to denote their final resting place. Regardless, both humanists and believers need a moral framework of some kind to live by, to avoid a world of complete anarchy.

On the other hand, assuming God exists, what is the grading system? If only a very tiny group of morally devout A+ students make the cut, then there is little hope for the rest of us who may be cutting up in class or not paying sufficient attention. Can you squeeze through the pearly gates with a report card showing a D-? Or if God decides on a sliding scale of life challenges, then the blessed and comfortable on earth may find themselves in big trouble when God grades their term papers.

If heaven is predicated on the paradigm principle of "to whom much is given, much is required" framework, it follows that the rich, gifted, or lucky will be judged by a much more brutal grading scale. Only a tiny few will make the cut. Furthermore, if heaven is determined by the obstacles one has overcome, the distance traveled in life with a giving and unselfish heart, the makeup of heaven, as to who gets there and who does not, may be very shocking. For a baby born into the most unforgiving conditions of life, having the very grit to survive and to show a gracious spirit is amazing. A baby who even makes it up to bat in life against staggering odds and quickly strikes out, much less makes it to first base, is a miracle in itself. It is a far greater achievement than another with all the advantages in life, who was born on home plate and believes, sanctimoniously no less, they hit a home run.

What's more, if God heavily considers omissions vs. commissions, the grading system may be even more daunting and discouraging. If one committed no traffic violations on the great superhighway of life and was smug about their good driving record yet failed to show compassion to help others out when they could, does one get their passport to heaven revoked? What about one's failure to speak up, intervene, or lift a finger when one has knowledge of lying, cheating, stealing, or the ability to alleviate suffering that could have made a world of difference?

Considering all the possibilities of God's grading system, it becomes clear that grace becomes an even more critical factor regardless of one's privileged birth, humble birth, or checkered background. The anthem "Amazing Grace" may be closest to the mark in this regard.   Perhaps the quote attributed to Mark Twain was right on the mark when he said, "Heaven goes by favor; if it were by merit, your dog would go in and you would stay out."

The definitive answers to these questions, one way or the other, will not be found here. But for fourth-quarter people with any or no belief system, it helps to contemplate such profound questions to calibrate our own moral compass by informing our lives as to where we should be going in a complicated and contradictory world. It has value in setting your life G.P.S. compass.

Faith, like the concept of God, is also a tricky thing. But not knowing something or not understanding something does not make it provable one way or the other, which is why it is called faith. Still, there is a difference between faith and blind faith, which are not the same. Far too many people of any belief system put on blinders and are wedded to the orthodoxy of black and white, right and wrong. Nuance, doubt, and dissent are to be banished. This is indeed unfortunate since, for an intelligent human being with a brain, it is important that hubris and irrational superstition not be substituted for a lack of rational analysis, even among the faithful.

On one hand, it is self-evident the incredible, unselfish work people of faith have done for others over many centuries to uplift mankind by their commitment, dedication, and self-sacrifice, true missionaries in every sense of the word. Such noble work of unselfishness and devotion in building hospitals and schools along with reaching out to the poor is simply astounding and should always be recognized and honored. Its positive force for good is undeniable. However, it is equally true that fundamental fanatics of many faiths and persuasions over many centuries have inflicted untold suffering, death, and sorrow upon millions of "heathens, infidels, heretics, and "others" in the name of their God. It is evil under the mask of religion. It is maddening to try and reconcile the incompatible. Perhaps it is this Gordian knot of trying to untangle good and evil that has perplexed mankind forever.

In our sophisticated and scientific twenty-first-century world, it is an interesting question to pose whether the biological makeup of mankind contains a God gene or perhaps a worship gene as part of one's genome. To a geneticist or biologist, such speculation has no rational basis and may be considered ludicrous. But some sociologists and anthropologists will observe that most of the world believes in God, maybe not always in religion per se, but in God as a higher being in a spiritual sense, a personal feeling of connection in life that is transcendent and largely unexplainable.

Interestingly, even non-believers in God could be said to have a worship gene. A driving secular force of worship is seen in the quest for money, power, sex, status, prestige, or a passionate, consuming quest in a particular field of endeavor. Like believers, most unbelievers are driven and animated by some core drive, and everything else revolves around this quest to give their life meaning. For unbelievers, this driving secular force is, in a sense, their mission, and on some level, it is their religion though not rooted in a deity. Generally, but not exclusively, it tends to be more rooted in expressions of self-interest than in altruism.

Faith based on a belief that cannot be validated, verified, or proven in any conventional scientific sense is faith in the unseen and unknowable. For postmodernists, it is hocus-pocus. Yet the intersection of faith and science can also miss the larger point of a meaningful life. While the world tends to see things in materialistic terms as a determining factor of the good life—like money, success, and the attendant power and trappings that come with them—it is a myopic view. Poverty is seen as the ultimate enemy, an evil curse to be conquered and a tragedy to be averted. Of course, financial independence and a sense of personal success in one's life are natural goals to strive for and to attain. But if one suffers deficits of generosity, laughter, love, cheerfulness, or sharing, there is a poverty of the soul that sucks the real joy out of life and leaves only a shell of an individual clutching their bank statement along with some assorted rusting metal trophies that make their success very hollow. They have the potential to slowly turn into Scrooge.

Poverty is more than just a lack of money. This is evident in the lives of millions of people of very modest means who are nonetheless rich in friends, humor, and an infectious enthusiasm for life. They openly look to the sunny side of life. They are a joy to be around. They are, in a very real sense, indeed rich.

What does it mean to be noble today? In centuries gone by, it was simply a title that one received by being very lucky to be born into the right family. All that was required was to be the end result of the right combination of a merged sperm and egg. But today the word noble has a different flavor, feel, and context. It is more about "doing" something noble, rather than "being" born noble. It is doing an act of sacrifice of some kind for others and the greater good. Because self-centeredness (the me generation–it's all about me) is mostly a given in the hurly-burly of modern life, those who give of their time and money to champion good causes are lauded in the public square because this is an ideal that all should aspire too. Being truly noble is not for applause or self-promotion; rather, in its pure form, it is an intrinsic desire to lighten another's burden.

Morality is essentially a code of conduct, an ethical set of principles to govern one's behavior. Living a decent, moral life requires following some rules. Yet, everybody and every group screams about their "rights" with passion, anger, and self-righteousness. Turn on the TV news and there is always a march or protest about something. Americans proclaim with gusto and conviction their feelings about freedom, liberty, justice, and not being told what to do. Politicians harp on these general themes incessantly like a broken record. We like those words so much better than duty, responsibility, citizenship, and self-discipline.

One reason why everyone hates government on some level is because mostly all they do is make up zillions of laws, regulations, and rules that are enforced by an ever-increasing bureaucracy that costs a fortune. Most all of us resent it and doubly so if any of it restricts us in our daily activities, but not so much if it applies to "them," whoever "they" may be. Of course, when you think about it, ninety percent of government rules are a result of dealing with the ten percent of the population that constantly screws up and causes trouble for everyone else. James Madison's observation that "if all men were angels, no government would be necessary" is the crux of the matter.[49]

Consider for a moment the Ten Commandments. The first four commandments are said to relate to God and the last six to man's relationships with one another. We will set aside the first four and the mystery of God for your own personal review to come to terms with as you wrestle with your own convictions. Turning to the last six we will look at them as an abridged version of only fourteen words. They are: 5) Respect your parents. 6) Don't murder. 7) Don't cheat. 8) Don't steal. 9) Don't lie. 10) Don't be jealous. With some added pretentious hubris, the inclusion of two extra admonitions to these commandments may be suggested. They would be the Hippocratic admonition of "Do no harm" alongside that of "Follow the Golden Rule." That would make up a total of twenty-one words. What kind of a world would it be if everyone just adopted and lived by these twenty-one words? Yet millions of laws around the globe have been written to deal with essentially these twenty-one words.

To make our analogy complete, these twenty-one words are just guardrails on the highway of life to prevent harm to oneself and others and to avoid pain or regret. As long as one stays on the highway of life, he or she can go slow or fast, change lanes, take side-roads, enjoy the scenery, or even stop for a picnic on the side of the road. It is like having seat belts, air bags, and four-wheel braking all designed to keep you safe. These twenty-one words are meant to keep everyone from leaving the road and driving off a cliff. Like dealing with gravity, if you defy it, the end result will not be pretty.

For humanists who basically believe "you only go 'round once in life," and that's the end of the story, reflection is also in order to contemplate the meaning of life and your gift to subsequent generations. Likewise, for people of great faith, a greater sense of tolerance, understanding, and aspiration is laudable. Good people of great faith and good people of no faith alike have made significant contributions to the advancement of mankind. The mystery of it all will remain a partial mystery but deserves everyone's time for consideration and contemplation. Everyone should strive to "keep the faith" beyond themselves.

43

SEVENTY... WHOOSH!

Don't count the days–make the day's count.

You glance at the milestone sign on the side of the road reading seventy (years) as it whizzes by you in a flash. You don't even tap the brakes. You shake your head from side to side in disbelief as you barrel on down the road, realizing that you are already halfway through your fourth quarter on life's journey. The only word that comes to your mind is surreal.

For the first time in your life, you are called a strange name, a septuagenarian. Is it a swear word? You laugh to yourself that you would be hard pressed to even spell it correctly. You don't like how it sounds, but perhaps it is just being overly sensitive about being pigeonholed by other people. However, it dawns on you that no other prior decade has a moniker attached to it in the same manner. No one is called a quadragenerian in their forties or a sexagenerian in their sixties, although the latter at least sounds sexy. Name designations only start in the seventies, followed by octogenarian, nonagenarian, and the pinnacle of being labeled a centenarian, a feat along the lines of climbing Mount Everest. These terms, in their benign form, are akin to getting a blue ribbon at the county fair.

In 2016, the leading-edge frontier boomers reached seventy. Born in 1946 after "The War," they may not have seen it all, but they have seen plenty. Boomers have lived through more revolutions and movements than any generation in all of history. There have been political, medical, technological, sexual, and scientific revolutions in a host of fields. There have been movements of civil rights, women's rights, gay rights, disability rights, and animal rights, among a host of others. Causes addressing climate change, sexual abuse, domestic violence, children's welfare, elder care, recycling, crime, education, and many, many more all ask for our attention. Charities abound for every disease, condition, and circumstance around the globe. In just one lifetime, the world went from local to regional to national to international to global very quickly. The world has changed—and is changing—in profound ways. In retrospect, so much change so fast does take one's breath away in wonderment. It is like that first big drop of a roller coaster where you feel you are in free-fall.

Seventy is a time to double down. A lifetime of experience and observation should inform those headed into this new decade that one's first priority is their health before anything else. Lifestyle choices matter greatly regarding diet, exercise, and mental agility. But nearly everyone knows that already. The trick is keeping the knowing part and the doing part in sync.

Being smart about what you can and can't, or to be blunt, shouldn't do, is also imperative. Showing off to the grandkids at the park or your friends at the tennis court may need to be dialed back a little bit. Just because you can still climb on the roof of your house to clean the gutters in the fall does not mean this is a good idea. Hubris, pride, and stubbornness (not to mention being cheap) can easily override rational analysis of what is the smart choice to be made. Such an activity is also a sign of denial and rebellion against Father Time by giving him the middle finger. Father Time is rarely amused and knows how to get even when you are not looking. He may even be your unseen helper, holding the ladder for you, and should not be trusted.

Being wise is not attributable solely to age, but it often comes later in life to those who can sort out the wheat from the chaff of what is important in life. The wise old owl who observes everything from his perch on a high limb of a tree got there by being a good student of his environment in the forest and adapting accordingly. The owl's motto is "Don't do anything stupid."

There is some good news for the majority of those cruising down the septuagenarian road. Only thirty percent of people ages seventy-five to eighty-four report disabilities, the lowest on record.[50] So the odds are in your favor at seventy percent, better than two to one, and even higher if you are taking care of yourself. Accidents, genetics, and disease are a fact of life and are out of our control. But it is also a safe bet to assume that a sizable plurality of the thirty percent who do struggle with disability is directly related to their past and continued poor lifestyle habits over decades. Those who abuse or neglect their health should not be surprised when a day of reckoning shows up. Like a home or a car, it will deteriorate much faster without any repairs or careful maintenance.

Deciding on keeping your priorities in balance is more important with each passing year. Family, play, travel, hobbies, causes, or even continued work in some manner will be different for everyone. But planning is key. As a newly minted septuagenarian, one good idea you can do at this stage, if you have not done so already, is to get out a five- or ten-year calendar and start filling it in. This does not have to be a frenetic schedule of events and commitments at all. If you are so inclined, write in a number of down days to enjoy hanging around the house for projects or a Netflix afternoon. But a schedule helps one focus. By looking at your week, month, and year ahead, it helps you avoid time slipping between the cracks. If you want to take a long-thought-about trip somewhere, force yourself to choose dates today, put it on the calendar for three or six months in advance, and buy the nonrefundable tickets this week. You are going–no backing out. And you will rarely, if ever, be disappointed upon your return from the experience. Now is not the time to put things off or to dilly-dally.

Consider planning out your entire yearly schedule even if it says next Tuesday you will be hanging out with the dog, reading a book, and cleaning out the garage. The dog will be happy, the book will be great, and the garage project may be unrecognizable if for no other reason that you can now park your car in it. The most important thing is to stay engaged with family, friends, and community. You should have something to look forward to each day marked on your calendar, whether staying in or going out. It becomes your handy reference to inform and guide your life. If you are stuck with a blank date, write in a friend's name and invite them over for ice cream. You have just done them a favor by helping them to fill in a blank date on their calendar.

Remember, regret is mostly tied to the things we did not get around to doing because we suffer from a lack of focus. So, whatever your bliss, it demands that you put it on your calendar. There is no time like the present. Seventy? Keep the pedal to the metal as you speed along life's journey. And keep singing to the tune on the radio with a smile on your face.

44

THE GIFT

"It is more blessed to give than to receive."

Acts 20:35

Gifts are hard to shop for. Consider a husband who has been married for thirty years, looking for a Christmas present for his wife. He doesn't have a clue, and for most men, walking the mall is more of a dreaded chore than a delight. He has been down this road many times, and it never gets easier when he considers the Big Four. Those would be the yearly gift-giving events of anniversary, birthday, Christmas, and Valentine's Day. Multiply that by thirty years of marriage, and the number one hundred twenty pops up. Wow, the husband reflects as he racks his brain to find something special, pleasing, and heartwarming for his wife. But he still has no clue. He is also desperate as he has again put this off to the last minute.

It gets even more complicated as he has been informed earlier by his wife with gentle hints. "No jewelry, as I have a few nice pieces and enough costume jewelry already. No perfume, as I still have ten bottles from your previous gifts. No expensive flowers since they die quickly, and no chocolate or candy to spoil my figure. Don't buy any clothes either since you lack fashion sense, and... Oh, by the way honey, surprise me." He keeps trudging the mall, shaking his head while muttering to himself, "No pressure," and still feels clueless. Wives, even though they may be wise and veteran shoppers, can also struggle with this search for a husband who says he "doesn't need anything."

One of the greatest final gifts a loved one can give to their spouse or children is to have their affairs in order. A will or trust, funeral arrangements, finances, and detailed instructions of important information along with any special requests are a priceless gift at a difficult time. What peace of mind for a spouse to say with serenity, "This is what he or she wanted" or for a child to say, "I really appreciate Mom or Dad for their foresight and making this easier on the family" No scrambling, no arguing, no guessing, and no second-guessing as to what to do or not to do in the hours and days from your passing.

There are a number of variables when dealing with any end-of-life issues. Did the end come unexpectedly, or was it foreshadowed after a long illness? The age at passing, from sixty to a hundred, also makes a difference. Regardless, having all your ducks in a row is a great act of love and compassion. Funerals can be a very stressful time and doubly so in some dysfunctional families with larger personality dynamics and historical baggage issues being played out by the grieving spouse, children, and extended family members.

Money is also a factor for many families of limited means with the median "basic" funeral costing over eight thousand dollars for a traditional funeral home.[51] And since that's the median figure, it means that over half of funerals can cost far more. Plus, a dinner provided after the service, plane-ticket assistance for a distant family member or two, and unanticipated costs can escalate the price very quickly.

For those with modest means it is a double tragedy if a family is stuck making monthly payments to a funeral home long after you are gone. Every month is like a mini-funeral all over again in scraping up enough money to pay off the debt. No one would wish to leave such a burdensome legacy to those they loved. Yet millions leave no instructions at all, leaving a mess for family members to try to cope and sort things out on their own. It is grossly unfair, and in some cases, the fallout can be more serious and contentious after one has passed on than during one's lifetime. Indeed, resentment can build and even taint one's memory even though you are lying six feet under or watching from your urn on the fireplace mantelpiece.

Funeral expenses are one of the greatest wastes of money in America. Most people have little or no experience with the whole process until it is thrust upon them by tragedy or circumstance. Vulnerable, confused, and unsure of themselves, it is just a default response to call up a funeral home and dump everything in their lap and worry about the bills later. After all, there are lots of phone calls and notifications to be made and so little time to even process what has just occurred.

Religious considerations also play a role, and "family image" plays a bigger role than most people will admit to since this is a mini-stage production, and one does not want to be unfairly judged by those who gather together. No one wants to be called cheap. In addition, family members may feel they are displaying an act of great love on their own part by giving the departed a lavish send-off, or at the other end of the scale, there is guilt over the past, and the added expense is a measure of contrition.

Even those who have financial resources to fund a very expensive funeral should reconsider. It is said that funerals are for the living, not the dead. The living are the ones who come to see the "one time only" show, grieve, pay their respects, and follow standard protocols of expected deportment. It is often a highly-scripted occasion and follows traditions laid down by preceding generations. But it is over in a flash. Even the deceased would object to paying big bucks for mostly a one-hour service.

Most of these issues that arise can be dealt with by preplanning. It does not have to cost a lot, and there are alternatives to the traditional way of doing things. Cremation should definitely be considered and is the current trend, approaching nearly fifty percent of funerals and, in the Western U.S., over seventy percent.[52] If possible, skip the funeral home altogether and just have a small service in a church or local hall for a nominal fee. The first impulse should be about legacy and the ability to do something wonderful that transcends the passing of the departed.

One suggestion is to have a very low-cost funeral and, with the savings, help fund a grandchild's education or the child of a deserving friend or neighbor by asking guests for contributions in lieu of flowers. One big bouquet is enough. And the ripple effect of that one life changed over generations is incalculable. The basic concept here is to fund your grandchild's education, not fund the mortician's kid's education by having a lavish funeral. This is foolish. There are more noble ways to spend the money. This is not showing disrespect to the deceased but an acknowledgment of proportionality of what is appropriate. One should never go overboard.

Do you want to be talked about for a long time after you are gone? Well, if you have the means, include this one idea in your will for your memorial service instead of spending big bucks on a traditional funeral. At the end of your service, request a couple of trusted ushers to hand out an envelope (with explanation of its intent) with a Benjamin Franklin (one hundred-dollar bill) tucked in it to every mourner who came. Have it announced that this memory gift in your name is not for them, but they must give it to some charity or deserving person who is not a friend or family member of theirs. They decide.

This is your way of giving to a host of unmet needs. Suggest gently that those who are able should consider matching your gift. Sure, a couple of people may just pocket the money and spend it on themselves, but this speaks more to the poor moral character of your family or friends and their false allegiance to your wishes than it does to anything else. It is what it is. However, have it also announced that anyone who pockets it for themselves will be subject to you coming back to haunt them and not putting in a good word to God when their time comes. A little justified shaming and humor never hurts. People may attend scores of funerals in their lifetime, but they will certainly remember yours, and they will also certainly remember who they gave the hundred (or two hundred) bucks to. Guaranteed!

Another idea to consider is to be the emcee at your own funeral. To some, this may sound a little creepy, but let the idea sink in for a while, and it may grow on you. Making a video stored in a safety-deposit box could be a great opportunity to address family and friends who have gathered together one last time. A short ten to twenty minutes to express your love and affection for family and friends, along with a little appropriate humor and some words of wisdom, can sometimes bring a lot of comfort to those left behind. In a strange way you are still with them speaking from the great beyond. In addition, consider one or more private videos just to a spouse or children. Most all families will be appreciative that you took the time to do this for them. Still don't think this is a good idea? Poof! You are gone tomorrow. What did you leave unsaid and undone? At least give it some serious thought and then act on your decision.

A side benefit is that such an exercise can do a lot for your life as you live it, no matter what your age. It allows you to reflect on your life, your relationships, and your mortality even if you live to be one hundred fifteen and outlive all the family and friends you are making these testimonials for. It keeps you rooted and connected to those who mean the most. It also makes you think about your values and future plans. And for a child left behind, whether forty, fifty, or seventy years old at your passing, to see you and hear your voice on video that can be played many times over is so much better than just some simple lifeless keepsake.

The reason why this is a good idea is because family and friends can have a piece of you. Plus, you have the last word. It is a form of immortality that can someday touch the hearts of children and adults still unborn. Think of actors in movies that are long gone who have left a legacy in their films that millions still enjoy generation after generation. At Christmas season, the Jimmy Stewart classic film, It's a Wonderful Life, is a family tradition for many and probably will still continue a hundred years from now. It touches lives.

Imagine if you could see and hear your great grandparents and great-greats as well. It is also a fun idea to tape record or video parents and grandparents around a kitchen-table setting for several hours and listening as they relate funny stories about their childhood and life events along with their laughter. People forget. If you really want to spice it up and make it even more interesting, add some aunts and uncles to the mix. When they are gone, many questions about family lore are lost forever. Then do the same for your kids as part of the next generation, to help them understand their roots.

Many will not appreciate such a gesture until later in their lives. Some will never care much at all, but others will greatly treasure such a window into their past.

The problem is that while a majority of readers of these words will wish they had such a thing to treasure from people they have lost along life's journey, only a tiny fraction will do it for their loved ones. Why? Inertia and procrastination! Take that assurance to the bank since it does require a little planning and rehearsing what you want to say.

In your own case, reflect upon a passed loved one whom you wish had done it for you. But we need to go shopping and check out a movie for the weekend along with a hundred things to accomplish on our "to do" lists. Maybe, if I can get around to it. We'll see? I have absolutely no time this month, and the next few don't look good either. But if misfortune falls, your family will be grateful for it. The ball is in your court.

45

THE CIRCLE OF LIFE

Okay, that's a wrap…

"Coming full circle" is an expression often used to describe many things in life. Coming back home to our roots, finding a lost love again, or picking up an old hobby or passion that was laid aside for decades can often seem like one of those rhythms or at least mysterious rhymes in life. Seeing some traits and patterns being repeated, both good and bad, in one's own grandchildren is fascinating as we also contemplate some of our own habits and outlooks in life, both good and bad, handed down from our own parents and grandparents.

Of course, we are seasoned adults here at this stage of our lives and realize that life does not run in a perpetual loop cycle of a circle but rather in the distinctive cycle of nature's four seasons. In a way, life is like a Hollywood movie director who, after the last scene of a movie is shot, may exclaim, "That's a wrap," indicating the movie is over and all that is left is the editing process. The end! So too someday will it be in all our lives. Life has no dress rehearsals to get things right, and you only get one shot. You get to be born on stage and do your eighty-year gig (hopefully more?) of working, interacting with family, socializing, etc. and then exit stage left as the world takes a momentary intermission and waits for the next actor to take your place. Depending on your performance, the world is either sad to see you go or is looking forward to the next act.

Millions of tourists have on their bucket list a visit to Egypt to see the great pyramids. They are the oldest massive mankind project of the past that still survives today, going back thousands of years. They are awesome engineering marvels, considering the primitive technology of the day and the logistical requirements for tens of thousands of workers in order to complete them. But what is often forgotten is the nearly maniacal concern of the great Pharaohs regarding the afterlife. Almost as soon as they became Pharaoh, they started to plan on departing this world. Huge amounts of state wealth and planning were poured into these ventures, often with each subsequent Pharaoh trying to outdo their predecessor. It was the transcontinental railroad or man-on-the-moon project of its time.

It is amazing the lengths the Pharaohs went to in their concern for the afterlife. Likewise, some American Native Indians talk of going to "the happy hunting grounds"; young, militant Muslim men are being tricked and promised "seventy-two virgins" (but not being told about the accompanying seventy-two mother-in laws!); Jews are still looking for the Messiah; Shia Muslims watch and wait for the appearance of the "hidden imam"; Buddhists look forward to transcending to a state of Nirvana, and Christians are focused on the second coming of Jesus and heaven. They all seem to be looking beyond this mortal life.

If you had to sit down in a movie studio's editing room and make a two-hour movie about your life, what would you include, and what would you leave out? Cramming a lifetime into only 120 minutes may be tough to do. What would be the highlights, the lowlights, the drama, and the turning points, much less the ending? Would it be the unvarnished truth or largely a fictional movie in the way you edited it? What would your spin be on this very personal project? And would anybody even be interested in watching it? What kind of ratings would it get? Or would most people just change the channel?

A man walked through a cemetery on a lovely spring day and was reading tombstones when he came across these powerful words, which packed a punch:

Pause weary stranger
As you pass by,
As you are now,
So once was I,
As I am now
So soon you will be
Prepare yourself, weary stranger,
To follow me.

Origin unknown[53]

The admonition of these words encourages contemplation of our existence, but we generally want to avoid thinking about our own mortality. Of course, one cannot be trapped by the fears of tomorrow because it robs us of living a full life day to day. For the very religious, they often lose sight of the here and now, preparing so diligently for the next world. Some are so warped with their own blindness that they will go to church, synagogue, or mosque and pray for the blind rather than helping a blind person across the street. This is simply a fake form of religiosity without purpose. Jews, Christians, Muslims, Hindus and a host of others can get so lost in tradition, custom, and liturgy on some esoteric point of contentious doctrine that they cannot see the forest for the trees. More points are scored with God by people helped and comforted than by prayers said, penance offered, offerings given, or arguments won.

Back to our man thinking deeply about the tombstone epitaph; he was moved to add these lines to the epitaph:

To follow you I'm not content
Until I'm sure which way you went!

46

TRANSITIONS

The accent of "assisted living"
should always be on the LIVING part.

Transitions throughout life can be smooth or tough, depending on circumstances and the personality of the person making them. Getting married, having children, changing jobs, or relocating far away from familiar friends and community can all require new adjustments and routines. For those deep in the fourth quarter of life or those in overtime, dealing with change is harder, especially if one feels their autonomy is being threatened.

Most parents and teenagers dread "the talk" about sex. It is awkward no matter how it is approached. Similarly, adult children and their parents dread "the talk" about taking the car keys away from Mom or Dad for their own safety and that of others on the road. Those over eighty-five as a group are the most dangerous on the road, with each one firmly believing they are the great exception. The common reaction of advanced seniors in this discussion is that someone just dumped the first shovel load of dirt on their casket. Yet even here, there is good news for boomers. Car services like Uber and others may fill an important gap for seniors in increasing their mobility. And before you know it, just over the horizon and in the nick of time for boomers, looms the potential of driverless cars. Already, online ordering for a zillion products through Amazon and other vendors is a common fact of life. Take-out restaurant orders delivered by drones to your driveway is already a fantasy come true technologically, being held up only by government, business, privacy, and insurance issues to make it viable.

The world of tomorrow may offer options to boomers undreamed of by seniors in previous generations. The Japanese are out in front in trying to develop intuitive companion robots to assist seniors with simple chores and medications. They are being designed to converse, play games, and generally interact in different ways throughout the day. New wearable medical devices are becoming more sophisticated to allow remote monitoring of patients' vital signs and medications.

All of these changes may allow seniors to stay independent for years longer than the case would have been in years past. It would be a godsend for them and their families and even save money for the taxpayers. The world is a-changin'!

Most everyone wants to stay in their home. A feeling of independence, familiarity, and comfort gives us a sense of well-being. It is our nest and shelter from the outside world. Our view of a hospital, an assisted-living facility, or especially a nursing home is where we go to visit others, not a residence for us. The positive news is that the overwhelming majority of seniors do remain in their own homes or with family members. Yes, a portion of this group relies on others simply due to a lack of money, but equally, nearly all cling to a fierce determination to retain personal independence.

Still, like a game of poker, we do not know what cards we will be dealt. When it comes to our health we all hope for aces but will still be happy with face cards showing kings and queens. But someone will get dealt a jumble of low cards, which will put them at great disadvantage. So if the time ever comes when you or someone you love is in need of some basic assistance and decides that an assisted-living facility is appropriate, consider the following in your deliberations.

Like everything else in life, things have their trade-offs. Those with good but slightly compromised health who find themselves alone in an empty home or apartment can begin to slowly close themselves off to the world. Sometimes it occurs imperceptibly, without one even noticing the gradual drift as it is taking place. An assisted-living facility for a select few under these circumstances should be viewed as a genuine plus, not a negative. It can open up the possibilities of new friends, planned activities, and semi-independence that can be maintained, thereby adding years of joy and contentment to one's life. As they say, "to each their own" applies here in the sense that what is viewed with misgivings by one can be a lifeline for another.

Moving in with an adult child in a strange city is not always the optimum choice. Especially, if they, along with their spouse, both work and their grandchildren are in school and have busy-after school activities. Long days in an empty house where one feels like an intruder rather than a guest are not appealing for many seniors. And when the exhausted family returns home from a full day they often want their own space and "downtime" to recharge their batteries.

For an elderly parent who is still capable, there are always adjustments in these multi-generational family situations. There may not be enough money for an assisted-living facility, or by choice, parent and child initially don't want to go down that road, and so roles begin to blur. Adult children want their parents to "butt out" with advice on raising their own children, housekeeping issues, or on their questionable financial decisions.

Adult children are also uncomfortable continually reminding their parents that they are no longer children to be bossed around. On the flip side, adult children often become more outspoken and critical about their parents' choices and decisions as well, finding themselves playing the parent role to their parents. It can be contentious and hurtful, and both sides need to navigate carefully.

Then there is the issue of the son-in-law or daughter-in-law and his/her parents and family. Need we say more? Falling down the rabbit hole is easy to do, and the stresses and strains for all families can be tough. Personalities, agendas, resentments, in-laws, past history, and assumed expectations can all collide and lead to conflict and hurt feelings. For some families, things work out reasonably well. Much depends upon temperament and mutual respect. For others, they can range from stressful tension to outright disaster.

Many assisted-living facilities are set up whereby guests buy into their own small home in a community-type setting and retain most of their independence. They have their own living space, kitchen, and bedroom. More common, others are set up for apartment-style living. A common cafeteria is an option available if one wishes, and generally, some cleaning services or errand services are provided along with some activities. Residents are ambulatory and can generally take care of most of their own needs. They are relatively autonomous.

The major issue is money. Only the well-off or those who have planned ahead can usually afford this option although many more can make the switch by using the equity in selling their current home. Those with generous pension checks can also qualify. Many seniors or their family members are stunned to learn that Social Security or Medicare programs do not pay out for extended long-term care and that they are on their own. So what happens to people who do not have family support or their own resources? Well, after all assets (with some protections for a healthy spouse) have been pledged or spent down toward their care, in essence wiping out one's life savings, the government will step in to provide basic care under the Medicaid program for the indigent. However, one's options and choices in these situations can be greatly narrowed, and the level of care can be problematic and far less than desirable. That is why individuals and family members need to have a financial game plan if this path in life becomes their own. Most often, it is just left to fate.

On a positive note, one's environment in these home-like settings can be adapted to make life easier to compensate for some of these life challenges. It is not easy or pleasant to deal with the extra hassles, but life, security, and limited activities still have value. Having a purpose and staying engaged is critically important.

47

OVERTIME
80+
Years

"Today, I'm 80, Lord."

Today, dear Lord I'm 80
And there's so much I haven't done
So I hope, dear Lord,
You'll let me live until I'm 81?

But then, if I haven't finished
All I want to do,
Would you let me stay awhile until I'm 82?

So many places I want to go,
So very much to see.
Do you think that you could manage
To make it 83?

The world is changing very fast.
There is so much in store.
I'd like it very much
To live until I'm 84.

And, if by then I'm still alive,
I'd like to stay until I'm 85.

The world is such a swirl,
So I'd really like to stick,
And see it all unfurl.
When I'm 86.

I know, dear Lord, it's much to ask
(and it must be nice in heaven)
But I would really like to stay
Until I'm 87.

I know by then I won't be fast
And sometimes will be late,
But it would be pleasant
To be around at 88.

I will have seen so many things,
And had a wonderful time,
So I'm sure that I'll be willing
To leave at 89... Maybe.

I'm 90, Lord, my mind is sound
I like it here; I can still walk around.
My time is limited I know
And someday I'll have to go,

I'm not greedy or guided by fear,
I want to see what happens
In the next few years,
I'm sure you've heard this plea before,
But my bags will be packed at a hundred and four!

Author Unknown

Eighty! Wow again. Yep, there is no question that this is the land of overtime. Seniors are not dumb and can still add and know how to read a calendar. They know the score. Yet another milestone year has arrived, and the number eighty is repeated in one's head much as every other recent decade was greeted–with amazement. There is no way to fudge around this one very much. It is acknowledged even to oneself that a line has been crossed into the official land of old even if at earlier stages of life some mind games of denial were overtly or subconsciously in play. Yet there is a silver lining for most seniors who arrive at this way station in life.

According to some studies on aging, the happiest group of all is the one between the ages of eighty-two and eighty-five.[54] Of course, the big caveat to this is the state of one's health. Yet for the majority of those crossing this threshold, they are blessed with reasonable health, all things considered, and are still in the game. It may seem counterintuitive that this stage of life should be met with such equanimity, but, nonetheless, there is some rationality for it.

Social scientists attribute some of this happiness factor to an internal sense of liberation. Yes, there may be regrets, but these regrets are often put aside, as in "the past is the past," and there is no sense in rehashing them. Life takes on a simpler routine much more rooted in the present than living in the past or the future, which is freeing to one's spirit. Time does not lose its relevance, but it does seem to lose its hold on one. There is no need to impress, no pretensions, and generally a sense of enjoying the mountain you are sitting on rather than scaling the next peak. The view is still pretty good on your mountain as you look down below at the parade of life in the valley. Much as a kid who was mesmerized by the town parade, so too is the wonder of the human parade, with its tragedies and triumphs all from the vantage point of a full life. Aside from health issues, worry and anxiety for many is lessened, and long-term planning is set aside as problematic and not worth a lot of effort.

This does not mean being put out to pasture by turning eighty but rather getting to write yet another chapter in one's life book, an epilogue. It is kind of like a bonus chapter in a book to tie up all the loose ends. Eighty does not mean the end but just another phase in the transition game of life. While time marches on, overtime can be fulfilling in many ways if one just let's go and does those things nearest and dearest to their heart. A few will still keep their fingers in the pie of work, travel, and the pursuit of passionate interests. They are still fully engaged mentally and physically with all kinds of plans and activities. Others will treasure even more the time spent with family and good friends and contribute where they can. There is a sense of peace and acceptance of the "circle of life," much like one who has put together a complicated puzzle of a thousand pieces with only a small handful of pieces left on the table to complete the entire picture.

True, this optimistic scenario will not be the lot for others if health and memory become an ever-greater challenge facing us all as mortal creatures. Adjustments will need to be made, and prior planning is crucial to meet these new circumstances. Still, like a baseball player who is only allowed one or two strikes instead of the standard three strikes in the batter's box of earlier years, octogenarians in these situations are still delighted to take a swing or two as the case may be. They may be down in the strike count but still not out and still expecting a few more hits.

Hopefully, because of one's wisdom and foresight, all their external concerns have been dealt with in their sixties at the start of their fourth quarter. All of one's affairs are in order and up to date because nothing should interfere with enjoying these extra bonus sunset years. With some good fortune, they can be very sweet. It is like coming back on the stage of life for an encore. May we all be so blessed!

48

BLINDSIDED

"To suffer the slings and arrows of outrageous fortune..."

Shakespeare's Hamlet

Boom! Heart attack, stroke, cancer, car accident, or some other dreaded misfortune strikes you or someone you love out of the blue. What the heck is this? No lightning-bolt, out-of-the-blue, life-changing health event fits into any of our life scenario expectations. Maybe in double or triple overtime, somewhere around a hundredth birthday party, we may have to deal with it, but it is definitely not on our radar screen at present. Besides, I don't have the time to deal with this right now or any time soon either.

We all plan on good health, strong minds, and reasonable mobility until the end comes. That is everyone's plan. We also harbor strong illusions that should something bad happen, it will most assuredly happen to someone else, not to us. Perhaps denial is our way of coping with unpleasant considerations. Even though we all plan to win this lottery of long life, we do know that one can be in excellent shape on Tuesday and with a fall or sudden medical condition, be in an entirely different place by Wednesday morning. In a flash!

The late old-time movie actress Bette Davis said, "Getting old isn't for sissies." In essence, she meant that you had to be very tough and wily and make allowances over the advancing years. In his powerful book, *Being Mortal*, Dr. Atul Gawande highlights the shortcomings of modern medicine as it relates to elderly populations. Doctors are so focused on fighting disease and complications that the well-being of the patient is often lost in the shuffle regarding what is really in their best interest. Turning a patient into a lab experiment and a pincushion with very poor outcomes at best while chasing phantom cures should cause everyone to rethink end-of-life scenarios. Sometimes, doing nothing is the right course of action, save controlling for pain. The goal is to extend a decent quality of living rather than prolong the dying process.

Perhaps one of the most moving quotes ever came from Triple Crown winner, jockey Ron Turcotte. He rode Secretariat, arguably the greatest horse of all time, to glory and into legend. Several years later, he was paralyzed in a racing accident. He was quoted as saying he never asks "Why me?" but rather "Why not me?" It is a stunning insight to how one individual views a calamity that has come his way.

In the most moving memorable public moment in all of sports history, Lou Gehrig, thirty-six years old, baseball great of the famed New York Yankees, addressed the crowd at Yankee Stadium on July 4, 1939. He had recently learned of his diagnosis of amyotrophic lateral sclerosis, a particularly devastating and incurable disease. He said, "Fans, for the past two weeks, you have been reading about the bad break I got. Yet today, I consider myself to be the luckiest man on the face of the earth." Lou would die less than two years later, and this disease has ever since been known as Lou Gehrig's disease. What grit; what grace! Nearly eighty years later, when viewing his farewell speech (which you can view on YouTube), it can still cause a lump in one's throat when considering what he faced and what he lost.

It is an interesting part of myopic human nature that when good things happen, like someone winning the lottery or finding a special love in their life, people quickly feel left out and wonder, "Why not me?" But when bad things happen, the reaction is always its opposite, "Why me?" "What did I do to deserve this?" The gods are so unfair.

Life is often a crapshoot when it comes to the unexpected. We can only do our best to put the odds in our favor. Live a healthy lifestyle, eat better, wear our seatbelts, look both ways crossing the street like Mom taught us, along with practicing a hundred other little safety tips is all we can do. The rest is up to good genes and a run of good luck. Each of us can relate a number of scary "almost" disaster stories whereby our life and limb were at stake and only luck or divine providence spared us from tragedy. But insurance statistics bear out the numbers that we are more than three times as likely to be disabled (defined as three months or more) than to die in any given year of our lives.[55]

Preparation for such a life-changing event is almost always inadequate or doesn't happen at all. Hopefully, one has family or friends to lean on in such a time of need and panic. Sadly, some do not, and this puts them at the mercy of the kindness of strangers to make decisions that may not always be in their best interest.

As tragic as such a life-altering event can be, the positive news is that many people do recover and leave a rehab facility. As Winston Churchill said, "When going through hell, keep going." Sometimes a bounce-back to one hundred percent is not possible as the body attempts to repair itself the best it can. But an eighty-to-ninety-percent comeback return from a devastating accident or illness is a result many will take, considering the possible alternatives. There is still a lot of life that can be lived and enjoyed even under altered circumstances. It is tough to accept, but again, stuff happens.

In these situations, there is no magic guidebook to consult, only a narrow menu of choices. Naturally, your first thoughts are going to be "Am I going to die?" followed by "What shape will I be in if I come out of this?" and the inevitable "How much is this going to cost?" Without being too flippant about a serious issue, the question of your demise is simple: you will or you won't die, and that is that. If you die, end of story. If you live, all your energies need to be devoted to your comeback. It is a binary situation. As for cost, most insurance or Medicare will usually pick up most (not all) of the tab if it is medically related for your recovery. You will also be provided with several weeks of convalescent care, but after that you are on your own unless you are dead broke.

When searching for a nursing home to meet your needs or those of a loved one, you absolutely must look at things with a skeptical eye. The nursing-home industry is above all else a business (and a very lucrative one at that). All too often, it is more about the institution and its rules and regulations than about the patient. The company and staff want to run things in an efficient and profitable manner as smoothly as possible for themselves. But no one wants to be treated as an assigned number in a computer.

Perhaps the first consideration is location, location, location: All things being equal, you want to stay in your city, town, or close-by neighborhood if at all possible. First off, friends and family who are close by is the single most important factor for mental health. Day trips out into familiar surroundings of shopping, parks, church, and friend's homes gives one a sense of roots and place.

All care facilities are not created equal. Do not be swayed by looks alone. In the scheme of things, these mean little. Be highly suspicious of a relative or friend who says, "This looks like a nice place." Judging from exteriors of a well-appointed lobby with a piano and a lovely chandelier or a nicely laid-out room will bore you to death in a matter of days, which some may consider a blessing. You want five-star-service and care with a capital C, not a lifeless five-star hotel.

Aside from cleanliness, do not focus on the buildings, gardens, or the nicely-done interior decorating that attempts to give the place a hybrid approach between a cozy home and a high-end hotel. Focus exclusively on the quality of care. The nursing-home business is selling a product by trying to tie the nicest bow possible on their facility. Too often, mega-million-dollar facilities hire immigrant $12-an-hour health aides to do all the grunt work while $100,000-plus on-site administrators sit in their cozy office on the phone. Meanwhile, $30-50K-paid nurses manage their stations and boss the aides around while the off-site corporate office rakes in millions. Remember, this is not Club Med. On the other hand, there are some fine facilities who genuinely try to do their best, but one needs to do their due diligence to seek them out.

Consider the size of the facility in your review. Too large, and you or a loved one may feel like it's a dormitory and become lost in the shuffle. Too small, and you may not like any of the people, including the staff, there. On balance, a larger facility may be better. There are more people around, and you are more likely to find someone that you can relate too based on sheer numbers. Also, larger facilities can often offer more amenities and services because of a larger staff and economies of scale. Yet, they may also not be immune to corporate bean-counters and may skimp on staff to plump their bottom line.

The truth is some unscrupulous operations have an

administrative staff sales team act in a manner to recommend an immediate in-house medical procedure. This "operation" is designed to try to remove your wallet as quickly as possible. You or a family member must be vigilant. If your needs are not being met, find a better place.

Whoever the decision maker is regarding such a move to a care facility, one needs to review in detail the running of the place and what it has to offer in terms of adequate staffing, food, and personalized attention to an individual's wants and needs. When evaluating a nursing home or rehab center, few things are more important than referrals from others. Recommendations from inside staff members, who know what goes on, or trusted testimonials are preferred. This gets you the real scoop as opposed to being sold by some fancy brochures or a sweet-talking sales lady trying desperately to keep the facility's head-count census full so she can keep her job. More than anything, you want someone who listens, really listens, and treats their guests as guests, not warehoused people. Interview the staff, not the pretty building.

Being a staff member in such a facility is a tough job that calls for a special type of person with tons of patience. It is very easy to get frustrated with some cranky, grumpy old people who are out of sorts. It is human nature. Assess the best you can whether the staff members want to be there or whether they are just "clocking in and out" as a mere job dealing with human widgets. Also, remember that there can be large turnovers in staff, so ongoing reviews need to be made. The same is true if the facility is sold and changes hands with the new owners immediately looking to cut costs by cutting personnel.

Often overlooked are the intangibles of making an intolerable situation more tolerable. As pointed out in Dr. Gawande's book, the three plagues of a nursing home are boredom, loneliness, and helplessness.[56] People, even in compromised situations, need a purpose. Simple things like in-room plants to water and care for are important, and perhaps an outside garden to cultivate and grow-vegetables and flowers can be therapeutic for those who are ambulatory. Having a playground for children and inviting them in can be a mood enhancer. Pets can make a huge difference from singing birds to cats and small dogs. Many facilities dismiss pets out of hand and cite cleanliness and safety grounds from a scratch or dog bite and getting sued. While they have a point and this may be partially true, this excuse is sometimes a smokescreen. The real reason is they mostly don't want the hassle, the extra work, the clean-up, or the responsibility. Yet as Dr. Gatwande's book shows, many such changes can be transformative for some patients. However, too often, the facility is less concerned about the patient and obsessively focused on efficiency. It is shortsighted, and one may want to consider another facility with a less restrictive policy environment that provides more options and leeway.

Each guest's health condition can vary greatly, but it is also important to ask how many people are "nursed" back to health to the point they can leave the facility, if possible. While realistic expectations need to be managed by the patient and family, each patient leaving represents many thousands of dollars going out the front door each month as well. There can sometimes be a conflict of interest with some facility policies that may be less than ethical. Ask for second opinions where appropriate. Nursing homes are businesses, and they want to retain business and cash flow, so you or your advocate may need to "push" administrators to make sure the front door is capable of swinging both ways. Most are ethical and have standards. But, like everything else in life there are good and bad actors.

The bottom line is you are looking for a continuation of your life or that of a loved one as best as it can be achieved under the circumstances. Big dollars are changing hands whether from your own pocket or your insurance, and what you want to buy is empathy, caring, listening, and attention, not bricks and mortar. Be especially suspicious if it appears that patients are over-drugged (less work and hassle for the staff) and there is little stimulation or few activities available. Also beware of superficial oversight and engagement, which can be a sign of understaffing or a poorly accountable staff organization.

What everyone needs in an ideal situation is an engaged advocate. Ideally, a family member or trusted friend who can frequently check in to ensure the staff is doing their job. The staff quickly learns who is watching them and will act accordingly. Sadly, those patients without close outside monitoring can, and often do, fail to get the full attention they deserve.

49

THE TWILIGHT ZONE

A cartoon shows a middle-aged couple at home, lounging on matching recliners watching TV. The husband turns to his wife. "Just so you know, I never want to live in a vegetative state, dependent on some machine. If that ever happens, just unplug me." Next cartoon panel: His wife is shown unplugging the TV as the husband cries out, "Hey!"

Jim Borgman cartoon

In the 1960s, a cult television show, The Twilight Zone aired on the small screen with Rod Serling as its host. It was a science-fiction show that did not fit a traditional genre. A dramatic show, it was designed to engage the audience on several levels of the imagination. It was scary, bizarre, and often thought provoking, sometimes all at the same time. It usually had a "twist" in its storyline that served the larger purpose of making its point that would surprise its audience. While familiar, it was also otherworldly, somehow awry where normal rules did not apply.

Aging over time slowly reduces our mental and physical powers. It is like Superman unknowingly living with just a little kryptonite placed in his closet, not enough to kill him but enough to interfere with his powers. Even Superman may find himself in need of some assistance from Lois Lane and Jimmy Olsen.

Then there is the mind-body split: Some aging boomers are mentally sharp but are greatly compromised with some chronic or physical limitation. Others are relatively physically fit but have cognitive issues of decision making or comprehension. Some are sadly faced with both.

Cognitive decline resulting in dementia or Alzheimer's disease is the condition that frightens people the most. It can be described as a fatal car accident occurring in super-super slow motion, one frame at a time. It literally robs you of being you. Becoming a shell of a person in which the lights are on but nobody's home is terrifying to contemplate. In essence, one is dead but still alive, a zombie. Even if one is ambulatory and shows no other physical limitations, the game of life is over. For without one's mind, it is like trying to play a football game without a football. It doesn't work. As mentioned earlier, statistics tell us that this affliction will visit up to nearly half of all seniors over the age of eighty-five in varying degrees from mild to severe.[57]

With an aging population, families and government are unprepared for the relatively large number of boomers coming on the scene who will be afflicted with cognitive challenges over the next few decades. Everyone hopes that medical research will come up with some great breakthrough before then, but at the present, it looks rather bleak on that front. And until it begins to impact more and more families, the funding will not be there until the media's white-hot glare will force government and institutions to make it a higher priority. Research in this area is grossly underfunded.

It is uncomfortable but true nonetheless: people in this condition are warehoused where they can be monitored and stabilized as they wait for their clocks to run out. There is nothing else to do except to make them as comfortable as possible. For loved ones, it is literally the "long good-bye" to a family member who eventually no longer even recognizes them, cannot speak, and is vacant in look and emotion. Heartbreaking! Most people would pray to get hit by the proverbial bus rather than to suffer this fate. Yet, millions will do so. One of the more courageous stories being told is that of the famous country singer Glenn Campbell. He, along with his family, has been outspoken in this twilight struggle in drawing public attention to a very private journey.

Many seniors worry about the potential signs of Alzheimer's for themselves, a spouse, or a friend. The positive news for most is that they have little to worry about until perhaps deep in overtime. If you have misplaced your keys to the car, that is normal and is more a sign of disorganization or preoccupation with something else rather than being a sign of mental decline. Where you or a loved one may be in trouble is when you have the keys in your hand but you are not sure what to do with them. That is when you need to seek help.

While the brain is a wonderful organ and is perhaps the most complicated thing in the universe, it does begin to run a little slower with age, much like a great athlete who has lost a step or two but is still covering a lot of ground. Likewise, your brain still works fine and gets you to your destination, just perhaps a little later than before. The other thing to remember is that your brain is like a supercomputer with a huge database of information in its hard drive, collected over a lifetime. Year by year, we cram in more names, events, experiences, stories, and data. Storage and retrieval issues are sometimes caused by glitches in the system. It may be signaling that it is dehydrated or in need of more nutritious food or more sleep.

Sometimes your brain just needs to reboot its hard drive.

To put this in context, there is the story of the man who needed a new brain and asked the salesman in charge of the store what he had to offer. The salesman said he had some fine brains to show him and proceeded to the display case where he announced that the brain of a well-renowned doctor was on sale for $100,000. In the next display case, he showed the brain of a famous scientist who had won the Nobel Prize for only $500,000. Finally, he showed him the brain of a teenager for sale at a cool one million dollars. The customer was shocked and taken aback. "How can that be?" he exclaimed. "Simple," replied the salesman, "it's never been used!"

It is quite common for fourth-quarter people to be more forgetful of a name or a common fact that was second nature to them in earlier years since their hard drive is so full. This should provide some comfort, explanation, and excuse when these "senior moments" do occur. At least, that is the theory and story for all boomers, and we are sticking to it.

Doctors do have a standard questionnaire protocol to assess on a scaled basis an individual's cognitive functionality. It can be an early-warning system and may be helpful as a baseline as time passes and the test is repeated. While there is no cure for various forms of dementia at present, some steps can be taken to at least slow down any progression. Besides hoping and praying for a cure of some kind before you need it, the best medicine is to keep the human machine in good order and stack the odds on your side. Keep walking daily and try not to carry extra baggage, either physical fat or mentally draining worry and mind clutter. Watch your diet and be conscious to eat the healthy stuff as much as avoiding the junk. No, this is not meant as some joy-kill buzz response to live like a monk and eat like a chipmunk. Not at all! Life is meant to be enjoyed. Eat the cookie. Savor the ice cream. Just try to stop there by using good judgment and practiced moderation.

For loved ones placed in an Alzheimer's unit, it is a frightening time for the patient who knows that something is wrong and that they are losing their mental faculties as they slip deeper into their own personal "twilight zone." They are scared as their minds slowly retreat from their former selves. The mind waxes and wanes in clarity and lucidity for a while but cannot hold its grip of functionality beyond ever-shrinking periods of time. It keeps losing light, much like a flickering candle in the wind until the light is finally gone. But the candle remains. It is sadder still for loved ones who are helpless witnesses and can no longer reach their loved one anymore.

For family or friends, they are now heavily reliant on staff to care for their loved one. This kind of care is often a more difficult job than that found in a nursing home, where many patients can at least communicate on some level. As dementia takes its devastating toll, it is very difficult to attend to a patient's other needs, such as pain or discomfort, for they are unable to communicate in any meaningful way. A lot of professional and intuitive guesswork is in play.

In order to humanize a patient as much as possible, family members should try to display large pictures of their loved one's former vibrant self in their room in an attempt to show staff another side to the diminished individual in their care. Engage staff with funny and touching stories. Diplomas, awards, wedding pictures, etc. all need to be prominently displayed to depict a real person in a former life. Personalize them as much as possible. Hopefully, in some small way, all caregivers that come in contact with a loved one may show extra compassion and appreciation for a life that was cut short by this roadblock on the highway of life. In the meantime, pray, contribute, and work for a cure. One never knows whose future could be changed. Even yours!

50

THE END GAME

"It ain't over till it's over."

Baseball manager Yogi Berra

Hospice is God's waiting room! For the few who find themselves getting off at this way station on their life journey, there is no way to beat around the bush. Hospice is the last roundup, the last rodeo. When hospice is decided upon by patient, doctor, and family, it is an acknowledgment that the human body has met its limit to rejuvenate and heal itself. Modern medicine has used up all its wizardry in its bag of tricks to keep the body going strong. The roughly give or take six-month clock is set in motion. The goal is to arrange for one's last days to be the best that are possible under the circumstances. No more surgeries, radiation, chemotherapy, space-cadet zombie medications and vampire syringe stickers around the clock. A patient's mental haze and stupor may actually be lessened as the meds and side effects begin to diminish. For some, they perk up with a very small mini-rally. Sometimes, the best course of action is no intervention at all if there is no purpose to it. There is hope, and then there is merely the illusion of hope.

Hospice usually receives two types of patients. The first are people with an incurable illness of some kind like cancer. With pain management, they are still cognizant with most of their senses and are aware of what is going on sometimes to the very end. They are still "with it," as many would say. The second group is in more dire straits, suffering from a terminal stroke, severe accident, or end-stage dementia whereby they are "out of it," not being able to truly comprehend their own situation.

Is there any silver lining to such a turn of events? Hardly, but also consider the alternative–someone near and dear to us is taken in a flash in a car accident, suffers a heart attack, or becomes a victim of some other sudden tragedy. Here one minute, gone the next. We have all gotten "the" phone call sometime in our life, bearing the shocking news that someone we loved or knew met sudden misfortune and, like the snapping of one's fingers, were gone in a flash, funeral details to follow. We hang up the phone, shaken and often in a state of disbelief. It rattles our cage and unnerves our brain as we attempt to process this new information and place it in some kind of context. Our minds don't want to compute or accept the tragedy of shocking news. We walk into another room and sit down in a vain attempt to take it all in. Our constellation of people in our lives will have to undergo an adjustment, the degree of which depends on the closeness of the departed individual to us.

Hospice care is not a complete negative for those who still retain their mental faculties. Indeed, it could be considered in one way a mini-gift if pain can be controlled and kept in check. Some will recoil and say, "Come on, give me a break. A mini-gift? Let's call a spade a spade and cut to the chase: everyone knows the purpose of hospice. How could anyone put even the tiniest spin on such an event? That is true, and the point is well taken, especially if hospice is required for someone who is young or in the middle of life. Yet, even this most bitter pill requires some perspective. If one's health has been compromised or a less-than-rosy prognosis has been rendered, such a "heads-up" pronouncement can be a helpful thing. Armed with such information, we switch metaphors again from football to baseball. It is the coach telling you that you are making your final appearance at the plate. But you are grateful to have the opportunity to share bear hugs and treasured stories one last time with those who mean the most to you. A chance to say good-bye is bittersweet, with tears and heartbreak, but it is also an opportunity. Many are taken suddenly in the blink of an eye. Not everyone gets to say good-bye.

Of course, some of this will depend on one's condition: some are not pretty while others just fade away peacefully. Allowing family and friends a window of time to come together even under tough circumstances allows for last expressions of love and time together that a sudden and unexpected death does not permit. It also allows planning time for a smooth transition when one's clock finally stands still.

For those tragic souls in the second group—who are already mentally "gone," but their body is still here with a beating heart, waiting and waiting for the last "sands of time" to push through the hourglass—it is heartrending.

To little children, the phrase "a fate worse than death" is a puzzling one. After all, what could possibly be worse than death, since that is literally the end? As adults, we've come to understand that this usually applied to dark things like torture, slavery, or a slow and brutal death with lots of suffering. Sadly, in an entirely different context, this is what happens to some seniors—a life without memory or dignity, completely at the mercy of caregivers, spoon-fed and seemingly without purpose or hope. The whole debate over end-of-life care is a moral, legal, financial, religious, and an ever-so-personal issue. It is so convoluted and distressing we turn our gaze away from it quickly because the answers are often complex and disputed. Who gets to decide? This is the ultimate question. Yet no family member would wish to inflict pain on a loved one.

By large majorities, people don't want doctors or the government playing God for them or loved ones but wish to retain such decisions for themselves or designated family members. It is the murky world between "let me go" and the following request of "help me go" to end terrible suffering despite hospice care. Yet we treat our beloved pets with so much more respect and great love. We do not demand they suffer in agony on the way to doggy or kitty heaven. Indeed, in a rich, ironic twist, we would call that "inhumane" torture to make animals suffer. Animal-rights activists would, justifiably, be out in force to protest such heartless cruelty. Instead, with a lump in our throat and many tears shed for our dearest four-legged friend, we put them "to sleep." It is our last act of great love and true devotion for them.

However, this is not the same compassion case for people. No, human beings need to suffer excruciating pain to the bitter end, no matter how long it takes or what agony or indignities they must endure simply as a moral matter. If they have to go through hell, so be it. Suffering is noble—it is God's will, and only God can decide when it is time to go under any circumstances! What hogwash! What kind of loving God is this?

There is often rage from a patient or loving family caregiver at the stupidity of all these medical "heroics." For what? Another couple weeks or months of unspeakable pain and discomfort? Isn't this torture? When is enough, enough? What arrogance is shown by a refusal to let one truly, in every sense of the word, "rest in peace"!

As boomers continue to age, this will be an increasingly contested political issue much as civil rights, women's rights, the environment, and abortion have been over the past several decades. Boomers will want to decide this issue for themselves and will increasingly demand that government and the clergy "butt out" of personal and family life decisions. Yes, of course, there will need to be some boundaries and protections imposed, but the final decision should be exercised personally or in consultation privately with family members.

Dying with dignity should be more than a phrase or slogan. No one wants to be a pincushion hooked up to machines that feed us through a tube and breathe for us while monitoring all our failing vital functions every second. No one wants to be reliant on catheters and bedpans or routinely drugged into a stupor that puts us in la-la land or fogs our brain to the point we struggle to distinguish between a few lucid moments of reality and the troubled nightmares of our own subconscious.

In an added twist of conflict of interest, hospice care is also big business, and they walk an ethical tightrope. If one dies too soon, they lose a ton of money, so seeing you or a loved one pass on quickly is not a good thing for their bottom line. If you linger too much over six months, they can get in trouble with insurers footing the bill. Be aware that money can be a factor on some level, even among good and well-intentioned people. Most are honest and ethical, but there are always a few who only see a generic patient's chart and dollar signs, not you or your loved one.

Perhaps the best advice if you or a loved one is in this position is to talk to as many people as possible who have been down this road before you. Sorting through information and opinions can help guide you in deciding what is right for your situation. And if you are unable to speak for yourself, it is even more imperative that your wishes be formally expressed in writing with a notary and even videotaped as discussed in previous chapters and entrusted with your designated advocate. Your wishes need to be expressed in concise and unequivocal language. This is, after all, all about you.

51

CELEBRATION OF LIFE

Sam and his priest are sitting on a church pew, having a serious discussion about Sam's recent heart attack and the priest's prayers on behalf of Sam. Sam, a sports nut, thanks his priest for the prayers and asks out of curiosity if there will be baseball in heaven. His priest looks down and says to Sam, "Sam, I've got some good news and some bad news for you. First, the good news: There is baseball in heaven. The bad news is that next Tuesday, you're pitching."

Just the word funeral brings a mental picture of, well, black. It is a downer. If joyous pink and blue are symbols of babyhood, white the symbol for a wedding, and red for Valentine's Day, then black is for funerals. Mourners wear black, the hearse limousine is black, the undertaker wears black, the preacher wears black, the funeral director and his assistants wear black, the attending grim reaper with hoodie and scythe is always dressed in black, and very often the deceased is laid out in black. The next association with funerals is somberness, solemnity, seriousness, and sadness along with crying and a little sobbing, along with a sniffle here and there. Sonorous words with weighty gravitas from the preacher holding the service follow in due course. Can't you already hear the following in your head," Dearly beloved, we are gathered here today to remember our dearly departed…" And to complete this picture of discouragement is a graveside service with mourners huddled together on a bleak and bitterly cold winter's day with swirling gusts of wind compounded by menacing dark clouds threatening a storm at any minute. Who makes this stuff up? It's almost as if Alfred Hitchcock would pop the casket lid, sit up, and turn ever so slowly toward those assembled for effect with a pregnant pause and then in his deadpan manner and gravelly voice, intone the creepy words "Goouud eeeveenning."

Now, make no mistake, those souls who are struck down in the dawn or prime of life are a first-rate tragedy. Tears, anger, rage, and heartbreak are the defining raw emotions that play out in such circumstances. We rail and scream at the injustice and unfairness, and rightly so. Only time and distance will slightly blunt the blow at hand, but there is no way to alleviate the sorrow, soothe the pain, or explain the randomness of life. It is a calamity of the first order, pure and simple. For those left behind, the scars and hurt will linger for a very long time, and for some it will be a life-changing sentence they will never fully recover from. Words fail to express the void in one's heart. The sense of loss is nearly all-consuming.

Fortunately, the old rituals of the past for funerals, which had almost a ring of Halloween to them, are fading. The trend line for families today is to remake the entire final farewell process into something more positive and uplifting. Of course, this is especially tough to do for the young who have passed away before their time. Life is unfair.

But especially for an older person who has run out the clock of four healthy quarters or more in overtime, there should be an entirely different rulebook to go by. Increasingly, the word funeral should be banished and replaced with a memorial celebration of life. They were part of the lucky ones who got to play the entire game of life.

Many families are now skipping the whole funeral scene altogether. There is a memorial service with friends and family, photos, life sketches (often on a big screen), funny stories, touching stories, special moments, highlights, little-known facts, hopes, hobbies, dreams, and loves. Often the deceased is not even present and has already been buried or cremated, attended only by immediate family. Even the idea of an open casket–a bizarre viewing of the departed, when you think about it–is becoming passé. This should not be one's "last visual," of a loved one stuck in one's memory bank; rather, it should be treasured snapshots of memories shared with an active and living person who is now gone that need to be remembered. The accent is on the good times spent together in life.

Like everything else in the world, funerals, memorials, and celebrations of life are all evolving in the twenty-first century. Increasingly, families are choosing "theme" funerals to match the dearly departed's interests or personalities. Hobbyists, sports fanatics, movie buffs, animal lovers, and a rich imagination help loved ones say good-bye in their own special way. While traditionalists may find this a little troubling to perhaps a little disrespectful for the occasion, others see the alternative as a way to truly honor those who are gone. Perhaps in a hundred years from now, the word funeral itself will become arcane and fall out of general use.

Many years ago, the comedian Buddy Hackett was a guest on the Johnny Carson Tonight Show. When Johnny asked Buddy about his wishes for his funeral, Buddy immediately rejected the conventional funeral tradition and launched into a funny animated visual scene of wanting a party for his wake.

Buddy told Johnny he wanted the wine to flow, lots of food, dancing girls, balloons, a hot band, and the music to swing. Buddy wanted the whole works for a magnificent send-off party where everyone had a great and memorable time. Then Buddy paused for a moment, becoming wistful, and slowly turned and looked directly into the audience camera with pitch-perfect timing and deadpanned, "Gee, Johnny, I'm really gonna miss being at that party," all to the delight and hilarious laughter of the audience. But Buddy was on to something.

Is there anything sweeter that a departed loved one or friend could ask for than for those who come to pay their final respects to have a wonderful time together at a memorial reception? This is no disrespect to the one who has passed, not at all. It should be looked upon as if it were one last heartfelt gift from the one who has passed to everyone he or she loved. There is no right or wrong way to commemorate a loss, yet some imagination and alternative thinking should be considered. Each individual needs to be remembered for who they were and all the lives they touched.

52

LEGACY

Service is the rent we pay for the time we live here on earth.

Lord Halifax, paraphrased

What will your legacy be after you are gone? No one likes to spend much time imagining a future without them in it. It is disconcerting, but it doesn't have to be if approached in the right context and perhaps thought of in the abstract, much as a math word problem. When thinking of a legacy to one's children or to the larger community of society, too many think of it in monetary terms of how much wealth is being transferred after our life cycle is complete. But this is too limiting. Rather, think of the many gifts that we ourselves treasure that have nothing to do with money. No one is "dissing" money here. It has its place. But think of the traits and values handed down and molded into our character, both good and bad, that have had more to do with who we are than any big bank account.

Never feel trapped by inadequacy about your legacy unless in your heart you have not done your fair share. You do not have to live up to any grand or great thing to leave a meaningful legacy. Too many people put a heavy burden on their shoulders and feel their lives were too ordinary and mundane. They were not the famous hero or heroine who saved the world by curing cancer or bringing peace in the Middle East. Some lament they did not leave a mark in life as much as a smudge. Do not fret about any of this since that may not be your destiny in life but falls to others. You are responsible only for your role, large or small, in the big scheme of things.

In any epic play on the big movie screen of life it requires hundreds of roles for actors to play. Without them all, the star of the show is lost. Furthermore, there are hundreds of production staff members that are needed to create a completed movie who will never be seen or even be known except for a flashing name on the screen credits at the end of the movie. Yet each person is vital to the success of the movie. Your only legacy requirement is to play your assigned role as well as you can. Be proud of your contribution and know that without you, the show would never have gone on. The trick is to never be just a mere spectator in life. Keep learning, keep growing, keep doing, keep sharing while you are here and try to pass these traits on before you are gone.

The trappings of great wealth can be a trap. There is a reason why they call them "trappings": because it is like a mouse that has fallen into a giant vat of cheese. Yummy, yummy: the mouse is mesmerized, but there is a fatal price to pay since he cannot eat his way out. He is oblivious to his situation since all he can think about is eating all the cheese his little tummy can hold. Likewise, those with means fear losing what they have, and the more they worry, the more they think they need to hoard. It becomes a self-fulfilling loop and a full-time job just keeping track of everything.

Having class does not mean being a stuffed shirt and to the manor born,[58] living high on the hog. Consider someone like Warren Buffett, premier billionaire investor and one of the richest men in America. Unassuming and unpretentious, he could easily blend into a golf foursome as any aging duffer on the golf course. He could buy anything in the world one can imagine but lives in his old family home in Omaha, Nebraska, of all places. He eschews fancy cars and lives a pretty simple lifestyle. Glitzy and ostentatious are not words ascribed to him. It is critically important to remember that real class and wealth are not synonymous terms at all. Wealth differentiates people, but class is something that everyone can aspire to, even the very poor. Class at its heart is treating others with respect, good humor, fairness, and compassion regardless of one's station in life. It is being well mannered and considerate of others.

Buffett's legacy is to leave most of his wealth where it can do some good. While his children are generously provided for, the bulk of his fortune is devoted to making a difference and a change in people's lives. The actor Kevin Spacey attributes to the late actor Jack Lemmon's sage advice for those who have found success in life "to send the elevator back down."

For a parent, their greatest lasting legacy will be their children and grandchildren. Hopefully, they will be their biggest positive contribution as evidenced by how they were loved, trained, and molded with character and values. For these progeny to become solid citizens and to be inspired to make a contribution beyond themselves is a parent's job well done. A parental role model of honor and respect is one of the greatest tributes any parent can give a child and for a child to appreciate. Parenting is the hardest job in the world by far and comes with no manual and "how to" set of instructions since all children are unique in their own ways even when living under the same roof.

Give some real thought to your legacy. Don't be just generous but also magnanimous. If possible, think beyond your family and inner circle to the general common good. However, do your homework on any and all charities that you may have an interest in. Many, even prominent ones tied to religious or esteemed civic institutions are scams in which most of the money raised goes to big salaries, high overhead, and more marketing to keep the pipeline of cash flowing in. It is scandalous what they get away with. Unregulated, many are fronts for selfish crooks. Check with reputable on-line websites that monitor, rank, and watch over such shady behavior. Giving with your brain is often even more important than giving with a willing heart. Make any changes you feel may be necessary to accomplish these goals.

Consider the "ripple effect" that your legacy can have upon the future both in terms of your personal values and your financial contributions to others. By doing so you have touched the face of the future.

53

EPILOGUE: THE FOURTH QUARTER

Life is not a journey to the grave with the intention of arriving safely in a pretty and well-preserved body but rather to skid in broadside, thoroughly used up, totally worn out, and shouting, "Wow, what a ride!!!"

Hunter S. Thompson

"Folks, welcome back to your radio play-by-play of the big game here in the fourth quarter. There is not much time left on the clock and the crowd is on their feet and going wild. Wow, what a heck of a fourth quarter this has been. Everybody got their money's worth for this game, that's for sure. Folks, it just doesn't get any better than this. It has been an over-the-top, thrilling game, and this has to be one of the best fourth quarters ever played. The crowd is hoarse from screaming and cheering. The coaches are chewing on their clipboards. The refs are chomping on their whistles. The cheerleaders are dog-dead exhausted. Photographers are fighting one another for the best angle. The hotdog vendors are frozen in place. Can you believe it, even the flag is standing at attention?

Okay, here we go: The big boys are coming to the line. Now the quarterback steps up to the line. (Note: Imagine here that you, male or female, are the quarterback of your life.) The line sets. The quarterback looks to his left, now to his right while barking out the cadence count. The crowd is absolutely going nuts... AAANND the ball is snapped. The quarterback steps back into the pocket while dodging one tackler and shaking off another. The stadium is rockin' and the noise is deafening. He looks way downfield at his receiver and let's go a mighty heave. The ball sails through the air in a tight spiral as the receiver sprints in full stride toward the end zone. He is covered like a wet blanket by both safeties as all three leap high into the air, arms outstretched, and... Wow, what an unbelievable game!

What happened? It doesn't really matter; it's how you play an exciting game. Go and play the best fourth quarter in the game of your life with passion, excitement, and purpose. Make it a highlight reel of your best efforts—film highlights to follow. Best of luck!

ENDNOTES

[1] Ten thousand boomers are turning sixty-five every day. See "Baby Boomers Retire," www.pewresearch.org/daily-number/baby-boomers-retire/.

[2] Luddites: These were nineteenth-century English textile workers (generally between 1811-1816) who protested against the Industrial Revolution and the new technology of the day such as spinning frames and power looms by attacking and destroying these new machines.

[3] Monikers for the follow-on generations succeeding the Boomers: Generation X, Generation Y (Millennials), and Generation Z. See Jill Novak, www.marketingteacher.com/the-six-living-generations-in-america/.

[4] Child mortality ratio numbers calculated by the author using compiled statistics from the US Department of Health and Services. Gopal K. Singh, "Child Mortality in the United States, 1935-2007," www.hrsa.gov/healthit/images/mchb_child_mortality_pub.pdf.

[5] National Vital Statistics Reports, 58:21.

[6] Life expectancy for a baby born today at birth. Gender and racial differences will vary this some. See Centers for

Disease Control and Prevention,
http://www.cdc.gov/nchs/fastats/life-expectancy.htm.

[7] See Felicitie C. Bell and Michael L. Miller, Life Tables for the United States Social Security Area 1900-2100, "Table 10—Period Life Expectancies at Selected Exact Ages, by Sex and Calendar Year,"
https://www.socialsecurity.gov/OACT/NOTES/pdf_studies/study120 .pdf, 162.

[8] One website you may want to try in determining your life span, which comes with a short questionnaire from the University of Pennsylvania is
http://gosset.wharton.upenn.edu/mortality/perl/CalcForm.html. There are many others, so you may want to google "How long will I live?" Compare and contrast to come up with your personal number (or an average of several sites) and then make plans to beat it. Good luck!

[9] Life Tables for the United States Social Security Area 1900-2100
https:www.ssa.gov/oact/NOTES/as120/LifeTables_Tbl_7_105-.html

[10] National Vital Statistics Reports 62:7, 47. See Table 20.http://www.cdc.gov/nchs/data/nvsr/nvsr62/nvsr62_07.pdf

[11] www.ssa.gov/planners/lifeexpectancy.html

[12] Ibid.

[13] These numbers are just expressed as the inverse from the note above.

[14] The term "healthspan" is just a takeoff on the common word lifespan but much more accurately reflects the quality of life rather than just its length. Healthspan denotes how well we are able to function physically and mentally to do the things we want to do in life. So although many people live long lives, because of poor health, they live out their lifespan in the shadows of life. This is not the way anyone

conceives their own future.

[15] Determining your own healthspan is very difficult. Some people will ascribe different metrics. For example, being able to walk vs. climbing a challenging mountain are two very different things. We also recognize the older we are, the more problematic some conditions may become. In addition, fourth-quarter people are rapidly realizing how quickly our lifespan clock is running already, and to shorten it again through a disability or accident compromising our healthspan is something we prefer not to contemplate.

[16] This website breaks down in detail the varying degrees of independence and assistance that some seniors may require. www.seniorcitizensguide.com.

[17] See "Alzheimer's Disease," www.mayoclinic.org/diseases-conditions/alzheimers.../risk/con-20023871.

[18] "2015 Alzheimer's Disease Facts and Figures," https://www.alz.org/facts/downloads/facts_figures_2015.pd f.

[19] The "Greatest Generation" is a term ascribed to the journalist Tom Brokaw of the generation about Americans who came of age during the Great Depression and went on to help win World War II.

[20] Prime Time TV: This term is used by the media to describe the evening hours that result in the highest TV viewership of the day.

[21] See Mona Chalabi, "How Many Women Earn More than Their Husbands?", http://fivethirtyeight.com/datalab/how-many-women-earn-more-than-their-husbands/.

[22] This website gives a brief backdrop of how pension systems around the world got their start from the precedent-setting system established under Otto Von Bismark.in Germany. See "Otto von Bismarck," https://www.socialsecurity.gov/history/ottob.html.

[23] "Do it now" was perhaps the most important recurring theme in the life lessons taught by W. Clement Stone (1902-2002). He was one of the earliest pioneers of the self-help motivational speakers in America for many years. Reviewing his admonitions and insights is a worthwhile endeavor of anyone's time as a wise investment. See Forrest Wallace Cato, The Register 7:8, www.iarfc.org/documents/archive/2006/vol7issue8_000.pdf, 3-8.

[24] So intently focused on the game or task at hand that everything else around them gets blocked out.

[25] David Brooks, a columnist for The New York Times argues the importance of incorporating "eulogy" values in our life as more important than "resume" values in his book, *The Road to Character*.

[26] Psalm 90:12.

[27] Research indicates that that this story has been adapted and changed into many forms. The closest original inspiration to be found is "The Star Story" by Loren Eisely, an essay published in The Unexpected Universe.

[28] From a poem by William Ross Wallace published in 1865 in praise of motherhood.

[29] Incredibly, a fifteen-year loan term means the house is completely paid off roughly three years before the midpoint of a thirty-year loan. See Bret Whissel's Website, bretwhissel.net.

[30] See Brad Tuttle, "Brand Names Just Don't Mean as Much Anymore," Time http://business.time.com/2012/11/01/brand-names-just-dont-mean-as-much-anymore/.

[31] A biblical reference to the longest person who ever lived, 969 years.

[32] With sixty-five-year-old men and women living on average to eighty-two and eighty-five respectively, and considering

that most men have a wife that is several years younger, the odds that they will both be alive at the age of eighty is under fifty percent. And it may be even less if the wife's (or husband's) age differential is significantly larger.

[33] Sleep is all tied in together with stress, habit, nutrition, and exercise and is therefore hard to solve in isolation. A consistent and holistic approach will be the most successful in the establishment of new habits. The best is going to bed by ten o'clock in the evening. But "night owls" find it very hard to change their ways mentally (longtime habit) and to reset their body clock. See Melinda Smith, Lawrence Robinson, and Robert Segal, "How to Sleep Better," http://www.helpguide.org/articles/sleep/how-to-sleep-better.htm.

[34] Time Magazine, "One size fits none" September 11, 2016

[35] A reduction of one hundred calories a day alone translates into over thirty-six thousand calories a year, which is the equivalent to ten pounds. Since most people consume far more than just one non-water beverage daily, the losses in weight could be even higher.

[36] See National Center for Biotechnology Information, http://www.ncbi.nlm.nih.gov/books/NBK64422/.

[37] See National Center for Biotechnology Information, http://www.ncbi.nlm.nih.gov/books/NBK64422/.

[38] David Heath, International Handbook on Alcohol and Culture (Westport, Greenwood Publishing, 1995).

[39] The Veteran's Affairs Administration lists US Total War Dead from 1775-1991 as being 1,190,110. See http://www.va.gov/PURCHASEDCARE/aboutus/news/archive/Americas_Wars.pdf. Added to this figure is nearly seven thousand additional losses in Iraq and Afghanistan since 9/11. See Hannah Fischer, "A Guide to U.S. Military Casualty Statistics: Operation Freedom's Sentinel, Operation Inherent Resolve, Operation New Dawn,

Operation Iraqi Freedom, and Operation Enduring Freedom," https://www.fas.org/sgp/crs/natsec/RS22452.pdf. Amazingly, only 651,031 (plus uncited [not included] numbers from Iraq and Afghanistan) of this figure were actual combat-related deaths. Most of the rest are attributed to disease and accidents. Even considering every skirmish and small-fry operation in American history—see https://en.wikipedia.org/wiki/United_States_military_casualties_of_war—in which American lives were lost, drunk drivers still exceed all military deaths.

[40] See "List of Motor Vehicle Deaths in U.S. by Year," https://en.wikipedia.org/wiki/List_of_motor_vehicle_deaths_in_U.S._by_year. (Complete original analysis by author.) Records indicate that from 1899 to 2012, there has been a total of 3,551,332 million highway fatalities. The percentage of current accidents that are alcohol related were at a low of 31% in 2013. See "Impaired Driving: Get the Facts," http://www.cdc.gov/motorvehiclesafety/impaired_driving/impaired-drv_factsheet.html. However, during the postwar years of World War II, the percentage of alcohol-related deaths was much higher, soaring to as much as 60% in the 1970s (and at a time when "total deaths" were much higher than today) according to the National Institutes of Health. See "Alcohol-Related Traffic Deaths," (report.nih.gov/nihfactsheets/ViewFactsheet.aspx?csid=24). Or google "percentage of alcohol related deaths in the 1960s." Since 2012, we can add a total of approximately 31,000 more deaths yearly with about 31% still being alcohol related (midway between ten and eleven thousand deaths per year). Therefore, taking a conservative factor of 40% over the entire timeframe

(since 1899) of some 3,650,000 traffic deaths we get a figure of 1,460,000 alcohol-related deaths. This easily surpasses all of the American military war dead in its twelve major engagements (some 1.2 million died) throughout its history. Indeed, if one considers only battle deaths (approximately 660,000 resulting from combat), it is more than twice the figure. These are truly astounding numbers.

[41] There is no accurate information on the first fatality between two automobiles. However, Henry Bliss is listed as the first fatality by being struck by a car as a pedestrian getting off a streetcar in 1899 in New York. See "Henry H. Bliss," https://en.wikipedia.org/wiki/Henry_H._Bliss. There are some competing claims as accidents (pedestrian or bicyclists). It is probably safe to assume that vehicles running into one another did not occur till the turn of the twentieth century, at least to become a new concern for society, replacing deaths and injuries caused by horses.

[42] (Author's original analysis.) The victims from 9/11 totaled 2,977. Considering a fifteen-year period (adjusted-2001-2016 and counting), we have a total motor-vehicle fatality rate according to the National Highway Safety Administration of approximately 552,000 deaths. Taking the lowest and most conservative percentage of 31% accidents related to alcohol (552,000 times .31) we get about 171,000 deaths during this time frame. Dividing the 2,997 victims of 9/11 into the 171,000 number of drunk driver deaths we get a death toll factor of OVER 57 times. And the stunning fact is we continue to add another 9/11 equivalency to the total about every three and a half months. Hard to believe, but true.

[43] See http://www-nrd.nhtsa.dot.gov/Pubs/812188.pdf. (Original analysis by author.) The National Highway and Transportation Safety Administration cites 513,000 traffic

injuries each year. If we apply the same current very conservative 31% of accidents that are alcohol related, we get 159,000 injuries a year. Multiplying by fifteen years since 9/11, we get a total of 2,385,000 injuries. Imagine how many doctors and hospitals this requires, not to mention medical costs, lost work days, and strains on families.

[44] There are thirty-two NFL teams with an average of just over 68,000 fans per game. If every stadium were filled, this would comprise nearly 2,220,000 fans. Of course, in reality only half the stadiums are used every week as half the league is away playing the other half as a visiting team.

[45] See Alice G. Walton, "New Study Shows How Marijuana's Potency Has Changed over Time," http://www.forbes.com/sites/alicegwalton/2015/03/23/pot-evolution-how-the-makeup-of-marijuana-has-changed-over-time/. The THC-addictive part of marijuana that causes "a high" is in many cases up to three times as potent as it was a generation ago.

[46] See "Popping Pills: Prescription Drug Abuse in America," http://www.drugabuse.gov/related-topics/trends-statistics/infographics/popping-pills-prescription-drug-abuse-in-america. The United States consumes seventy-five percent of the world's prescription drugs.

[47] See Nic Darling, "So Many Square Feet, So Few People," www.100khouse.com/2008/10/20/so-many-square-feet-so-few-people/.

[48] See Self Storage Association, www.selfstorage.org. Fascinating statistics about the self-storage industry.

[49] The Federalist Papers 51

[50] See LeadingAge California, http://www.aging.org/14a/pages/Index.ctm?pageID=2107.

[51] Median costs of a funeral. See National Funeral Directors Association, http://nfda.org/about-funeral-service-/trends-and-statistics.html.

[52] See Tyler Mathisen, "Cremation Is the Hottest Trend in the Funeral Industry," http://www.nbcnews.com/business/cremation-hottest-trend-funeral-industry-1B8068228.

[53] This poem apparently has many derivations, and research suggests a couple lines of it trace back to early gravesites in New England in the eighteenth century, but there is no definitive attributable source.

[54] See David Brooks, "Why Elders Smile," http://www.nytimes.com/2014/12/05/opinion/david-brooks-why-elders-smile.html.

[55] See "Death vs. Disability," http://www.affordableinsuranceprotection.com/death_vs_di sability.

[56] Atul Gawande, Being Mortal (New York, Metropolitan Books, 2014), 116.

[57] See "2012 Alzheimer's Disease Facts and Figures," https://www.alz.org/downloads/facts_figures_2012.pdf. While there may be varied stages of cognitive decline, many in this group are still able to function and get by on their own.

[58] An English reference to being born into a titled or privileged upper-class home.

Made in the USA
Charleston, SC
30 January 2017